Salt-water Fishing from Boats

SALT-WATER FISHING FROM BOATS

by MILT ROSKO

COLLIER BOOKS, NEW YORK, NEW YORK

COLLIER-MACMILLAN LTD., LONDON

The Macmillan Company
866 Third Avenue, New York, N.Y. 10022
Collier-Macmillan Canada Ltd., Toronto, Ontario

Salt-water Fishing from Boats was originally published
in a hardcover edition by The Macmillan Company
as *Fishing from Boats*.

Library of Congress Catalog Card Number: 68–17203

FIRST COLLIER BOOKS EDITION 1972

Printed in the United States of America

Contents

To my father,
a fine fishing companion

Acknowledgments

Where do you begin to say thank you for the help in preparing a book such as this? A native Bahamian who showed me a way to catch bonefish contributed his share of knowledge, as did a Florida charter skipper who taught me the way to load up on dolphin offshore. A California party boatman who suggested I switch to a lighter line added to my know-how, as did a Down-East commercialman who showed me how to jig pollock.

Some were close friends, others casual acquaintances, and some just fellows sitting on a dock or standing alongside on a party packet. All contributed their share.

This book in effect is the result of many years of fishing from boats in many places in the Atlantic and Pacific Oceans and the Gulf of Mexico. I'd be remiss were I not to acknowledge the help of all the people I've met and fished with. This book would not have been possible were it not for them, and to all I say sincerely, "Thank you."

One person who rightly deserves a thank you is my father. When I was seven years old he woke me early one morning, and I sleepily accompanied him to the coast. There, after persuading the skipper of a party packet to permit me to go along—in those days they didn't usually sail with youngsters aboard—we put out to the offshore grounds together.

My first fish was a prettily hued weakfish, and as my father tells it my angling accomplishment was the hit of the day for all aboard. From that time on Dad seldom wet a line without me by his side, whether fishing from a party packet, a rental rowboat, a U-drive skiff, or an offshore cruiser.

There's a woman in my life who deserves a thank you too. She's my wife, June, who frequently, with our children, Linda and Bobby, accompanies me on fishing trips along the seacoast. Often she's busy with the camera while the children and I are catching fish, although she sets it aside and catches her share too. A great many of the photographs in this book are the result of her fine camera handling, for which I am grateful.

Milt Rosko

Introduction

For years men have gone down to the sea in ships. Some to earn a livelihood, others to enjoy cruising along the broad expanses of the oceans and gulf which are our country's natural borders.

Until quite recently—less than a decade ago—the sea and all its beauty was enjoyed by a relative handful of our population. Suddenly, however, a boating boom hit the seacoast. Almost overnight, it seemed, quiet small seacoast communities were transformed into bustling ports of call for a new breed of boatmen. The worker who toiled all week at a job and spent his weekend doing chores around the house suddenly started to plan his weekends so that he and his family could head for the seacoast.

At first most of these weekend sailors were content to make friends at dockside and to cruise waters close by. But soon they became restless, eager to do something more on the waters, where their boats could provide a useful role.

Everywhere there were people, fellows like you and me, who turned to the sea for recreation too. They may not have been as eager as those who bought their own boats, but they had just as much enthusiasm, employing the services of charter boatmen, or renting a small skiff from a U-drive livery. Many found it enjoyable to just drift along in a rowboat communing with nature.

As boating grew in popularity, so salt-water fishing grew in popularity. It was inevitable that fathers, wives and youngsters would tire of just cruising and that they would decide to wet a line, anxious to see what they could catch from the tidewaters.

We observed this transformation take place. Many boatmen turned to fishing and became so enthralled in the excitement and challenge our tidal waters offered that their boats simply became a means of getting to and from the fishing grounds!

With many other boatmen, however, it proved far less exciting. In fact, often it proved downright frustrating, expensive and dull. Some boating enthusiasts were fortunate enough to make the acquaintance of veteran anglers, who took them into their confidence. Far more boatmen stumbled about when it came to fishing in salt water, not knowing where to turn with respect to fishing equipment, techniques and the myriad details that must be mastered before one becomes adept at catching fish from the sea. Many lost interest in fishing, and some in boating too.

Having observed much of the frustration (a fellow and his family fishing for flounder with tackle suited for bluefin tuna; a boatman vainly trying to cast to a surfacing school of blues with an oversize trolling reel; a party boatman whose sinkers were so light his rig never touched the bottom; and so on, we thought there must be a way much of this misdirection and frustration could be overcome.

While thinking about this, we also reminisced of the many times we'd wasted countless hours employing the wrong equipment with improper techniques and even fished the wrong areas, all because we didn't know better.

With that thought in mind we set out to write this book. Its purpose is to inform the newcomer and possibly broaden the knowledge of the veteran coastal fisherman. If somewhere along the Alantic, Pacific, or Gulf Coasts there is someone who wants to go fishing from a boat and this book proves helpful towards that end, it will have served its purpose.

Within its covers we have compiled data drawn from experience of more than twenty years fishing from boats along the seacoast. Often we employed new techniques brought from faraway places. Trolling lures popular off Mexico's Baja Peninsula blitzed dolphin off Maryland; chumming techniques from Bermuda worked well on Florida's Gulf Coast; while bottom-fishing rigs used on the East Coast worked just as well bouncing on the bottom of the broad expanse of Pacific.

In compiling the data for this book we've fished all three coasts: the Atlantic and Pacific Oceans and the Gulf of Mexico. We've traveled to Mexico's offshore islands in the Pacific, to the Virgin Islands in the Atlantic, Puerto Rico and Haiti. Bermuda provided exciting deep-sea challenges. There were wonderful experiences and exciting fishing from many of the islands of the Bahamas.

We must, however, in all fairness say that this book offers only the fundamentals of fishing from boats along the seacoast. We attempt to cover the major techniques, equipment used, and favorite fifty species of the boatmen, but essentially this book is only a primer of fishing from boats along the seacoast. To call it more than that would be an exaggeration, for in all honesty we must say that an entire book could be devoted to any one of the topics we cover.

We do believe that the serious boatman who studies what is written within the covers of this book will come away with a broader knowledge of salt-water fishing. We have often proved that fishermen in some areas are creatures of habit. The wise boatman who breaks from habit and hand-me-down tradition will see his catches and enjoyment improve many times over. Make certain to count yourself as one of those, for the sport-fishing horizons know no limits.

When the manuscript for this book was nearing completion, we passed it on to one of this country's leading boat builders, who had fished many of the areas we'd fished. His comment might prove of interest, for while many of his boats sell well into the tens of thousands of dollars, he said there wasn't an item on any of his craft that could offer as much help, for the cost involved, as this book. We hope you'll agree.

1 Boats for Fishing

OVER the years we've fished from a wide variety of boats. We've drifted down a tidal estuary in a tiny pram where fat flounders were the quarry, and we've dropped a bait off the stern of a troopship to catch husky groupers! We've had fun from every type of boat from which we've fished. Some boats were better suited to salt-water fishing than others, but in a pinch all served their purpose —to put us within range of feeding fish. After that it was up to us.

While the two extremes we cite above are exceptional, we should like to note that there are a great many different types of boats available to the angler who wants to wet a line in salt water.

One of the things which has lead to the great popularity of fishing from boats along the seacoast is that there is a type of boat fishing to suit most everyone's pocketbook. The pleasures of fishing from boats sort of grow on a person over a period of time. Many anglers become acquainted with boat fishing when they're young and on a summer vacation at the seashore. They sail out onto a coastal river or bay and catch whatever happens to take their bait. As they grow older they progress to a party packet or charter boat, then perhaps to a U-drive skiff. Many go on to purchase their own boats.

We will here include in broad categories the different types of boats which are utilized for salt-water fishing. We would like to point out that there are many kinds of boats whose features and designs overlap. There are also many individual one-design boats built for a specific purpose in use along the coasts today. We make no attempt to include these, preferring to discuss only those which find broad use among sport fishermen.

Party Boats

Most anglers are introduced to offshore salt-water sport fishing aboard party boats. A party boat is a fishing craft where you need no reservation. You simply arrive at the dock before the prescribed sailing time and step aboard to take your place at the railing. With few exceptions, it is a first come, first aboard proposition, and the boat sails when a prescribed number of anglers are aboard.

The passage, or fare, to fish from a party boat is based on a fixed fee per head. Because of this, party packets are called "head boats" in some areas. In some sectors party boats specialize in bottom fishing, and they are frequently called ground-fishing boats because of this.

Fares range widely for fishing from party boats. The fare is most often dependant upon the type of fishing being done. By far the highest fares are aboard the party boats which fish off southern California. These boats make trips of several days to a week's duration. The fuel and bait expended is considerable, and the skipper charges a sizeable fare.

Most party boats, however, have a nominal fare and specialize in basic types of fishing. Along the middle and north Atlantic Coast sea bass, porgy and flounder are the species most sought during the summer months. In Florida and along the Gulf Coast the packets specialize in groupers and snappers, although frequently king mackerel, little tuna and Spanish mackerel are landed. The California party-boat anglers look for yellowtail, barracuda, bonito and kelp bass to fill their bags.

Party boats range in size from about 40 feet to upwards of 100 feet in length. They are comfortable craft, ideal for the newcomer who may need assistance or for the father who wants to take his son or daughter fishing. Some of the boats even have lounge decks for the ride to and from the fishing grounds. Many have small restaurants where the angler may obtain soup, sandwiches and items from the grill, as well as coffee and cold drinks.

Those boats which sail for several days duration have bunks

This party boat is typical of hundreds which sail from West Coast ports each day. Sometimes they find fish close to shore, but occasionally they travey fifty miles or more seaward in search of elusive albacore.

Mexico's Baja Californa peninsula forms a backdrop for these anglers fishing aboard a party boat out of Ensenada. The boat is anchored just off from the thick kelp beds which hold great numbers of gamefish. The fish are coaxed from the kelp by a liberal spread of live anchovies used as chum.

Most party boats have a pool or jackpot for the biggest fish. Each angler on board usually contributes a dollar to the pool, and if he's lucky enough to catch the biggest fish, determined by placing it on the balance, he may return to port with enough jackpot money to pay for several trips. This packet is returning from a trip to Block Island off Rhode Island. The deckhand has a big pollock and codfish on the balance, with the former being the larger of the two.

which may be rented for a nominal fee. Tackle may also be rented, and terminal tackle purchased.

In addition to the licensed skipper, who is responsible for piloting the party boat, there is usually a crew of from one to three mates, or deckhands, who assist the passengers in any way they can.

Most party boats sail on a daytime schedule, usually leaving dockside between six and eight in the morning and returning around four in the afternoon. There are, however, boats which sail on a half-day schedule, with a trip in the morning and another in the afternoon. Additionally, some boats sail early in the evening, returning in the wee hours of the morning.

Party-boat anglers often make fine catches, for the professional skipper is on the water almost every day, and he is able to follow the movements of fish, putting his patrons into the best fishing locations available.

The tackle most often used by anglers fishing from party boats falls within the general-purpose category. An exception is the regulation-class tackle used for some trolling and chumming which is done from party boats for heavy gamefish such as school bluefin tuna, yellowfin tuna, wahoo and other tough fighters.

Charter Boats

Charter boats are smaller in size than party boats and are most often of a basic boat design called an offshore sportfisherman. These boats range from 30 feet to a top of 50 feet in length and are more luxurious than party packets.

As their name implies, the boats must be chartered by anglers who wish to fish from them. This is usually accomplished well in advance of the date you plan to fish. Many experienced top-notch charter

The Skip II, *skippered by Walter Drobecker, Jr., out of Montauk, New York, is typical of many charter boats along the coast. It can comfortably accommodate six anglers who can fish for any species they might care to fish for, right from bottom feeders on up to gamefish such as school tuna and white marlin.*

skippers have their entire season booked solid many months in advance.

Most charter-boat skippers prefer to fish with only four or six people, although some boats may accommodate eight or more. Too many anglers make it difficult to fish, as it is seldom possible to fish more than six lines at a time.

While some charter boats will do whatever type of fishing you prefer, most charter skippers much prefer to specialize in game-fishing. Along the middle and north Atlantic Coast they set their sights on striped bass and bluefish for inshore fishing, while school bluefin tuna, bonito, little tuna, dolphin and white marlin are the targets when they head for blue water. Southern and Gulf Coast chartermen set their sights on sailfish, dolphin, amberjack, king mackerel, tarpon, snook and redfish. West Coast anglers look towards albacore, striped marlin, white sea bass, yellowtail and king salmon.

All equipment and bait is supplied by the charter boat. Usually, however, the tackle used is somewhat heavier than that which might be used to obtain maximum sport. The reason for this is that inexperienced anglers often fish from charter boats, and were the skipper to supply light tackle, it would too often become broken or smashed.

Most captains are accommodating, though. They'll permit you to use your own tackle, providing it appears to be in mint condition and adequate for the fish being sought. Remember that a charter skipper's livelihood depends on the fish he deposits on the dock, and he isn't about to have his reputation suffer from an angler who brings inadequate tackle aboard.

On by far the greatest majority of the charter boats from which we've fished, regulation-class tackle has been used. Were you to take aboard your own 20-pound or 30-pound-class tackle we'd say most charter captains would be happy to accommodate your sporting interest, although they'd be quick to say that the light tackle would curtail the day's catch somewhat, because of the added time required to land each fish.

Charter-boat fishing is understandably more costly than fishing from a party packet, but it is favored by many small groups of anglers who like to fish together.

While most boats are chartered on a daily basis, some skippers charter their craft on a weekly basis, permitting the anglers to live and eat aboard during the entire week. We chartered for a week-long fishing cruise through the out-islands of the Bahamas recently, and it proved to be an exciting experience, with fishing far beyond our expectations. While the cost of such a charter runs to a thousand dollars or more, when split between two couples it really isn't too costly. Particularly when one stops to consider that meals, on-board lodging and fishing are all included in the charter rate.

Guide Boats

We include guide boats because this type of service is increasing in popularity along all seacoasts. The guide boats which we speak of are usually small boats in the 15-foot to 18-foot range, with a guide who accommodates a maximum of two anglers. These boats are most often used for inshore fishing, particularly when seeking tough gamefish.

In the main the guides offer specialized services, seeking such fighters as striped bass, bluefish, channel bass, snook, tarpon and bonefish.

The rate for these charters, on an individual basis, is by far the most costly type of fishing you can do. This is understandable because of the limited number of anglers involved.

Most anglers obtain the services of a guide because they like to cast to feeding gamefish. While the guide provides casting tackle, as well as trolling and bottom-fishing tackle where necessary, most anglers prefer to use their own gear. Light spinning tackle, popping outfits and fly-casting tackle are the most popular for the species of fish mentioned.

Rental Boats

In this age of do-it-yourself, the popularity of rental boats has grown tremendously. Today you can rent almost any type of boat imaginable along the seacoast and be your own skipper. If you like offshore trolling you'll find seaworthy sea skiffs in the 24-foot to 30-foot range available as U-Drives at many major fishing ports.

Most rental boats, however, are smaller in size and best suited to inshore and sheltered water fishing. In the main these are skiff or runabout types, powered by outboard motors in the 9.5- to 20-horsepower range.

Not to be excluded from this listing are the rowboats or rowing skiffs, which are rented in great numbers at almost every fishing port along the coasts. A great deal of fishing enjoyment can be obtained from these fine small boats, which can be propelled either by oars or with a small outboard motor. They're ideal for the family man who wants to fish in the protected reaches of bays, rivers and estuaries with his wife and youngsters, for they constitute perhaps the most economical type of fishing boat there is.

Private Boats

Few people just go out and buy a boat on the spur of the moment. Boat buying is often a gradual thing, with an apprenticeship

Here Pete Perinchief poles the author across a Bermuda bonefish flat. The boat being used here is typical of those used by private owners for fishing in shallow water. Many bonefish guides use the same type of craft.

Sturdy boats such as this one may be rented for a few dollars per day. They're ideal for the family man who has his own outboard motor and who likes to travel from spot to spot. Here the family is about to spend a day fishing the Indian River in Delaware.

served on a party or charter boat, or while fishing from a rented rig or on the craft of a friend.

But once the decision is reached to purchase a boat, there are three basic types which will prove of interest to the sport-fishing enthusiast. These are general boat types, and it must be remembered that many of them can be used for a wide variety of fishing situations.

OFFSHORE SPORTFISHERMEN

The offshore sportfisherman is, as the name implies, a boat designed expressly for fishing far from shore in quest of big gamefish. While many anglers who own boats of this type in the 30-foot to 50-foot class specialize in big game, including the giant bluefin tuna, the blue and black marlins, the broadbill swordfish and giant sharks, there are as many more who are content to fish for the medium-sized offshore gamefish which we include in this book.

Boats of this type include the larger conventional sea skiffs com-

Offshore sportfishermen such as this specialize in catching big gamefish. They can go many miles to sea and usually troll or chum. Most boats of this type are privately owned, although many are available for charter for extended trips of a week or more.

plete with cabins and a flying bridge. Most are equipped with outriggers and fighting chairs in the cockpit. Because their design is expressly for fishing enthusiasts, they have been called "fishing machines" by their builders.

In the main, these are boats for regulation-class tackle, as most people who use them are concerned with trolling and chumming for gamefish, as opposed to other types of fishing.

SEA SKIFFS AND INBOARD-OUTDRIVES

Falling into the 20-foot to 30-foot category are perhaps the greatest assortment of boats used by salt-water sportsmen. These are usually called sea skiffs or runabouts by their builders and are powered by either inboard or inboard-outdrive propulsion.

They're fine, seaworthy boats, capable of fishing on the broad reaches of the ocean, providing you don't stray too far from shore. They're the basic boat for the weekend sailors, and each season sees many fine catches brought back from these medium-sized boats.

While regulation-class tackle is used by many anglers who own boats of this type, by far the most useful tackle is that which we discuss under the heading of general-purpose tackle, for this may be used for the many types of fishing which the small-boat man enjoys, including trolling both offshore and inshore, chumming, bottom fishing and boat casting.

One good aspect of a boat this size is that it's small enough to fish bay and river water, yet large enough to head seaward when offshore species beckon.

Many owners take these medium-sized craft and customize them, putting a fighting chair in the cockpit, along with outriggers, and rod holders, which makes them a smaller version of the offshore sportfisherman, creating the ideal family boat for fishing fun.

OUTBOARD BOATS

Outboard boats are another large group which is extremely popular among the salt-water fishing fraternity. Here too there is a wide range of designs, from 12-foot aluminum skiffs on up to roomy wooden skiffs often powered by a pair of 50-horsepower outboards.

Speedy sea skiffs such as this one, with a small cabin and sheltered cockpit, are popular on all of our coasts. They're ideally suited to a wide variety of fishing, both in the open reaches of the ocean and in protected bay waters. The boat is returning from a trip off the Delaware coast.

The fog-shrouded hills bordering San Francisco Bay form a backdrop for these anglers about to bring aboard a big striped bass they hooked while drifting in their inboard-outdrive runabout. Boats such as this, built of fiberglass, are economical to purchase, run and maintain.

Al Anderson and Howard Beyer use Al's outboard-powered runabout as a casting platform while fishing off the Rhole Island coast. It is typical of many boats in use on all three coasts, in that it can be hauled from the water onto a trailer in a matter of minutes. Many anglers who own rigs such as this travel up and down the coast, literally following the movements of fish.

These three anglers are fishing for winter flounders on a blustery winter day on Barnegat Bay in New Jersey. Their boat is light in weight and may be trailered or carried on a cartop carrier, giving them mobility to travel to wherever the fishing is good.

The outboard propulsion system on a boat is favored by many, for it is economical and requires a limited amount of service. It is just as dependable as an inboard power plant, which has also added to the popularity of the units attached to the sterns of a wide variety of small boats.

While some boatmen keep their outboard-powered craft at coastal marinas, a great many anglers prefer to carry their outboard boats on trailers. In this way the driveway or back yard becomes their slip, and they can work on their boats at their leisure. The trailer rigs make them completely mobile: the angler who owns one is ready to go wherever the fish are cooperating at an instant's notice. Many trailer-rig owners like the idea of fishing in different places, instead of being limited to a certain radius from one marina.

What has added to the popularity of boats of this type is the fact that most marinas have launching ramps, and many states have built public launching ramps to accommodate the small-boat men who visit their coastal areas.

Indeed, it is not uncommon to see an enthusiastic angler trailer his boat a thousand miles or more on vacation, so that he may enjoy sport-fishing from his own rig, using his own tackle, in waters he'd heard about but never before visited.

Among trailer boatmen more than any other breed, there is a camaraderie that defies description. If you're a visitor from far-away you can often learn the fundamentals of an area just chatting with the natives who are about to put in at the same ramp you're using. We've found that most small-boat men have a togetherness that builds good sportsmanship on the water.

Outboard-powered boats do have their limitations, however. We've occasionally observed them on the offshore scene while trolling for big game. But we do not recommend that craft of this type be taken beyond a sensible range, for in doing so you toy with danger. Most outboard boats are not built for rugged offshore duty, so the wise owner uses them for inshore coastal fishing, where protected waters are only a short run from the fishing grounds.

SAFETY AND COMFORT ESSENTIAL

We have not delved into the many facets of boats and boating, except as they apply to fishing. However, it should be noted that safety and comfort are essential in any boat, whether it is used for fishing or otherwise. The sea is unpredictable, and a boatman must always have respect for it. His fishing boat should always be equipped with the standard safety items required by the Coast Guard, whether it is his own boat he fishes from or a party, charter or rental craft.

We like to look at a boat as a piece of fishing equipment. In order to obtain maximum enjoyment from it, the boat must perform flawlessly. When it does, then one cannot help but enjoy fishing from it, whether it is a small rental outboard runabout or a big offshore sportfisherman.

Center-console boats, both outboard and stern-drive-powered, have become increasingly popular on all coasts. This one is rigged for offshore trolling, complete with outriggers.

2 Selecting Basic Tackle

IN order to obtain maximum enjoyment while fishing from a boat, it is important that you equip yourself with the finest quality fishing tackle you can afford. Quality tackle is a wise investment, repaying you many times over, whether you use it while trolling many miles offshore or drifting through a tidal estuary.

Because there are so very many different types of tackle available, many anglers become confused as to just what tackle they should purchase. Therefore we shall discuss throughout this chapter and the balance of the book what we believe to be good, functional tackle suited to specific types of fishing. Much of the tackle discussed may be used for several types of fishing. In this respect it is wise to make your first tackle selections with the thought of adding to them later, so that you get the best possible set of balanced tackle as a start. Your ultimate goal should be to have your tackle locker or boat equipped with the tackle best suited to each type of fishing you may do.

In this chapter we are making tackle recommendations with the average angler in mind. We like to think that most anglers like to go fishing just for enjoyment and aren't interested in doing trick fishing. We'll not even touch on the extremes of stunt fishing, for we feel that few fishermen are interested in catching marlin on a fly rod or tuna on ultra-light spinning tackle. By the same token, the tackle recommendations made here are not compatible with those used by charter boatmen. They of necessity must use heavy tackle in order to accommodate the needs of the wide variety of anglers who use their equipment, from the tyro to the seasoned pro. To many old-time chartermen our tackle selections may seem to lean toward the light side, which they do. But this is because we feel greater enjoyment will be derived by giving an even chance to the fish being sought.

Over the years we have fallen into a pattern of purchasing our own tackle in matched pairs. While initially this may seem unnecessary, if you own a boat you may find it the practical thing to do. With matched regulation trolling tackle it will be much easier for you and your guests to switch from outfit to outfit, always using the same drag settings, knowing exactly how much pressure the tackle can bear, and not being confused with a different type of reel every time you pick up an outfit.

This is true for inshore fishing in protected waters as well, and especially for the family man. In fact, wives, children and newcomers are more likely to enjoy fishing and to develop confidence when using the same outfit trip after trip. Matched sets of tackle keep the youngsters from all wanting to use one particular outfit.

We are dividing our discussion of a selection of basic tackle into three groupings: regulation-class tackle, general-purpose tackle and casting tackle.

Each of these basic groups has an application for the angler who fishes from a boat, whether it be his own craft, a charter boat or a party packet. While the discussion of regulation-class tackle is limited to one basic type of tackle, several types of tackle are included within the framework of the other groupings.

Regulation-Class Tackle

There are many names given to the tackle here described as regulation-class tackle. We've chosen this heading for the basic group because tackle of this type falls within the framework of various classes of tackle recognized by the International Game Fish Association. The I.G.F.A. has set sporting standards for various tackle classifications. By using tackle which falls within the ranges established by them, you may qualify for a world's record within a given line classification should you be fortunate enough to hook a

Regulation 20-pound-class tackle was used to land this little tuna while trolling along the edge of the Gulf Stream off Florida. The little tuna provides great sport on light tackle such as this, but would hardly be a match for 50-pound-class tackle.

heavyweight. While this may seem of small significance and highly unlikely, there are hundreds of instances where record fish were landed on tackle not qualifying as regulation tackle, and these records were not recognized by I.G.F.A. Specifically, rods which are too short, lines which test over their marked breaking test, wire lines, and use of prohibited terminal tackle will automatically rule out an otherwise record fish.

Unfortunately, each manufacturer gives a different label to the tackle which falls under our heading of regulation tackle. So that you're not confused, we'd like to point out that the tackle which we are discussing here will be listed as big-game, class tackle, trolling tackle and deep-sea tackle by various manufacturers. The thing to keep in mind when purchasing an outfit is to make certain it falls within the framework of regulation-class tackle. Most manufacturers have indicated this either on the rods or in their catalogs.

In the main, the species of fish discussed in this book are those which are most apt to be caught by small-boat men. We'll not even touch on giant bluefin tuna, blue and black marlin, the broadbill swordfish and giant sharks, for these species are in a class all their own. As such, specialized tackle and techniques are required, and one most often finds that professional skippers are employed to go after them. The tackle most often used for these is 80-pound-class and 130-pound-class regulation tackle, which is far too heavy for the average fishing situations you'll encounter.

The recognized tackle classes which fall within the usefulness of the small-boat man include 12-pound, 20-pound, 30-pound and 50-pound class. Personally, we prefer to eliminate 12-pound-class tackle from our tackle locker, as this is extremely light. It is most often used when tournament fishing or when out to break a specific record. On the other end of the scale, 50-pound-class tackle tends to be a little on the heavy side for fish on the offshore scene. Just about the only time tackle this heavy would be necessary is when fish are consistently running to 100 pounds or more. Fifty-pound-class equipment is fine for big-school bluefin tuna, wahoo, amberjack, yellowfin tuna and white and striped marlin; although even here, there are many anglers who prefer tangling with these heavyweights on 30-pound-class tackle, for the sport is then superb.

What this all narrows down to is a matter of personal preference. For all-around offshore fishing with tough gamefish on the agenda, you'll not go wrong in selecting 30-pound-class tackle for a starter, or 20-pound-class if you're an experienced angler. With a good boat, a qualified helmsman and patience on your part, you can land any fish up to 100 pounds without too much difficulty.

RODS FOR REGULATION-CLASS TACKLE

Quality is of paramount importance in selecting a rod in this tackle category, for more than any other type of tackle, tremendous pressure is brought to bear on it by big fish, particularly while fishing in deep water.

In recent years fiberglass has become the standard material from which all types of rod tips are made. Bear in mind that while outwardly many fiberglass shafts look alike, there is often a marked difference in the quality, which is most often borne out by the price of the rod.

The majority of the regulation rods measure six feet ten inches in overall length. Tips usually measure five feet six inches. Each manufacturer, of course, varies his design to conform with what he believes to be important, while still staying within the limit of regulation tackle.

Among some of the important things to look for in a 20-pound, 30-pound or 50-pound-class rod is an overall look of durability. Everything should have a solid look to it, for as stated earlier, tremendous pressures are brought to bear.

Roller Guides and Tiptop

While it will cost several dollars more to purchase a rod with roller guides and a roller tiptop, these are far superior to a rod equipped with ring guides and a ringed tiptop. The roller guides permit the line literally to roll in and out, with no friction applied to it and so very little chance of it fraying. The design of the roller guides is such that they are mounted high off the rod, permitting the line to run from the reel directly into the guides in a line almost paralleling the rod, thus not causing undue pressure where the line meets the first guide.

These guides should be mounted so that the strain is distributed throughout the entire length of the rod tip. There are some rods on the market which have too many guides mounted too far forward; this causes the tip to bend severely, and often the line touches the rod midway between the reel and the first guide, which is undesirable.

With a light, flexible shaft, such as on a 20-pound-class rod, the first roller guide should be close to the forward grip for best results, as this permits you to put maximum pressure on a fish by bringing the lower section of the tip into play, which because of its design has more backbone. The majority of the better made rods have a total of six roller guides.

Rods used to fight medium-sized gamefish for prolonged periods of time must of necessity have a comfortable foregrip, preferably six to nine inches long. For while fighting a fish, the angler most often holds the rod with one hand on the foregrip, while turning the reel handle with his other hand. You can well understand that comfort here is important, for you may be holding onto the foregrip for half an hour or more while fighting a big one.

The foregrip should have a non-slip quality. Extremely smooth finishes tend to become slippery when wet. Select neoprene, specie cork, or felt-covered specie cork, as these are less apt to become slippery. None of these materials is as hard as wood, which should never be chosen, and they cushion your hand, preventing calluses or blisters from working up due to prolonged pressure and rubbing.

Reel Seat

Where the tip meets the butt there should be a top-quality combination reel seat and ferrule. The male ferrule on the tip section should be keyed for exact alignment, so that the roller guides are upright in relation to the reel, and it should lock into place, so that there is an absolutely solid grip. Under no circumstances should pressure against the tip cause the male ferrule to work loose or the tip section to twist, placing the guides out of alignment.

The reel seat should be of a screw-lock variety, preferably with a double ring, so that the reel, when placed in the seat, can be held as firmly and securely as possible. Prolonged pressure occasionally causes some screw locks to work loose, making the reel wobble within the seat, which can become frustrating when fighting a big fish.

Inasmuch as the reel seat is exposed to salt water—as is the rest of the rod—it should be of fine quality chrome.

Hickory Butt

At first glance, the butt, or handle, of a rod looks just like an ordinary piece of wood. On a cheap rod that's all it is, an economical piece of pine or other wood which has little or no strength.

In a top-quality rod the butt should be turned from a piece of select straight-grain hickory. It shouldn't be a thin butt, but should have a diameter and weight which gives heft and balance to the lower section of the rod. This keeps the rod from being tip-heavy and balances the whole unit nicely as you hold it to fight a fish.

The hickory butt is hard and strong, whereas other woods are either hard and brittle or just plain soft and weak. Remember that often you will relinquish your rod to a rod holder. Should a strike occur at that time, practically all of the pressure is transmitted to the butt. Over a period of many years we've observed a number of butts of inferior quality which simply broke where the wooden butt met the reel seat when a big fish hit. In several cases this resulted in the tip section and reel being lost overboard. Granted, a properly adjusted drag on the reel could have prevented this. But had there been a quality butt, perhaps the line would have broken instead.

A gimbal nock is a must on a regulation-class rod. When the rod is set in a rod holder, it holds the rod in an upright position, so that when a strike is received the pressure is brought to bear in an even manner, with the line rolling against the roller guides. The cross-slotted gimbal nock is designed to fit the fighting chairs of most boats and the rod belts which many anglers wear.

You will find that quality rods have the gimbal nock attached to the butt with a small screw. This prevents it from working loose and turning. Gimbal nocks which are glued to the butt have a habit of coming loose at the most inopportune times, resulting in undue hardships to the angler.

While each component of the rod is important, the overall quality of a rod may be judged by the quality of the workmanship that goes into the finished product. Windings which hold the guides should be neat, with all guides underwrapped. Guides and tiptop should be in perfect alignment, as should the reel seat. The gimbal nock should fit neatly into the butt, and the butt should be smoothly finished. Color preserver should be applied to the windings so that they feel smooth to the touch and not bumpy. The butt and windings should also have several protective coats of rod varnish or of the newer plastic finishes to protect the rod, which is constantly exposed to the action of salt spray.

There are no two rod blanks alike. Some are very soft, while others are rather stiff. Here it's a matter of personal preference in making a selection. The happy medium is a tip which bends enough to help wear out a fish, yet has sufficient backbone to pump it up from the depths when necessary. Although many anglers prefer the stiffer type of rods, we greatly enjoy using a tip that bends a lot, especially in the 20-pound and 30-pound-class rods. In our way of thinking this adds a lot more of the thrills to fishing, whether you are tangling with a 5-pound bonito or a 75-pound tuna.

REELS FOR REGULATION-CLASS TACKLE

The boatman doesn't have as much of a problem in making his reel selection as he does with a rod. While there are many manufacturers of rods, who make a wide variety of models, for reels there are fewer manufacturers and a limited selection that are clearly designed for regulation tackle.

In salt-water reels designed for regulation-class tackle, the majority of the manufacturers designate the size of the reel with a numerical code, the first number of which denotes the size. This number is followed by a diagonal slash and the letter "O," which means ocean. The sizes which are most often used with the rods discussed earlier are either a 2/0 or 3/0 with a 20-pound-class rod, a 3/0 or 4/0 with a 30-pound-class rod, and a 4/0, 5/0 or 6/0 size with a 50-pound-class rod.

Essentially, the smaller reels are lighter in weight, balance well with the lighter rods and have approximately equal line capacities for the line class they are intended to carry.

It must be remembered that each manufacturer designs his reel and its spool somewhat differently, which results in each holding a somewhat different amount of line. So that you understand the general sizes we're speaking of, we'd call the following line capacities of various reels about normal: 2/0—425 yards of 20-pound-test line; 3/0—375 yards of 30-pound-test; 4/0—450 yards of 30-pound-test; and 6/0—400 yards of 50-pound-test. These figures are based on monofilament line of average diameter. Should you elect to use either Dacron or braided nylon, the diameter of the line will vary somewhat, and as a result so will the reel's capacity.

It should be noted, however, that all the reels discussed here have capacities in the general range of 400 yards. This means that a reel filled to within a quarter-inch of the cross bars will have about 1,200 feet of line on it. This is a long length of line; believe us when we say it takes a strong fish to rip off this much line and clean you out. In the hands of an angler who doesn't get excited, and with good boatmanship, some mighty big fish are landed on this combination of tackle.

Fortunately, there aren't too many inferior reels on the market today. If you're uncertain which to buy, the best bet is to stick with well-known manufacturers who have been in business for some years.

Reel Drags

Reels are equipped with drag mechanisms so that a strong game-fish can take line under controlled tension without breaking it. In order to perform satisfactorily the reel must be equipped with a smoothly functioning drag that permits the line to slip from it without sticking or binding. A gamefish making its first powerful run should be able to take the line very smoothly, without a jerking effect being felt by the angler on the rod. Even after a prolonged battle the drag setting should function smoothly, so that should a gamefish make a last-minute bid for freedom the line would slip from the reel just as easily as when the fish was first hooked.

There are several different types of drags, and these are adjusted in several different ways. By far the most popular is the drag which is used on most moderately priced reels, which is actuated by a star wheel and most often called a star drag.

The star wheel is mounted on the reel adjacent to the handle, so that with a finger motion the angler may turn the star clockwise to tighten the tension on the drag washers within the frame of the reel or counter-clockwise to reduce tension. Because of its design and location it is very easy to tighten or loosen a drag of this type accidentally. But still it remains a favorite, and in the hands of an experienced angler it performs extremely well.

It is very important that the drags be tested regularly while on the fishing grounds to ensure that they are properly set. Settings vary with different types of fish and fishing. We will discuss the correct ones later under the various fishing methods.

On the more expensive reels there are drags which may be pre-set and actuated by lever-action drag controls, which range over an arc of more than 100 degrees, lessening the chance of applying too much pressure. Reels of this type usually are equipped with a drag lined with automotive-type brake linings which ensure trouble-free performance under the most trying conditions.

Free Spool Lever

The reel should be equipped with an easily actuated free spool lever, which is often brought into play when hooking some kinds of fish or doing some types of fishing. Most levers are positioned on the top of the reel at the right, where they are readily accessible.

There should also be an audible click mechanism on the reel, with sufficient pressure so that it prevents line from leaving the reel when it is under a slight amount of tension and the reel is in free spool. The button engaging the click should be positioned so that it does not come in contact with your hands or arms when fighting a fish. There are reels having the click button poorly located, and when an angler fights a fish for a prolonged period the button can actually chafe so much that his inside forearm or wrist will bleed.

Sizeable Handle

Select a reel that has a sizeable handle. You'll be holding onto it for up to an hour or more at times, so you want it to fit into your hand comfortably. Several manufacturers make two or three different sized handles for their reels, and if you've a big hand you should select a large handle.

Quite a number of reels come equipped with reel clamps, which may be used to secure the reel firmly to the rod. These aren't really necessary with 20-pound and 30-pound-class tackle, however.

Harness lugs are generally built onto reels of size 4/0 and larger. They are placed on the top of the reel and are used to snap your harness to the reel. The lugs serve a useful purpose when fighting big fish in long battles and are helpful for youngsters who may have difficulty controlling the rod and reel when fighting a sizeable fish, but they are seldom used otherwise.

One-Piece Spools

With reels called upon for heavy duty, it is important that they be equipped with strong spools. A majority of the major manufacturers equip their big-game reels with one-piece spools, which are either cast or machined and are far stronger than reels made of several pieces. Keep in mind that tremendous pressures build up on the reel spool when the line is being reeled in under heavy tension. A cheaply constructed spool will simply burst, even when used with lightweight 20-pound and 30-pound test lines.

LINES

Today's anglers are fortunate in that they have available excellent lines that give very fine service on the fishing grounds.

While braided nylon was common many years ago, as was linen line, today these lines are seldom seen on the offshore scene. They've been replaced by far superior lines of nylon monofilament and braided Dacron.

Both monofilament and Dacron are excellent lines. Here we can discuss the merits of each, but each type has a great many devotees, each convinced that one is superior to the other.

Monofilament

Monofilament line is an extruded line, and as such is smooth and offers great wear resistance. It is also almost invisible in the water, particularly in the lighter 20-pound and 30-pound tests. It also possesses a considerable amount of stretch.

The stretch quality is favored by some anglers, for they believe they are less apt to break a line if the fish makes a run. This built-in stretch also acts as a cushion, preventing a rod from breaking or the hook from being straightened if the drag is set too tight.

Captain Russell Young and mate Alfred Basden of the Sea Wolfe *strain to hold the 83-pound, 14-ounce amberjack landed by Mrs. Eddy Perinchief while fishing at Challenger Banks off Bermuda. She landed this beauty while using regulation 20-pound-class tackle and broke the women's world record for this tackle category—proof that light tackle can land big fish.*

Dacron

Of the many lines sold by your tackle dealer, you'll find Dacron has the least amount of stretch, with the possible exception of wire line. Because of this quality, which many term no-stretch, it is favored by many anglers who fish for tough-jawed gamefish, especially billfish such as sailfish or white and striped marlin.

It is the feeling of many anglers that the limited amount of stretch in Dacron permits them to strike home more quickly and get the barb to penetrate faster than were they using a line that stretched.

Here it is a matter of what you get used to. Many anglers prefer the monofilament because it wears well, whereas Dacron has a tendency to fray and must be handled more carefully. Also "mono" is the more economical of the two, which adds to its popularity.

Over a period of many years we've used both, and we feel that for day-in-day-out fishing, and with rough handling, monofilament is perhaps the best line for the average angler.

BALANCE IMPORTANT

Balanced tackle is important, for with proper balance you can get far more enjoyment out of fighting a fish. We must add however, that occasionally we use tackle that is somewhat out of balance, because we've found it more to our liking.

As a case in point, we frequently employ 30-pound-test line loaded on a 3/0 reel on a rod rated for 20-pound-class line. While this may make manufacturers and the International Game Fish Association shudder, we do find it a pleasant outfit to use, and there's absolutely nothing wrong with using it. We prefer the lightweight 20-pound-class rod because of its very flexible tip, yet we like the 30-pound-class line because we can apply more pressure without fear of popping a line by a miscalculation or too much drag pressure. The 30-pound-test line takes practically twice the abuse of the lighter line, and when handling fish at boatside it gives a far more comfortable feeling than would the lighter line.

Here it should be noted, however, that were the spread of tackle too great, say a 50-pound-test line with a 20-pound-class rod, there is a good chance you'd smash the rod due to the imbalance of tackle.

John Mason waits with the gaff ready as the author leads a big albacore to boatside. The albacore is being fought on regulation 30-pound class tackle after having been hooked while trolling almost a hundred miles off the coast of Mexico.

So bear in mind that any variations from the basic tackle should be minimal, so as not to throw it out of balance.

PRIMARILY FOR TROLLING AND CHUMMING

By its very design, the tackle we've described here is suited primarily for offshore trolling for what are popularly called blue-water species, among them the smaller marlin, the tunas, king mackerel, albacore, dolphin and wahoo, to name but a few. There are inshore applications, however, for this tackle, including fishing for big tarpon, or even bottom-fishing after giant black sea bass or lunker jewfish.

The tackle is ideally suited to chumming and drift fishing as well, and the boat fisherman will find it extremely useful whether angling in Atlantic, Gulf or Pacific Coast waters.

General-Purpose Tackle

Within the framework of general-purpose tackle fall two basic rod-and-reel combinations which find more applications for the boat angler than any other types. As the name implies, their design is general and they may be brought into play for a wide variety of fishing situations for a great many species.

Here, as with regulation-class tackle, we have a great variety of names given to the basic components of the outfits about to be discussed.

BASIC BOAT OUTFIT

In the catalogs of most manufacturers you'll find the rods within the framework of this category referred to as boat rods, sinker-bouncing rods, drift-fishing rods, jigging rods and live-bait rods, to name only a few. Some even call them trolling rods.

With reels much the same is true, with such classifications as deep-sea, ocean, trolling, casting, fast-retrieve and jigging among the more popular names.

RODS

Bear in mind that here we are looking for a rod which may be called upon to perform a wide variety of services, as opposed to a specialized rod designed for a specific type of fishing. In selecting such a rod we must look for the characteristics that will provide maximum sport while catching two-pound porgies, yet have sufficient backbone to handle striped bass weighing 25 pounds or more, or albacore of comparable size.

A rod which measures in the range of seven feet overall, plus or minus about three inches, fills the bill nicely. The action should be rated for either 20-pound or 30-pound-class line, preferably the latter, for often the rod may be called upon for heavy-duty fishing in deep water or other situations where big baits, heavy sinkers or strong currents necessitate a sturdy outfit.

In selecting such a rod, make certain you flex the tip and choose one with a shaft that has a nice arc to it. Stay away from rods which have a soft or sloppy action, as well as those which are so stiff that it takes excessive pressure to put any kind of bend in them.

Ring Guides

A quality rod should have either four or five graduated ring guides on the tip section to distribute the strain properly. Shy away from rods having fewer guides.

Guides should be of the finest quality obtainable, as those with economical chrome plating will quickly become grooved and useless.

A number of manufacturers put guides with tungsten carbide rings on their rods, and these hold up very well. Tough monofilament and even wire lines will not cause them to become pitted or grooved.

As to a tiptop, one having a ring of tungsten carbide is fine. Several manufacturers put a small roller tiptop on some rods, but depending on the type used, they can become a handicap when casting may be necessary. However, some of the newly designed roller tiptops are made in such a way as not to impair casting; these are fine.

Foregrip Essential

The rod should have a comfortable foregrip, about four or five inches in length, placed just ahead of the reel seat. Neoprene, some of the softer plastics and specie cork are among the favored materials. The foregrip should feel comfortable in your hand, for often you'll be holding onto it for prolonged periods while fighting a fish.

Sturdy Reel Seat

You can almost always tell the quality of a rod by looking at its reel seat. If the reel seat is hard chromed and of a screw-locking variety with a locking ring which holds the male ferrule secure in the reel seat, you can be assured that it's what you're looking for. The male ferrule should be keyed to fit the reel seat, thus assuring perfect alignment of the guides in an upright position.

Butts Vary

Rods of this type come equipped with a variety of butts. Among the more popular models in lightweight rods are those which have a butt section made of a piece of fiberglass shaft, onto which are glued either specie cork or neoprene grips, one just below the reel seat and the other at the extreme end of the butt, with the fiberglass shaft exposed in the middle.

Other butts have specie cork around the entire length of the handle.

While butts of the aforementioned types are light in weight, the most practical butt is one turned of straight-grained hickory. We've found that the length of the wooden segment of the butt should be about 14 inches, giving an overall length, including the reel seat, of approximately 19 inches.

A butt of this length is ideal for most rod holders aboard a boat, it handles well when fighting a fish from a belt socket, and it can be comfortably tucked under your arm while chumming or bottom fishing.

June Rosko landed this big silver salmon just brought aboard by Captain Gene Grimes while using a live anchovy bait and a general-purpose rod typical of those used on the West Coast. Note the long, lightweight tip and large number of guides preferred by anglers who use live bait and fish the broad expanse of the Pacific Ocean.

On the end of the butt there is either a slotted gimbal nock or a protective rubber butt cap. The slotted gimbal nock is necessary if you do a lot of trolling, for it permits ease for fighting a fish when wearing a rod belt or fishing from a chair. When the fisherman is seated, it holds the rod upright. Much the same is true when the rod is placed in a holder.

However, for bottom fishing the hard-chromed gimbal nock is not as comfortable to use as a rod equipped with a protective rubber butt cap.

Many anglers select a rod having a butt equipped with a small gimbal nock, and when they use it for bottom fishing or light casting they simply slip a rubber butt cap over the gimbal nock, which works out extremely well.

Bear in mind that a rod of this type in the hands of an experienced angler can be used for almost any salt-water boat fishing where the fish are of reasonable size. Some anglers who do a lot of bottom fishing in deep water may prefer a shorter, stiffer rod for use when fishing for cod or grouper and the like. Anglers employing live bait and fishing from coastal party packets may find a longer, more limber rod to their liking.

REELS

There are literally dozens of reels on the market which match up perfectly to the rods we've just described. Some have narrow, wide-diameter spools and fast retrieve ratios, while others have wide spools with narrow diameter. Many have metal spools, and quite a few have plastic spools. All of the better-quality models work extremely well, depending on what your particular needs are.

There are a handful of reels, however, that may be used for almost every boat-fishing situation, from the lightest on up to the heaviest fishing you're apt to run into while angling from a small boat.

Take-Apart Feature Is Important

The reels we like to use are general-purpose reels having a take-apart feature. This is mentioned first because, for the angler with a limited amount of tackle, having a reel with this feature enables the reel to be brought into play in a wide variety of fishing situations.

The take-apart feature is nothing more than one to three thumb screws which can easily be removed from the right-hand side plate of the reel, which permits the easy removal of the side plate, enabling you to change spools.

With this feature an angler can have as many as three or four different spools of line, and each may be placed in use as conditions dictate. A plastic spool may be loaded with a lightweight braided-nylon squidding line for casting situations, or with monofilament for casting and light trolling. The metal spools may be loaded with wire line for deep trolling, or perhaps lead-core line for intermediate levels and Dacron for normal trolling.

You can see the tremendous versatility a reel with a take-apart feature gives you, and we recommend it highly.

The reel, of course, should be one of the better quality models. Select one that has either a three-to-one or a four-to-one retrieve ratio, preferably the latter, as the higher ratio enables you to retrieve line effortlessly and quickly.

Star Drag Standard

In reels of this size star drags are the standard type in use. The drag pressure is adjusted by actuating a star wheel mounted adjacent to the reel handle. The drag should be smooth and permit line to pay out effortlessly and without binding, no matter how it is set.

A majority of the reels in use today have smooth drag systems; the greatest number of problems when fighting fish stem from angler error rather than malfunction of the drag.

The free-spool lever on most reels is located on the same side as the handle, and may be quickly engaged by throwing the lever to the forward position. Some reels, however, have a lever which is depressed for free spooling and is automatically engaged when you turn the reel handle. Both work very well.

What was said about reel handles earlier in this chapter applies equally to the general-purpose reels. Make certain the torpedo or ball grip is of a size that comfortably fits the palm of your hand.

Line Capacity

Almost all of the reels which we've used in these intermediate salt-water sizes have a line capacity far in excess of what you normally would use. Having the reel filled is good insurance though, should you hook a big one.

The reels have a line capacity of approximately 300 yards of 30-pound-test monofilament and 400 yards of 20-pound-test monofilament. If you spool other types of line, such as wire or lead core, the capacity is reduced considerably because of the wider diameter and the loose and irregular spooling characteristics of the line.

LINES

Earlier we mentioned the distinct advantages of having reels in intermediate sizes with take-apart features. Often fish feed at different levels, and in order to reach these levels different types of lines prove helpful. A reel that can accommodate several lines simply by changing spools puts you at a distinct advantage.

Monofilament a Good Choice

Because you'll be using this outfit in a variety of situations, we'd suggest using monofilament line as your basic line, with 30-pound test being perfect for most angling situations, especially when used with the rod and reel described earlier.

We'll not repeat the various merits of monofilament as opposed to Dacron, as these were covered under regulation-class tackle. Here again, however, if you like Dacron for surface trolling, you can always load an extra spool with either 20-pound or 30-pound test and just slip it into the reel whenever the mood strikes you.

Wire Line

For deep-sea fishing situations where you really want to get down near the bottom while trolling, wire line is the answer. While it is not as sporting to use as other types of line, and the I.G.F.A. will not recognize fish caught while using it for world-record purposes, the wire line very definitely has its place.

Indeed, there are many types of fishing where wire is almost a necessity, particularly in deep, swift water where fish habitually hug the bottom.

Rather than fill an entire reel with heavy wire line, many anglers load the reel to about two-thirds capacity with either monofilament, Dacron or braided nylon, and splice or tie in a long trace of the heavy wire. The general rule is that it takes approximately 100 feet of wire line to get a lure trolled at moderate speed to a depth of 15 feet. To reach twice that depth you need just a bit more than twice that amount of line, say around 225 feet of wire line to go down around the 30-foot mark. In depths in excess of 25 or 30 feet, you'd have to troll at least 100 yards of wire line.

Mention of wire line immediately causes many anglers to think of springy, stiff wire, such as the stainless steel used for leader wire. However, the wire line used for trolling is Monel soft-drawn wire, with a .021-inch diameter being the most popular, since it tests out in the range of 35 pounds, which is more than adequate for most fishing. The Monel is relatively soft and spools well on the reel, but you do have to be careful when letting it out so that it does not overrun. When retrieving or reeling in a fish it is very important that the line be spooled evenly to prevent a build-up in one spot, which can cause a problem by slippage, resulting in a mess when you let the line out again.

Lead Core Line

Lead-core line is a rather unique type of line. It is actually a lead core which is sheathed in a very strong, tightly braided nylon sleeve. The lead core is naturally very heavy, which takes the line much deeper than conventional monofilament or Dacron lines, but not quite as deep as solid-wire line.

Most manufacturers put it up in 18-pound, 25-pound, 40-pound and 60-pound tests. Because of its core the line tends to wear quicker than other types of line of the same test, so we prefer using 40-pound test, which gets down very deep and has plenty of strength besides.

A great length of this line isn't necessary. Most anglers simply use a 100-foot length of the lead core, which is attached to their basic monofilament line by way of a modified nail knot.

Bay or Popping Outfit

We are including the bay or popping outfit under general-purpose tackle because it can be used for a wide variety of light-tackle fishing situations, including casting, trolling, bottom fishing, chumming and practically anything else you might think of doing.

MODIFIED NAIL KNOT

STEP 1—*Position the lines and tool as shown, allowing yourself about eight inches of free monofilament end to work with. The monofilament and lead core lines should be reasonably close in pound test strength.*

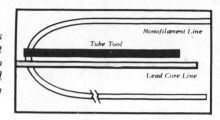

STEP 2—*Take three turns of monofilament around the tool, lead core, and the standing monofilament. Make the coils snug for easier handling. Hold them between your thumb and forefinger.*

STEP 3—*Bend the lead core up out of the way and take a turn around the tool and standing monofilament only.*

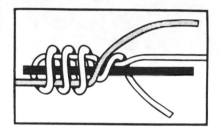

STEP 4—*Bend the lead core down to its former position and take three turns around the standing monofilament, tool and lead core. Hold all the coils securely.*

STEP 5—*Pass the free end of monofilament through the tube and then withdraw the tube slowly.*

STEP 6—*With your free hand, pull gently on one end of monofilament, then pull on the other end. When the coils are tight, pull hard on the two mono ends. Then pull the lead core against the standing mono to test the knot. Trim off the free ends and the knot is completed.*

The popping outfit is lightweight and affords the angler maximum sport with even small fish. These tasty winter flounders were landed on the outfits pictured while fishing in Long Island Sound.

It is actually a scaled-down model of the basic boat outfit we just discussed.

It too goes under a variety of names. Some anglers refer to it as a bay outfit, while fishermen along the Gulf Coast prefer to call it a popping outfit, for frequently it is employed while using a popping cork for spotted sea trout. It is actually more similar to a fresh-water baitcasting outfit than anything else. Beefed up, of course, for salt-water use.

RODS

Most popping rods are in the six foot six inch to seven foot range. They have a very light fiberglass tip, designed for use with light terminal tackle, yet have sufficient backbone in the lower section of the tip to subdue big fish.

A check of a manufacturer's catalog or the label on the rod will most often indicate it is intended for use with lines in the 10-pound through 17-pound-test range.

On the tip are mounted either four or five small ring guides, with a ringed tiptop. Some manufacturers use guides and tiptops with rings made of tungsten carbide, which hold up very well when used with lightweight monofilament lines.

The rod should be equipped with a foregrip just ahead of the reel seat, for comfort while pumping a big fish.

The reel seat on most popping rods is considerably lighter than those on the various types of rods just discussed. Some are made of anodized aluminum, while others are chrome plated. All have a screw-locking feature.

Trigger Grip on Reel Seat

The majority of the popping rods have reel seats with a comfortable trigger grip. This is simply a small curved piece of metal which extends downward immediately below and behind the reel. You can hook your index finger around it for added leverage when casting.

Lightweight Butts

Almost without exception, popping rods are equipped with lightweight butt sections which measure 10 inches in length, or 15 inches including the reel seat. The majority are made of specie cork over a fiberglass shaft or over a piece of lightweight aluminum tubing. Some are built of non-slip neoprene, which makes for a comfortable grip.

The end of the butt is fitted either with a permanent butt cap, or a removable protective rubber butt cap.

This basic rod varies from one part of the country to another. A plug caster using it for snook around mangroves often prefers a stiffer tip, while a northern flounder fisherman likes a lighter, more sensitive tip to feel the light bite of these bottom feeders. But basically the design and purpose remain the same.

REELS

Most anglers prefer using a small casting reel with a popping rod, as it can be cupped comfortably in your hand while casting or trolling. On the average, reels designed for such light fishing have a line capacity of approximately 200 yards of 15-pound-test monofilament, so be guided by these capacities in making a selection.

Level-Wind Feature Favored

With a light rod many anglers prefer using a light reel which has a level-wind feature. While not a must, you'll find such a feature adds to your fishing pleasure. The level-wind feature proves a distinct advantage, for it lays the line back on your spool with a back and forth motion, preventing line build-up in one spot, which could hinder your next cast. The feature also proves advantageous when you've youngsters or inexperienced anglers aboard.

Star Drag

There are some small bay-fishing reels which do not come equipped with a drag feature, but these are not recommended, for you never know when you're going to hook into a big one, and then a drag is very helpful.

The star drag is by far the most popular, employing the familiar star wheel discussed in this chapter. It should be particularly smooth, because you'll be working with a light rod tip and light lines, and a sticky drag could result in trouble after a prolonged battle.

Lightweight Spool

We recommend you stick with those reels which are equipped with a lightweight spool. Spools made of either aluminum or plastic are fine. They permit casting with ease, for during a cast the lightweight spool starts rotating faster than a heavy spool and is less apt to overrun and cause a backlash.

Some reels come equipped with braking and anti-backlash devices, but these aren't essential. An educated thumb is far superior to any mechanical devices we've yet to see.

Although it is only available on a few of the higher priced salt-water casting reels, we much prefer using those which have a quick take-apart feature. This makes changing spools quick and easy and enables you to carry an extra spool or two of different test lines to suit a wide variety of conditions.

LINES

There is little doubt that somewhere along the seacoast an angler is using an outfit such as we've just described and using any one of the number of lines which are made, including monofilament, braided nylon, linen, Dacron, fine Monel wire or lead core.

While we admit that unusual situations may require a specific line, in the main you'll find that using either monofilament or braided nylon line will suit the great majority of conditions. If you have a reel with a take-apart feature you can load one spool for casting with braided nylon, and the other spool with monofilament for trolling, bottom fishing or jigging.

A combination which we've found to our liking includes loading the reel with 225 yards of 12-pound or 15-pound-test braided nylon line for casting, and another spool with upwards of 200 yards of 17- or 20-pound-test monofilament. While the 20-pound test is admittedly a little on the heavy side for this outfit, it must be remembered that if the equipment is occasionally used by inexperienced anglers, the heavier line provides more latitude for error. Also, it results in your losing less terminal tackle due to snagging it on the bottom.

Casting Tackle

The two general-purpose outfits we've discussed are unquestionably the most useful outfits for the boat fisherman. Armed with them the angler can enjoy maximum sport with the greatest number of fish species.

Initially many people think of casting tackle as being employed in salt water only by anglers who fish from the surf, jetties or bridges. Quite to the contrary, casting tackle most certainly has a place in boat fishing. For in certain situations it is far better that the angler cast his line rather than troll or drift it.

Basically, casting tackle falls into three distinct categories: The first type includes all outfits employing conventional multiplying reels, such as the lightweight and medium-weight tackle discussed under the heading of general-purpose tackle. Casting with this type of tackle is the most difficult, for it requires careful thumbing of the reel spool. Consequently, it is used by a limited number of boat fishermen in casting situations.

Second, by far the most popular type of tackle used by boatmen is spinning tackle. The spinning reel has a fixed spool, and in casting the line slips off the edge of the spool, permitting even an inexperienced angler to cast considerable distances with a minimum of instruction.

Third, there is fly-casting tackle. Within this last casting category falls the ultimate in salt-water casting. In fly casting the angler casts an almost weightless tuft of feathers or bucktail which resembles a baitfish, using the weight of the flyline to cast, instead of the weight of the lure as in other types of casting.

Spinning tackle and fly-casting tackle are designed expressly with casting in mind. We believe best results are obtained by using this tackle expressly for casting, not attempting to use it for bottom fishing, trolling, or what have you.

LIGHT SPINNING OUTFIT

Of the two general types of spinning tackle useful for boatmen, specifically light and heavy spinning tackle, the former finds the most use, for it may be brought into play in a wider variety of casting situations.

RODS

Rods which are designated as one-handed rods fall within the light-spinning category and will range anywhere from six to seven feet in overall length. They're listed in many tackle catalogs in the section featuring heavy fresh-water tackle, for they are much the same in design as those rods used by fresh-water bass and trout anglers, with the exception that they're made a bit heavier for salt-water use.

Sturdiness is an important quality to look for in rods of this type. There are many rods on the market with agate guides that are susceptible to breakage, or fine-diameter wire guides which bend easily. Also, all hardware should be of anodized aluminum so that it doesn't become pitted due to the constant exposure to salt.

Backbone a Must

The tip section of the rod should be light enough to handle lures in the eighth-ounce and quarter-ounce sizes, yet there should be sufficient backbone to handle a two-ounce or three-ounce live bait or artificial bait of the same weight.

Shy away from rods billed as having a light action, for these are most often too soft to be brought into play when fishing from boats.

A majority of one-handed rods are jointed in the middle with a ferrule, which should be of sturdy construction as tremendous pressure is often brought upon it.

Guides Distribute Strain

Select a rod having five or six high-quality graduated spinning guides. Remember that too few guides will not distribute the strain properly. The better quality rods have hard-chromed stainless steel guides which hold up very well under exposure to salt water. Some manufacturers put guides on their rods having bridges to give added support to the large rings of a spinning guide, and these prove helpful in keeping the rings from bending or breaking off.

Reel seats of anodized aluminum are pretty much standard on light rods of this type. They do a good job of withstanding the effects of salt on fine equipment.

When fighting a fish with a spinning rod, one hand is usually clasped around the reel seat, with two fingers before and two behind the arm extending to the reel's housing. Accordingly, there is little use for a foregrip when fighting a fish. So on most spinning rods there is only a two-inch or three-inch foregrip to balance off the rod.

The butt section proper is lightweight and narrow and made of either specie cork or neoprene. We've found that a butt length of about nine inches, or fourteen inches including the reel seat, is ideal on this type of rod. It's short enough for one-handed casting, yet sufficiently long to fit into a rod belt.

REELS

Two basic reel sizes may be used on the rod just described. Many anglers use a standard fresh-water spinning reel, simply employing a salt-water spool having a large line capacity. Others prefer a somewhat heavier reel with more capacity, and for this they use the intermediate-sized reels.

The reel's line capacity should be at least 200 yards of 12-pound-test monofilament line, preferably a bit more, for while using light casting tackle it is not uncommon for a fish to run off more than 150 yards of line in a single shot.

Unlike rods and multiplying reels, which are fairly standard, in spinning reels there are a great many varieties, each acclaimed by its manufacturer as the finest. Having used many of them, we find that most of the medium-priced spinning reels on the market today are well made, whether imported or domestic.

Smooth Ball-Bearing Action

The reel should have a smooth ball-bearing action, resulting in effortless retrieves. Its gear ratio should be at least 3.5 to 1 or more, so as to give you a fast retrieve, which is often important with speedy salt-water gamefish that want their lures moving fast.

The reel should be equipped with a sturdy bail mechanism, for in rugged salt-water fishing a weak part that might be adequate in fresh water just won't hold up.

As you're using monofilament lines while spinning, there is a tremendous cutting action of the line against the bail's line roller. Here a tungsten carbide roller will last far longer and give superior performance to rollers of other types, with the possible exception of agate.

As some anglers won't trust bails, they remove the bail completely and switch to a manual finger pickup, which most manufacturers have available for their reels.

Strong Anti-Reverse Lever

The spinning reel should be equipped with a strong anti-reverse lever, for when fighting a fish this is in the "on" position and it keeps the reel handle from spinning backwards.

Flawless Drag Necessary

Most spinning reels have their drag mechanism located on the front of the spool. In most cases adjustment of the drag is accomplished by turning a finger-grip disc clockwise to increase pressure and counter-clockwise to decrease it.

Inasmuch as spinning tackle affords the angler the opportunity of using light-test lines—which are a must in order to accomplish reasonable casts—it is of utmost importance that the drags are smooth and do not bind, no matter how much pressure is brought to bear. For with light lines, the slightest tightness or jerkiness will result in a broken line.

Some of the smaller-sized spinning reels have handles which may be comfortable on a trout stream, but are a downright hardship while fighting a big gamefish of the sea. Select a reel having a large-size circular or torpedo-type handle, so that you can get a good grip on it.

LINES

The best part about using spinning reels is that the spools are removed more easily than with any other type of reel. On many it's just a matter of pushing a button, and off pops the spool. Because of this convenience most boat fishermen carry several spools with them, each loaded with a different size of line.

The light spinning outfit just described will often be brought into

Frank Ray, Jr., unhooks a big yellowtail snapper hooked by the author, while June Rosko fights another yellowtail. Both are using light one-handed spinning outfits while fishing a shallow reef off Bermuda.

play while poling across the bonefish flats, at which time a six-pound or eight-pound-test monofilament line is just perfect. While pitching plugs at tarpon rolling on the surface of a swift river, the angler often feels more comfortable when his reel is loaded with 15-pound mono.

In light spinning, even with an intermediate-sized reel, it's not practical to go much above 15-pound test, for the line would then become extremely difficult to cast.

Over the years many types of lines have been tried with spinning reels, but monofilament line remains the only practical line to use with a fixed-spool reel.

HEAVY SPINNING OUTFIT

The heavy spinning outfit closely resembles the light spinning outfit just described, except that it is bigger overall.

In the main it is brought into play while casting for big striped bass just offshore from crashing breakers, or while tangling with amberjack and cobia with cast jigs worked along the bottom, or when gingerly casting a live anchovy bait for wary albacore on a live-bait boat.

Seldom is this outfit used for fish weighing under 20 pounds. It is a formidable weapon and in the hands of a skilled angler it can land fish up to a hundred pounds, admittedly with a little luck on the part of the angler.

RODS

The heavy spinning rod is a two-handed rod, meaning in effect that you've got to hold it with both hands while casting. This is primarily because of its size and weight. In design it closely parallels rods used for jetty casting, and some manufacturers recommend that they be used interchangably for all types of heavy salt-water work.

Some of the heavy rods have a ferrule in the middle, while others are joined where the tip meets the butt. Made in either fashion they work out equally well, providing good hardware is used.

Because of their length, many manufacturers put seven or eight graduated spinning guides on them in order to properly distribute the strain. Heavy-duty chromed stainless steel guides which are bridged for added strength are by far the best type on a rod of this sort.

Strength in Lower Section

While many of these longer rods appear to have very light tips, it must be remembered that this lightness is necessary in order to handle lightweight lures and baits. But note the strength in the mid-section and near the butt. When fighting a fish the entire arc of the rod is brought into play, with the lower section supplying the power to whip big fish.

A comfortable butt length both for casting and fighting fish is around 14 or 15 inches, 19 inches if you include the reel seat. There are a wide variety of butts on heavy spinning rods, with specie cork being used on some and neoprene, or even hickory, on others. This last is for those who like the weight of the hickory to balance the rod.

REELS

Much of what was said earlier with respect to spinning reels for light spinning applies equally to heavy spinning reels. Actually, there's little that can be added, except that the reels are bigger and stronger, and have a much greater line capacity to subdue the ocean fish.

Many of the big reels are identical to the smaller models, so we'll not repeat our recommendations.

LINES

Most heavy-duty salt-water spinning reels have a line capacity in excess of 250 yards of 20-pound-test monofilament line, which is usually quite sufficient, even for big gamefish. Seldom do anglers employ lines lighter than 15-pound test on a reel of this type, and not too often do they go above 20-pound test, which is pretty much standard.

It is always best to keep your reel properly filled with line, for if you do not your casting may be severely hampered.

FLY-CASTING TACKLE

During the past few years fly rodding along the seacoast has come of age. What was once the passing fancy of a handful of anglers has come to be a standard fishing method for a group of dedicated fishermen who do not measure their enjoyment by the number of fish they catch.

Fly casting is a method employed by boatmen which is an entity within itself. Unlike other types of equipment discussed earlier in this chapter, much of which is interchangable, in fly fishing the outfit includes not only rod, reel and line, but leader and flies as well. Because of this we will expand discussion of fly-casting tackle to include all its components.

However, before proceeding, we feel it best to explain briefly the difference between fly casting and other types of casting. In most casting situations, whether with spinning tackle or using an outfit with a multiplying reel, the rod provides the power to send the lure to its target. The weight of the lure is an important factor, for when

During the past few years the Salt Water Fly Rodders of America has done a great deal to popularize the sport of fly-rod fishing on all our coasts. Balance is extremely important in fly-casting tackle, for a caster must often present an almost weightless fly to a feeding fish 50 feet or more from where he is standing.

balanced properly with the rest of the outfit it may be cast a long distance.

In fly fishing the weight of the lure, in this case a streamer fly or popping bug, is practically nonexistent. So in reality you do not cast the fly, but instead depend on the weight of the fly line to execute the cast. The line is cast and it in turn carries the leader, onto which is tied the fly.

From this we believe you can understand the importance of perfect balance for the equipment, as well as the development of casting skills in order to present the fly to feeding gamefish properly.

RODS

Most salt-water flyrodders are in agreement that a rod measuring nine feet overall and weighing about six ounces is ideal for use from a boat. Bear in mind that in salt water you're using big flies which offer a considerable amount of resistance, and often they'll be cast in windy weather, which necessitates a big, powerful rod.

Until a few years ago salt-water anglers used what was commonly referred to as a bass-bugging rod, which was designed for use in fresh water but worked out reasonably well on the salt-water scene.

Today, however, most major manufacturers build fly rods expressly for salt-water use. Although the finest quality fly rods are made of split bamboo, they often carry a price tag beyond the reach of many anglers. Fiberglass continues to improve for fly-rod action each year, and in the eyes of many experienced flyrodders it's just as good, and in fact more serviceable than split bamboo.

Among the characteristics to look for in a fly rod is a powerful, yet responsive action. Remember that the rod will be called upon to pick a long, heavy fly line from the water, and with a minimum of false casting it should have the power to shoot a line anywhere from 60 to 100 feet to the target.

Big Stripper Guides

Select a rod having large stripper guides, seven or eight in all, for this will permit a smooth flow of the heavy fly line through the guides, which is particularly important when attempting to shoot a long line. Shy away from those rods employing tiny snake guides, as these can actually hamper casting effectiveness.

On a fly rod the reel is mounted on the reel seat located at the very end of the rod. The butt section, which you hold while casting, is immediately forward of the reel and usually constructed of specie cork, although some rods have butts of neoprene.

Extension Butt Helpful

As it is difficult to get leverage on a fly rod while fighting a big fish, many anglers prefer using a rod equipped with an extension butt. This is a two-inch or three-inch butt which has a male ferrule that fits into a female ferrule located within the reel seat. This short extension gives you something to work with when fighting a fish, and it can be rested either against your forearm or against your body.

All fly rods are of either two-piece or three-piece construction. Most are joined with metal ferrules. However, one company makes a fine line of rods which employ no separate ferrule, but simply a fiberglass-to-fiberglass joint which gives continuity of action and a strong connection as well.

REELS

When used on a fly rod, the primary purpose of a reel is to store the line. Only when a fish is hooked is it brought into play, at which time it must perform with a smooth drag that permits a tough game-fish to make a determined run with no undue strain on rod, line, leader or fly. In casting, the reel is not brought into use at all.

Single-action fly reels are the most popular types in use by salt-water fly rod enthusiasts. Single action means just what the name implies: one turn of the reel handle results in the spool turning only once, for what might be termed a one-to-one ratio. There are fly reels which have a faster retrieve ratio, but these are not in as widespread use as the single-action models.

Look for reels having a strong, one-piece frame, for these are sturdier and take more abuse while boat fishing than those with other types of construction.

We'd recommend staying away from automatic fly reels for salt-water fishing, as the springs used for automatic retrieving often rust easily and the various moving parts have a tendency to break down under exposure to salt water.

The standard-size fly reel for salt-water use has a spool which is four inches in diameter, and because of this the reel is commonly referred to as a four-inch fly reel. The width of the reels vary from seven-eighths to one and a quarter inches, depending on the individual features of the reel. Most weigh from nine to ten ounces, with the custom-machined models or those having special drag systems weighing a bit more.

The reason for using a reel this large is that only with such a size do you have sufficient capacity for 30 yards of fly line as well as 200 yards of 20-pound-test backing line.

Simple Pressure Drag

Although some fly reels have anti-reverse mechanisms which keep the handle from turning while the line is going out, these are in the minority. A few fly reels also have sophisticated drag systems.

The most popular single-action reels have a simple braking system, by which the angler adjusts a lever, applying pressure to a spring which gives more than enough tension to the line as a fish is making a run. You don't need the type of heavy drag system found on multiplying reels and spinning reels, for if you were to exert too great a pressure with the light leader, it would break.

LINES

Salt-water fly lines come in two basic types, floating lines and sinking lines. The former have a specific gravity of approximately 98 per cent, whereas the latter's specific gravity is in the range of 120 per cent.

The well-equipped boat flyrodder makes certain to carry one of each type with him, so that he is in a position to use whatever line conditions dictate—a floater when dolphin are chasing bait on top, and a sinker when probing the depths for amberjack.

Salt-Water Taper

The weight of a fly line can be distributed in several ways, including a double taper, level line, or weight-forward taper. In addition, some manufacturers produce a salt-water taper, which in effect puts the greatest amount of weight well forward, so that a caster can get by with a minimum of false casting and shoot the heavy line to cruising fish with ease.

The American Fishing Tackle Manufacturers Association has set up standard weights for fly lines, with each weight range being assigned a numerical designation. Salt-water flyrodders using the type of rod and reel described earlier will find that lines in sizes 9, 10 and 11 usually balance best.

To assist you in distinguishing between the various types, tapers and weights, the lines carry a clear designation. A weight-forward line—which a salt-water flyrodder is most apt to use—carries a WF designation, meaning weight forward. This is followed by the weight of the line, in most cases 9, 10 or 11. Next comes the designation F for floating fly line, or S for sinking fly line. Together they look like this: WF-10-F for a weight-forward number 10 floating line; or WF-11-S for a weight-forward number 11 sinking line.

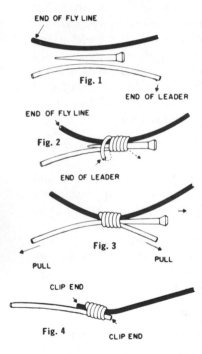

END OF FLY LINE

Fig. 1

END OF LEADER

END OF FLY LINE

Fig. 2

END OF LEADER

Fig. 3

PULL

PULL

CLIP END

Fig. 4   CLIP END

Nail Knot. The nail knot is used to tie the butt end of your leader to the forward end of your fly line. It is also used to tie backing to a fly line. This knot gives a smooth, streamlined connection, and the flat-lying knot will move freely through the guides of your rod. If tied properly, this knot cannot slip, cut or pull out. The knot is tied using either a tapered nail or a piece of small tubing. We often use a discarded plastic or metal cartridge from a ballpoint pen. Here's how to tie it: Hold the line, leader and tube or nail alongside each other as shown in Fig. 1. Allow ample overlap. Then wind leader downward around both line and tube or nail six times. Run the end of the leader back along nail or through tube up under loops (Fig. 2). Pull both ends of leader tight. Slip knot down nail or tube, tightening by pulling both ends of leader as it goes. Slip nail or tube out and retighten by again pulling leader ends (Fig. 3). Finally, pull line and leader tight and clip end of line and leader close to knot (Fig. 4).

Name Brands

By sticking with well-known brands of fly lines you'll be assured of good quality lines that perform admirably while casting and wear extremely well. Most of today's scientifically designed fly lines have millions of tiny air cells trapped within their nylon coating, which keeps them floating indefinitely.

By the same token, sinking lines go deep quickly because of their design, but they, too, do not soak up water, permitting you to lift them from the water and to execute your casts with a minimum of effort.

Most fly lines are 30 yards long, which is more than ample for casting, but hardly sufficient once you hook a big ocean gamefish. This calls for backing line, and most flyrodders find Dacron ideally suited for backing. It is strong and has a small diameter. While

2½-ft.	2½-ft.	2-ft.	2-ft.
25-lb. (.018)	20-lb. (.016)	14-lb. (.014)	10-lb. (.011)

A salt-water fly leader tapered to these dimensions will turn over a large salt-water fly or popping bug with little difficulty. It should be constructed of stiff nylon monofilament leader material for best results.

some fishermen use 15-pound test, far more popular is 20-pound test. The average four-inch fly reel is capable of holding approximately 200 yards of backing, plus the fly line.

Accompanying this chapter is an illustration of a nail knot, which is the best method we've ever employed for attaching backing line to the fly line, as well as the fly line to the leader. Once you try tying this knot a couple of times you'll find it's really not too difficult to master, and it is one which makes an excellent, smooth connection.

LEADERS

You will notice that the butt end of a fly line is quite heavy. Were it to be attached to a piece of nylon leader material with very fine diameter, there would be a marked difference between the two. As a cast was executed, the fly line would lie out straight, but instead of the leader lying out straight, also, in direct line with the fly line, it would double back and lie parallel with the line.

So in order to give continuity to the fly line and leader and to enable the fly line to transmit its turnover power to the leader, it is necessary to use a leader whose butt section closely approximates the diameter of the butt of the fly line. Depending on the individual fly line, this may require 30-pound or 40-pound-test monofilament.

Taper Your Leaders

Naturally, you wouldn't want to use a leader this heavy, not when you're using a small fly that you want to present in a delicate manner. So you have to taper the leader from the heavy butt down to a lightweight tippet onto which the fly is tied.

Assuming that you add three feet of either 30-pound or 40-pound-test stiff nylon monofilament onto the fly line, you can then construct a tapered leader by employing approximately two and a half feet of 25-pound test, two and a half feet of 20-pound test, two feet of 14-pound test and a final two feet of 10-pound or 12-pound test as the tippet. These pieces are best joined by use of a blood knot, with the end result a perfectly tapered 12-foot fly leader.

SALT-WATER FLIES

Into the broad category of streamer flies and bucktails fall the lures which fly casters use to coax strikes from salt-water gamefish.

Until a few years ago there weren't more than perhaps a dozen standard patterns which were designed for salt-water use. But as fly rodding grew in popularity on the salt-water scene it was inevitable that thousands of amateur fly casters would create patterns to suit their particular bait conditions, or which they felt would do a better job of fooling a wary gamefish.

Were we to say there are several hundred patterns in use today we'd be conservative. But many proficient salt-water flyrodders carry a limited number of proven patterns, leaving their packed fly boxes more for show and conversation than for practical use.

Indeed, we recall an interesting chat with one of this country's finest fly casters, who confided that all he needed to catch any salt-water fish was a white fly tied on a size 1/0 hook, with the body dressed with a small amount of chenille and a sparse amount of bucktail.

Starter Set

For a novice salt-water fly caster we'd recommend a limited number of patterns as a basic set. While every flyrodder naturally expands his collection of bucktails and streamers, as well as the effective popping bugs, if you stick with the following basic starter set you should be able to catch almost any salt-water fish in the sea.

First on the list should be a selection of Blonde Bucktails. This highly effective fly has grown to be the standard of the salt-water flyrodder, for it has accounted for a great many fine record fish. For several years we used the Honey Blonde almost exclusively, but have since employed the Strawberry Blonde and Platinum Blonde patterns with good results. It's wise to carry a selection with you that are tied on size 1/0, 2/0 and 3/0 tinned or stainless steel hooks. The Blonde Bucktail group was originated by noted angler-author Joe Brooks and it is one of the truly fine salt-water flies.

That sparsely tied bucktail we discussed earlier as being useful in catching any salt-water fish is called a Bonefish Bucktail by most fly casters. The fly may be easily cast in a strong wind due to its small size, and it works extremely well in shallow waters. Of white, yellow, or blue and white bucktail, it is usually tied on size 1/0 hooks for best results.

An easy fly to see when retrieving, and one which breathes as it is stripped in, is the Multi-Wing Streamer. It has long saddle hackles, making it a big fly, which is very useful when out after big

The beautiful tarpon about to be released here was estimated to weigh over 100 pounds. The happy angler landed it in the Florida Keys.

dolphin, tarpon and other salt-water heavyweights. It is usually tied on a 1/o or 2/o hook, and has a small plastic head with painted eyes, which makes it closely resemble a small baitfish. The Multi-Wing Streamer is tied in every color combination imaginable. By including red and white, red and yellow, and blue and white patterns in your set you'll be well equipped for any whims of salt-water scrappers.

Include Popping Bug

Included in the starter set of the salt-water flyrodder should be several good popping bugs. Most of the better salt-water poppers are made of either balsa wood or cork, although many good models are made of tenite plastic as well.

These may be painted to resemble a small baitfish, although we've used a solid white model with a red head with good results—and it doesn't look like any baitfish we've ever seen. It's good to carry two sizes with you, one long popper and the other short. The primary purpose of the flyrodder's popping bug is to make a surface disturbance which attracts gamefish, so select models which float well and cause the water to gurgle and sputter as they're retrieved.

The tail of the popper may be dressed with either bucktail or a sparse tie of feathers. The body of the popper is in itself difficult to cast with a fly rod, so don't use poppers with a heavy bucktail or feather skirt.

With a selection such as this we honestly feel you can stand up with the best fly-rod fishermen on the coasts and catch your share of fish while casting from a boat. Remember that often it is not the lure, but the accurate presentation and the skillful retrieve that brings strikes from husky gamefish in this ultimate of salt-water sports.

Helpful Accessories

So far we've discussed only the three basic components of fishing tackle used by boat fishermen, namely the rod, reel and line. The angler who fishes from a boat will find that there are a number of additional accessories which will be useful while on the water, and which will add to his comfort and fishing pleasure.

If you fish from your own boat or with a friend, you'll find that

Herb Schoenberg just brought aboard this big dolphin landed by June Rosko while trolling at the tip of the Tongue of the Ocean in the Bahamas. She fought the big dolphin with the aid of a rod belt, which held the rod securely during the lengthy battle.

almost all of the accessories we discuss here should be included as part of your personal equipment. If, however, you do most of your fishing from charter or party boats, then it will not be necessary to include a net, gaff, billy or other items which would normally be included in the craft's tackle locker.

ROD BELT

A rod belt is one of the most useful accessories used by a boatman, whether he fishes inshore with light casting tackle, or far beyond sight of land.

The most popular general-purpose rod belt is made of top-quality leather and is designed like an apron, with leather belting attached to each end and a sturdy buckle to hold it securely. In the center of the apron there is a large cup which accommodates the butt section of your rod. To give added stiffness to the apron, some manufacturers line it with a piece of metal placed between the outer surfaces of leather. This results in maximum protection for your stomach and prevents serious injury or bruises which can easily be caused should you attempt to fight a big fish without wearing a rod belt.

The general-purpose belt is the most popular, but it cannot hold the slotted gimbal of a regulation-class type rod securely. So if the greatest amount of your fishing is with rods having a slotted gimbal, then it is best to obtain a rod belt which can accommodate it. There are several styles available, almost all of which are comfortable and provide the needed protection for your stomach area. The advantage of a rod belt with a gimbal is that when the slotted gimbal is seated the rod cannot be twisted.

Look for a rod belt where the gimbal points upward at approximately a 45-degree angle, and which has a wide mouth into which the slotted gimbal can be slipped with ease.

Most of the better quality rod belts are well cushioned for maximum protection.

SHOULDER HARNESS

When either trolling or chumming for big offshore species a shoulder harness is extremely helpful, for it relieves the angler of the task of holding the weight of his outfit with his hands alone. The shoulder harness permits the weight of the rod, reel and line to be distributed to the shoulders and back. It also brings the strength of the back and shoulders into play while pumping a big fish.

A harness may be used while fighting a fish from a fighting chair equipped with a gimbal. It may also be used in conjunction with a

A shoulder harness such as this takes the pressure off your arms when fighting a fish for a long period of time. All the straps can be adjusted to an individual's frame so as to insure comfort while playing big fish.

rod belt that is fitted with a gimbal for situations where you wish to fight your fish standing up.

The most basic shoulder harness is nothing more than a pair of heavy leather or web straps which cross behind your back and come around your arms. To these are joined a pair of rings, onto which are fastened a pair of straps. On the end of each strap is a heavy-duty brass or stainless steel snap, which fasten onto the harness lugs on the tops of reels of 4/o size and larger.

One of the most comfortable shoulder harnesses to use is the vest type. It is made to fit much like a vest, with a solid leather or canvas back that distributes the strain across the entire upper portion of your back and shoulders. On this type of harness, all leather straps are adjustable for maximum comfort and positioning of the rod and reel while fighting a fish.

A shoulder harness of this type is particularly useful when you consistently encounter fish weighing over 50 pounds, especially when you fish for them with light tackle. It is practical with large school bluefin tuna, yellowfin tuna, wahoo, amberjack and other deep-sea fighting fish that usually require long periods of time to land.

LANDING NET

Almost any boat fisherman you're apt to speak with will recall a honey of a fish that was finning alongside, spent and ready to be brought aboard. But how to do it? For the net had been left ashore, or the boatman just didn't feel one would be necessary. Trying to lift the lunker aboard resulted in the leader breaking or the hook pulling out.

A landing net is a must for every angler that fishes from a small boat, especially those who do their fishing in sheltered waters. Although you may never expect to catch a lunker, there are often occasions when a big sea trout just happens to inhale your shrimp offering, or a husky striper engulfs your tiny fly which had been intended for smaller game. Lifting any big fish aboard invites disaster, for when using light tackle the test of the leader or the hooks is often less than the weight of the fish. Attempting to lift the dead weight aboard will often result in losing the fish.

Even with species that don't weigh much, it is best to net them. The weakfish, for example, has a tender mouth which rips easily, often resulting in a loss. Fish such as flounder often thrash wildly as you bring them to the surface and start to swing them aboard, resulting in their getting the leverage of their broad, flat bodies against the water, which often pulls the hook free.

A good landing net for use in salt water should be of very heavy construction, able to lift aboard fish up to 20 pounds without fear of the frame of the net bending at the handle. The frame of the net should be approximately 20 or 22 inches wide, and the bag should be approximately 30 inches deep. The bag should be made of nylon mesh, as this is far more durable in salt water than cotton.

The length of the handle will depend on the size of the boat you fish from. In a small outboard boat you may get by with a four-foot handle, but on a big inboard boat a handle five or six feet long is more convenient. Remember that you should be able to lead the fish alongside and net it with ease. Using too short a handle on a landing net results in your having to bend too far over the side to net a fish, which is not only uncomfortable, but dangerous.

A landing net is a must in landing tough gamefish, especially when using light tackle and particularly if the fish is to be released. Here Pete Perinchief lifts a big Bermuda bonefish into his waiting net as the author watches. Moments later the bonefish was unhooked and released to fight another day.

Gene Grimes gaffs a nice sand bass for the author while fishing off Newport Beach, California. Note the length of the gaff, which permits the gaffer to reach the fish to be gaffed with little effort.

GAFF

While tussling with big gamefish at boatside, fishermen have found a gaff to be the most useful tool in bringing them aboard. A gaff is actually nothing more than a big, sharp hook on the end of a long handle. When the fish is brought alongside, the angler lifts the gaff into the fish or with a chopping motion slams it into the fish, quickly swinging it aboard once the fish is gaffed.

Construction must be of the best quality materials. Remember that a tremendous amount of pressure is brought to bear on the entire gaff when it is slammed into 50 or more pounds of twisting, thrashing gamefish. Select gaffs with quality hardwood handles or with strong anodized aluminum handles. The gaff hook should be strong, and recently most boatmen have come to favor stainless steel, for it never rusts. The gaff hook should be securely fastened to the handle with either stainless steel wire or strong line wound to keep the hook firmly in place.

Many gaffs have the handle wound with heavy cord where you grasp it. This gives a slip-proof hold, which is important. For a big fish can rip a slippery, wet gaff from your hand with ease as it lunges to gain its freedom.

As with nets, it is important that the gaff have a handle length that doesn't require you to bend over too far. A gaff we've found to our liking for almost all inshore and offshore situations has a handle measuring 48 inches in length, with a sturdy three-inch gaff hook. When properly used it will bring aboard all the species covered in this book.

UNHOOKER

There are many devices on the market today for unhooking fish. Some are slipped around the leader and pushed down into the fish's mouth to get at the hook. While these unhooking devices work, by far the best device we've seen for this operation is one which closely resembles a pair of long pliers with a pistol-grip handle. Such an unhooker can extend fully six or eight inches into a fish's tooth-filled mouth, grasp the hook or lure with the plier-like

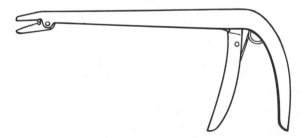

Of the many unhooking devices in the market, this type is by far the most popular with salt-water anglers. The jaws of the unhooker are activated by the pistol grip, which permits you to reach into a fish's toothy mouth and extract your hook with little effort and no fear of getting your finger bitten.

grippers and work it free. While you are working with them, your hand is holding the pistol grip of the unhooker, far from the snapping jaws and sharp teeth.

A small item like this costs only a couple of dollars, but it's worth many times that amount in the cuts, scratches and possible infections it saves you from.

Unlike many types of unhooking devices, the type we use and recommend may be used with either single hooks or lures with fine results.

BILLY

It might sound like the days of sailing ships when a billy was kept close at hand to quiet a drunken seaman, but today too the billy has a place on a boat. Many a big fish when brought aboard is wild, shaking furiously and practically beating you to pieces as

Stan Gibbs uses a billy to quiet a thrashing bluefish he hooked while casting a popping plug in the water of Nantucket Sound off Massachusetts. Only once the fish has been quieted with a couple of taps from the billy does Stan attempt to remove the hooks from the tooth-filled jaws of the bluefish.

you try to wrestle it into the fish box. The solution to this problem is to employ a billy to quiet the fish down. One or two sharp blows with it will settle even the greenest fish.

The billy, or club, doesn't have to be anything elaborate. It should be made of hardwood such as hickory, and measure anywhere from 12 to 18 inches in length, with a diameter of one and a half to two inches. Some are shaped like a baseball bat, while others have a plastic form-fitting handle for a secure grip. There are even some with a hole drilled in the head, into which lead is poured, and then smoothed off. A single blow with such a formidable billy immediately quiets down the wildest gamefish, permitting you to handle it with ease.

SIDE-CUTTING PLIERS

A pair of side-cutting pliers has many uses on a fishing boat. They are most often used for routine holding and cutting chores, such as cutting wire or bending the hook of a plug back into place. Occasionally they may be called upon to push a hook back out of a finger where it became imbedded, and then used to cut off the point and barb so that the hook can be backed out of the flesh.

While almost any pliers may be used for most chores, one can well understand that it requires a sturdy pair to cut through a strong hook should you or someone aboard have the misfortune of becoming hooked. Accordingly it is wise to obtain a pair of strong six and a half inch side-cutting pliers, for only with a heavy-duty pair can you expect to cut through a large-size hook.

Select a pair having a chromed finish, or any other rust resistant finish, as ordinary pliers will quickly rust when exposed to salt water.

Several manufacturers produce handy small leather holsters which fit on your belt, where the pliers slide in easily and are always ready on your hip when you need them.

KNIFE

During the course of a day's fishing a knife is called upon to do a variety of jobs. It starts off the day being used to cut bait, then it may be used to cut the hooks out of fish, and back at dockside it is used to clean the catch. In every instance a razor-sharp knife makes the job more easily done.

Much to the salt-water angler's delight, there are today many high-quality stainless steel knives on the market. These withstand the onslaughts of salt water remarkably well. Unlike the stainless steels of years ago, the newer types hold an edge extremely well.

A knife I've found much to my liking measures ten inches over-all, with a gently curving semi-hollow-ground flexible blade, which makes it ideal for filleting. On the top of the blade there is a scaler edge for those occasions when you want to scale your catch. It has a strong, smooth handle which is impervious to salt water. The knife comes in a leather sheath which totally encloses it, thus preventing damage to the knife or serious injury which could occur were it not sheathed in a tackle kit or locker.

As important as the knife is a honing kit, which should be regularly utilized to keep the knife sharp. Most honing kits come equipped with one coarse cutting stone and one finish stone for a final razor edge. A can of oil is supplied with most honing kits, and should be used on the stones to insure a fine edge.

Remember to keep your knife sharp at all times. A sharp knife is safer than a dull one because it cuts easily where you want it to.

GLOVES

Gloves may seem like an insignificant item to mention. Initially many newcomers to the salt-water fishing scene seem to think that they're not really necessary. Well, we'd guess they're not really, not if you don't mind getting your hands cut while handling a leader wire with a wild fish on the end of it, or while attempting to hold a fish by the gills to remove a hook.

There's no need to get expensive gloves for a fishing boat. The first time you use them they're apt to get slimy, bloody and maybe even ripped. So just buy the cheapest cotton work gloves available. Most coastal marinas keep them in stock.

Once you have them aboard, make a habit of using them. They should always be worn when handling a fish on a leader wire close to the boat, while gaffing fish, and most certainly when holding a fish by the gills to unhook it. Almost all fish have sharp gill covers and equally sharp gills. Many have sharp teeth too.

SUNGLASSES

Regardless of whether you do your fishing in the North or South, inshore or well out to sea, you're certain to encounter a strong sun at times.

There are many types of sunglasses on the market, ranging in price from extremely economical to very expensive. Price alone does not necessarily determine the quality, for much of the price is determined by styling.

Over the years we've tried many different types of glasses and have found that ones with Polaroid lenses are the most effective glasses for the fisherman. Glasses of this type screen out reflected glare by polarization. Because of this they not only prevent eye strain, but enable you to see fish in the water that might not otherwise be seen. They are especially useful in tropical climates when fishing on the flats for bonefish, where spotting the quarry before casting to it is of paramount importance.

Although some anglers wear a safety line on their sunglasses so they don't fall off, there are many models which hook around the ears and cannot fall off. For maximum eye protection from the sun, make certain the lenses are of a size that completely blocks out the glare.

SUNTAN LOTION

A tube of suntan oil or lotion takes a tiny amount of room in the tackle box, yet it is surprising how few angler boatmen carry it with them. Usually they make the mistake only once, for after having experienced a bad sunburn, they're certain to carry it in the future.

It is particularly wise to use a liberal amount of suntan lotion early in the season, especially if your body hasn't been exposed to the sun for several months. Remember that while on the water you not only have the direct sunlight to contend with, but also the glare off the water. You'll burn up quickly if you don't take a few moments to apply plenty of oil or lotion.

Anglers who may be heading to southern climates for the first time and plan to do a lot of fishing on boats should be especially careful. We've seen people burned severely in a matter of just a couple of hours in the Bahamas. So don't try to get a lifeguard tan in one day, but expose your body to slow doses of sun, with plenty of lotion at all times.

STORM SUIT

Practically everyone who's done a lot of fishing can well recall leaving dockside on a beautiful summer morning with bright sun and not a cloud in the sky. Shortly after noon the wind comes up and the sky fills with clouds, and shortly thereafter the sky opens up and a torrential downpour rained out an otherwise perfect day.

Admittedly, nothing spoils a day's fishing like a rain squall. But if you're equipped for it with a storm suit, then things aren't half bad, for you can continue to fish, yet stay dry and comfortable.

Thanks to modern synthetics such as nylon and Dacron, storm suits are now made of lightweight material, and do a fine job of keeping you dry in even the worst downpour. Another advantage of the synthetics is that they can be folded up into a small package barely the size of a cigar box, which takes hardly any room, yet is well worth the room it does take when a storm is suddenly upon you.

While the prime advantage of a storm suit is to keep you dry, you'll find it is comfortable to wear when the weather suddenly turns chilly, or an unexpected wind develops.

Most storm suits are of two-piece construction. The pants are either of a bib type or of the drawstring variety. The parkas are usually hooded and come in either regular or extra-long lengths. The longer parkas are best, as they keep the wind from blowing water in underneath.

We never leave dockside without our storm suit, and recommend you develop the same habit too.

HEAD LAMP

When you fish from big boats at night there is usually ample illumination, especially on party and charter boats and big offshore sportsfishermen. But if you do your night fishing from a small boat you may not have anything more than your running lights. Many boatmen employ regular flashlights, but this can become a handicap, for there are times when you'd like to use two hands to complete whatever you may be doing.

For situations such as this we've found a miner's type headlamp to be ideal. Most headlamps receive their power from four size D dry-cell batteries or one lantern-size dry-cell battery. In either case they give a fair amount of illumination to the scene and permit you to work with your hands free. While the lights are designed to be worn around your forehead, most anglers slip the elastic headband around their necks, which works out extremely well.

The technique of deep jigging, employing either spinning tackle or conventional casting tackle, has gained in popularity during recent years, with the heavy bucktail jigs—some with a sparse dressing of Mylar— readily bringing strikes from bottom feeders and gamefish on all coasts.

3 Trolling

OF the many different techniques which a boatman may employ to catch gamefish, trolling ranks among the most exciting and most productive. By trolling along the coast, a boatman may cover mile upon mile of productive water in a single day's fishing. The greater the area covered, the more apt he is to score.

On the surface, trolling seems to be a very simple technique to master. It appears that all you do is let your lures out behind the boat and tow them around, waiting for a fish to strike. But trolling varies considerably from towing. To tow something behind a boat requires no skill. But to troll does require skill—to attract fish from the depths to your lures, to cause a lure to swim in a lifelike manner, and to tell you when you should speed up your motor to get strikes from a roving school swimming just below the surface.

Offshore Trolling

There is a marked difference between the trolling which is commonly referred to as offshore trolling, and trolling close to shore or in the protected reaches of bays, rivers and estuaries.

For purposes of this chapter we'll distinguish between the two by first discussing offshore trolling, which in some sectors is refered to as blue-water trolling. This will deal with the pelagic species, among which are our finest gamefish, the status symbols of the trolling fraternity. The smaller billfishes, the tunas, bonito, mackerel, the fighting jacks, dolphin and a host of other species which call the waters far from shore their home are the targets of the offshore set.

The wahoo is one of the greatest gamefish found in the coastal waters of the U.S. June Rosko landed the beauty being held here by Herb Schoenberg while trolling over 50 miles at sea off Ocean City, Maryland. It was taken on regulation 30-pound class tackle and a balao skip bait.

These party-boat anglers sailed aboard the New Lo-An *out of San Diego, California, and are trolling for albacore. Once an albacore is hooked on the trolled lines the engines are quickly shut down, and chumming with live anchovies commences from the live-bait tanks pictured in the foreground.*

TACKLE

Regulation-class tackle was designed expressly for offshore trolling. Those boatmen who may not have this specific type of equipment aboard may, for the medium-sized pelagic species, bring a basic boat outfit into use with satisfactory results.

Terminal Tackle

In our discussion of terminal tackle for offshore trolling, we'll begin with threading your line through the guides, and then step by step, cover each piece of gear required, including lures and baits, before proceeding into actual trolling techniques.

Before even a single piece of terminal tackle is attached to the line, many anglers prefer to double back anywhere from 10 to a maximum of 15 feet of line. This is accomplished by using a knot commonly referred to as a Bimini bend. It is a strong knot which doesn't slip or cut into itself.

There are a number of reasons anglers prefer a double line. Once an angler reels the double line onto his reel he has in effect almost twice the line strength that he would with a single line. This is particularly useful when a tough fighter puts up a wild struggle at the boat. Also, the terminal end of a line naturally gets the greatest amount of wear, just from periodically being reeled in, if nothing else. Thus the double line is as much an insurance factor than anything else.

Ball-Bearing Swivel

There are a great many different types of swivels which may be tied to the end of the double line. The purpose of a swivel is to prevent the line from twisting, even though a lure or bait may be twisting or spinning in the water. If the swivel is to perform properly, it must prevent line twist regardless of whether you're trolling a tiny spoon or a heavy mullet that may weigh half a pound or more.

The finest swivels we've ever used for this purpose are ball-bearing swivels. They have positive swiveling action, and your line will never twist when using them. They come in a wide variety of sizes, and while they are somewhat more expensive than other types of swivels, they're the best investment you can make, for they'll save you many times their cost in ruined lines.

The size 4 swivel has a breaking test of 100 pounds, while the size 3 swivel tests out at 80 pounds. Both are very small and extremely strong, being more than adequate for most offshore trolling situations where light or medium tackle is employed.

Select those ball-bearing swivels which come equipped with a coastlock snap, as this facilitates changing leaders and is one of the strongest snaps made.

If ball-bearing swivels aren't available, key-chain type swivels or barrel swivels may be used. With both, we'd recommend sticking to those which test out for 100-pound breaking strain and which are equipped with a coastlock snap.

Attach with Clinch Knot

Some anglers simply slip the swivel onto the loop of the double line. But this method is not recommended, for with a loop of this type there is a cutting action, where the line can actually cut through itself when under pressure.

By far the best way of attaching the swivel is with a clinch knot. The end of the double line is simply run through the eye of the swivel, and the clinch knot is tied, giving a very strong connection.

It is important that a good swivel always be used to join your line with your leader, to prevent a twisting or spinning lure from twisting your line. The ball-bearing-type swivel with coastlock snap pictured here is by far the finest swivel obtainable, for it has perfect swiveling action, thus assuring trouble-free trolling with most any lure or bait.

The Bimini bend is popular among boatmen, who find it an ideal way of doubling their line without weakening it appreciably. It may be used with almost any line, such as Dacron, braided nylon or monofilament.

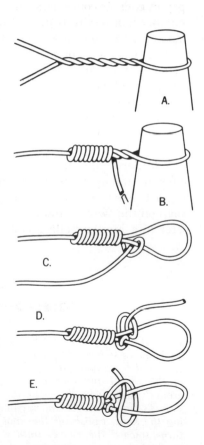

A. Allow yourself as much line as you wish to double back, and place the looped end around some fixed object such as a cleat or reel handle. Take around six turns to the line, keeping tension on the line and the turns tight.

B. While holding the coils tight with your hand, wrap the free line over the first twists. Keep the coils close together and use as many as you need until you come up to the "V" of the loop. In making a long double line, you would have to pull the "V" up toward the end where the line was being twisted.

C. While still holding the twisted line tight with your thumb and forefinger, take a half hitch around one side of the loop and pull it up tight.

D. Next take a half hitch around the other side of the loop and pull it up tight also.

E. Finish off the Bimini bend by taking a half hitch around the base of the loop and neatly clip off any excess line.

LEADERS

The leaders used most frequently by offshore trollers are made of stainless steel wire, nylon monofilament, stainless steel cable, or stainless steel cable coated with nylon.

By far the most popular are stainless-steel wire and nylon monofilament. Both materials are economical and easy to work with, which accounts for their popularity.

Stainless Steel Wire

Stainless steel leader wire is available in 25-foot coils, and quarter-pound coils. It comes in a great many sizes, but for offshore trolling number 8 or 9 wire is ideal. Number 8 wire has a diameter of .020 inch and tests out at 86 pounds, while number 9 wire is .022 inch with a test of approximately 104 pounds. Because of their fine diameter they are very easy to work with, and in the new pre-straightened types, which are torsion-straightened while being manufactured, there is little chance of kinking.

Select wire which has coffee-colored or dull coating. The dull color reduces visibility and is far superior to wires with a bright silvery color.

A leader length of approximately ten feet is a good average for offshore trolling. Many boatmen cut up several dozen lengths, making a twisted loop at one end (which is attached to the coastlock snap on the swivel) and leaving the other end plain, to be attached later to a lure or trolling bait.

The improved clinch knot is strong and very easy to tie, ideal for joining your line to swivels, or leaders to swivels, snaps and other terminal tackle. It is tied by running about three or four inches of line through the eye of the swivel and then doubling it back and taking at least six turns around itself. You then put the end through the opening next to the swivel's eye. Then the end is run through the big loop formed while making the knot. Finish off the knot by pulling on the end and sliding the turns toward the swivel until it comes up tight. Clip off any excess, leaving about a quarter inch of line or leader extending.

Although some anglers use a 15-foot leader while billfishing, because of the extreme length of these species, it isn't necessary for the smaller pelagic species. Bear in mind that if you're fishing for species other than billfish and employing 15-foot leader, you'll have to handline the wire the last 15 feet in order to gaff the fish or swing it aboard.

Because billfish do not have teeth with which to bite through leader material, many anglers now employ nylon monofilament leaders in preference to wire when trolling for them. Much the same holds true for other pelagic species which do not have teeth. But for sharp-toothed adversaries such as wahoo, king mackerel, barracuda, sharks and other residents on the offshore scene, stainless steel leader wire is a must.

Nylon Leaders

The one distinct advantage of nylon monofilament leaders over wire is that nylon leaders are almost invisible in the water—a distinct advantage when seeking wary gamefish.

Remember that a leader takes a lot more abuse than the line to which it is attached. Therefore, while using a line testing out at 20 or 30 pounds, it is altogether proper to fish with a leader of nylon monofilament that tests anywhere from 50 to 75 pounds. Heavy tests such as this are less apt to be cut by sharp gill covers, fins or the scales of a fish as it twists, jumps and fights to get away.

There are several ways in which the nylon leader may be fastened to the swivel and coastlock snap. Some trollers simply use a clinch

It is rather easy to form a loop or eye in a piece of stainless-steel leader wire. First you make a loop and hold it firmly between the thumb and index finger of one hand. Next you take the thumb and index finger of your other hand and evenly twist the wire around itself at least three times. Then make three or four turns with the short end of the wire neatly around the standing part of the wire. The excess wire should not be cut off. Simply bend the wire back and forth until it snaps off cleanly. When done in this manner the break is clean and close and you won't rip your fingers while handling the leader wire.

knot, which makes a permanent fastening. This, however, can be inconvenient at times, especially when you want to change lures.

The next best bet is to use an improved end-loop knot on the end of each leader; this can be slipped onto the coastlock snap with ease. The improved end-loop knot, incidentally, is the best knot to use for an end loop, as it is by far the strongest.

In some areas, particularly on the West Coast, stainless steel cable leaders, often covered with nylon, are popular with many boatmen. But these require sleeves or the fusing of nylon in order to make, and they are by no means as popular as the materials discussed earlier.

A word of caution regarding any leader material. Remember that your lure is attached directly to the leader, preferably without a clip or snap. Should you use too heavy a leader wire, or an extremely heavy-test nylon monofilament, it could and often does detract from the action of your lure, particularly the smaller lures.

Snaps and Clips

Some lures are so designed that they may readily be attached to a leader with a clip or snap, which makes it convenient to change lures quickly. However, on the offshore scene you're often

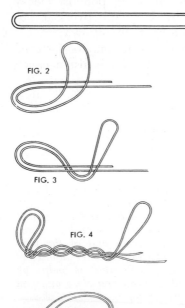

FIG. 1

FIG. 2

FIG. 3

FIG. 4

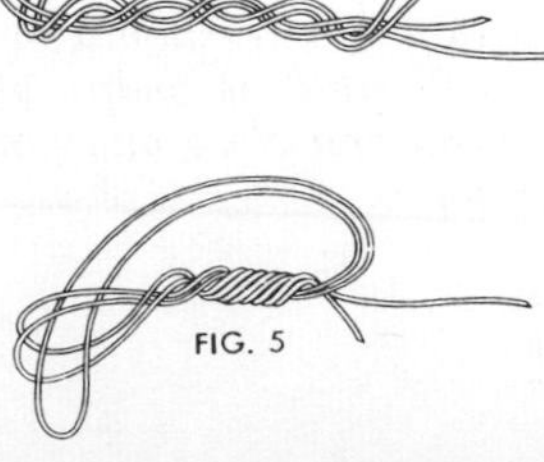

FIG. 5

The Improved End Loop is the strongest loop knot you can employ while using monofilament leaders. A nice feature of it is that it's very easy to tie:
1. First bend over the strand of monofilament about four to six inches from the end so that you have a "U" as shown.
2, 3, & 4. Then bend the "U" backward and around itself at least three to five times, depending on the thickness of the line.
5. Next, insert the end of the "U" bend through the first loop made by its backward turn and pull the knot up tight. By pulling the knot up slowly and smoothly you'll have a strong, neat knot.

Bob Stankus gaffed this big African pompano for the author while fishing off the Berry Islands in the Bahamas. The 26-pound heavyweight was taken on light regulation-class tackle, and one can well understand that all of the knots in the leader and line had to be at full strength during the half hour required to bring in the gladiator.

tussling with very tough, heavy fish that have a great deal of power. Because of this it is best to keep terminal tackle to a minimum. We much prefer to make direct connections, using a pair of side cutters to remove a lure and then twisting or tying on a new lure.

If you're fishing for smaller fish and like the convenience of changing lures quickly, then we'd recommend you use stainless steel clips or snaps only. Use those types which lock or have a interlocking safety snap to prevent their opening. The single-wire dual snap, which locks around itself, is a fine snap which is small in size yet extremely strong.

DEEP-TROLLING AIDS

There will be occasions when you may want to add weight to your line to take lures down to deeper levels or to keep them from skipping out of the water at fast trolling speeds. There are a number of ways in which this can be accomplished, among them the use of wire or lead-core line, although these are seldom employed with regulation-class tackle. The other alternatives are to use either trolling sinkers or planers.

Trolling Sinkers

By far the most popular sinker in use today to get trolled lures to various depths is the torpedo-shaped trolling sinker. These come in a wide variety of sizes, and for the practical use of the offshore troller it is wise to include one-ounce, two-ounce, three-ounce, four-ounce, and six-ounce sizes in the tackle locker. Weights heavier than this would be impractical to troll with light tackle. By far the most used weights are the two-ounce, three-ounce, and four-ounce models, which are used primarily to take the lures just below the surface, and to keep such lures as spoons and metal flashers from leaping out of the water.

Trolling sinkers usually come equipped with a swivel at one end and a snap at the other. Make certain the hardware on the sinkers is of high quality and made of rustproof material, preferably stainless

Of the many types of snaps and clips on the market, this stainless-steel single-wire dual snap, which locks around itself, is the strongest and most dependable. When used with a lure it is inconspicuous too.

The torpedo-shaped trolling sinker is the most popular sinker used by trollers, both inshore and offshore, to take their lures deep.

steel, for this becomes a connection between you and the fish, and any inferior quality here can mean a lost fish.

The trolling sinkers are attached directly to the coastlock snap and swivel combination on the end of your line. Then the leader is attached to the snap on the trolling sinker. In this way the trolling sinker is far removed from the lure, not visible to the fish and not affecting the lure's action.

Here, as with the case of leader wire, use dull-finished trolling sinkers. When they are new the lead is usually shiny, but after use in salt water it becomes dull, which is a good thing. There have been many instances where a gamefish has struck at a shiny new trolling sinker as it was trolled through the water, often severing the line with its teeth. This happens frequently in southern waters, where almost all gamefish have a wicked set of dentures and strike at almost everything that is shiny.

Keel-Shaped Sinkers

Several companies manufacture trolling sinkers which are keel shaped. These are intended for use with lures that tend to spin a lot. The theory is that the keel prevents the lure from twisting the line. But, as stated earlier, a ball-bearing swivel will do a good job of keeping any lure from twisting a line.

Deep-Trolling Planers

If you really want to send a lure down deep, use a planer, which is attached to your line much like a trolling sinker. This is a trolling device designed to plane your lure to a desired depth. There are a number of models on the market, some made of stainless steel and others of plastic.

Planers have adjustable arms which enable them to travel to various levels. They put a tremendous amount of pressure against your line as they dive for the depths. But they do get deep.

Most planers have a tripping device which releases the pressure against the line once a fish is hooked, permitting you to fight the fish directly, without undue pressure from the planer.

Underwater Outrigger

Still another method of getting a lure deep is to employ an under-water outrigger. This is actually nothing more than an ordinary planer, as described earlier, which, instead of being attached to the line above the leader, is tied to a heavy piece of handline, which is in turn tied to a cleat at the stern of the boat. To the planer is attached a snap-type clothespin by way of a short piece of line.

Your line is snapped into the clothespin, and both line and handline are eased out together. Once a fish strikes your lure, taken deep by the planer, it snaps out of the clothespin, and you don't have to contend with the bulky planer on the line. In many areas this rig, and several similar variations, is called a deep-diving outrigger.

TROLLING LURES

Within the wide general category of trolling lures come some which can be used only for trolling and others which may be employed for casting and jigging as well. There are literally thousands of different trolling lures, but we will include only those which, because of their long use and proven ability, are regarded as standard among boatmen on all our coasts.

Trolling Feathers

The first trolling feather we ever used, over a score of years ago, was popularly referred to as a Japanese trolling feather, because that's where it came from. Today these fine lures are made locally as well as imported. It is perhaps one of the most basic lure types, and one of the easiest to use to catch gamefish. The greatest majority are made with a torpedo-shaped head, roughly twice as long as it is wide. In the center of the head is a small hole, through which the leader passes. Molded into the lead head, which is either chrome-plated or nickel-plated, are a pair of eyes. Some are made of glass; others are imitation mother-of-pearl, plastic or a variety of other sparkling materials.

Molded as part of the head is a shoulder, onto which are tied a large number of feathers. Next a plastic or oilcloth-like skirt is tied to the head, folding over the feathers and covering the bulky tie. This makes a streamlined lure which closely resembles a small baitfish when it is drawn through the water.

The trolling feathers are rigged by running the leader wire or nylon leader directly through the hole in the head and attaching your hook. When pulled up tight, the hook is drawn firmly against the head, with the bulk of the hook concealed in the feathers.

Trolling feathers come in a great many sizes and an equally great
number of colors. In the main, however, trollers enjoy best results
while using heads weighing from a half-ounce to three ounces. On
some heads there are long feathers, while others have short feathers;
it is a good idea to have a supply of several sizes.

In the many spots we've sailed from, plain white feathers ap-

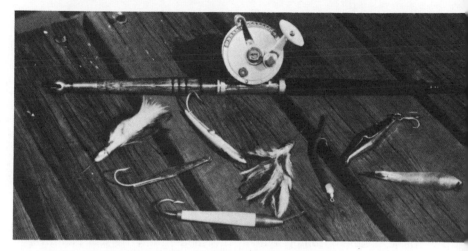

*Pictured here with a regulation 50-pound class outfit is a selection of
lures favored by offshore trollers. Included are, left to right: Japanese
trolling feather, chromed spoon, cedar jig, bone squid, Japanese trolling
feather in tandem, surgical tube lure, chromed jig and stainless-steel
spoon.*

*The Atlantic bonito is a formidable adversary on light trolling tackle.
This husky specimen was landed off the Carolina Outer Banks on a
Japanese trolling feather.*

peared to be most popular, with a red-and-white combination next. We've experienced times when tuna would strike only a black-and-white combination, and dolphin wouldn't look at anything but solid blue. We've made good catches on green and yellow and on solid black, too, so it's best to keep a good variety of colors and head sizes in your tackle locker.

Various Trolling Heads

You can well understand that tackle designers just won't leave a good thing alone, so there are many variations of the basic trolling head on the market. Instead of feathers, some are dressed with long nylon fibers, a few of which measure a foot or more in length. Other heads are dressed with plastic skirts encompassing every color in the rainbow.

One trolling head which gained popularity on the West Coast and which we subsequently tried on the East Coast and in the Bahamas consists of an aluminum trolling head with a scooped-out effect at the top of the head, giving it a wobbling action. Immediately behind the aluminum head comes a second head of molded plastic. Onto the plastic head are attached plastic skirts of various colors, over which is attached a metallic skirt. An offshoot of the basic Japanese trolling feather, this modern-day rig will take everything from amberjack to striped marlin, for it comes in a wide range of sizes, all of which work extremely well when trolled.

Forged O'Shaughnessy Hook Best

Before proceeding onto other lures, we'd like to make several recommendations as to hooks, for many of the lures, particularly those with feathers, require you to rig them with a hook of your own.

A good hook style that has served anglers well along all coasts is the O'Shaughnessy forged hook. This is a strong, fine quality hook, which is available in tinned models, as well as the new stainless steel models being offered by several prominent manufacturers.

A universally favored size, which we'd say you couldn't go wrong with, whether trolling for little tuna, white marlin, dolphin or albacore, is 7/0. Some anglers go to an 8/0 size when the fish are running on the heavy side, but on the light tackle you'll be using you should find the 7/0 more than adequate.

For basic rigging a ringed hook should be used. But some trollers like to sneak a pair of O'Shaughnessy hooks onto their lures, rigging in tandem to hook those gamefish which strike short of the primary hook. This is accomplished by using one ringed O'Shaughnessy hook and one needle-eye O'Shaughnessy hook. The needle-eye hook is slipped through the ringed eye of the other hook, and the leader is attached to the needle-eye hook. This results in the ringed hook riding on the curve of the needle-eye hook. The rig is easy to make up and works very well.

Spoons

The darting, twisting, shimmering action of a spoon flashing in the wake of a boat trolling many miles from shore has accounted for the capture of practically every gamefish you can think of at one time or another. Right behind the trolling feathers, it rates as one of the finest tools in the arsenal of the offshore troller.

There are a great many different styles of spoons on the market, but don't let them confuse you, for basically most are alike. The majority are shaped somewhat like a fish, having a tapered head and long, tapered tail. They are made of brass or stainless steel, with the former being either chrome-plated or nickel-plated.

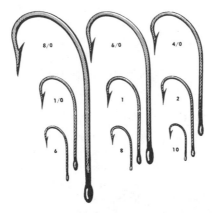

The O'Shaughnessy-style hook is a strong, forged hook favored by most boatmen for use on all trolling lures.

Affixed to the end of the spoon is an O'Shaughnessy-style hook, which is attached to the spoon with a screw, or in some cases with a small nut and bolt.

Because of the curvature of the lure, it becomes necessary to use a larger hook than that used on a trolling feather, and many manufacturers equip their spoons with forged 8/o O'Shaughnessy hooks.

In the main, the preferred spoons used by offshore trollers are between five and seven inches in length. These are popular because they closely resemble in size the many kinds of baitfish on which offshore gamefish feed, including anchovies, butterfish, mackerel, mullet, flying fish and a host of other forage species.

In most spoons the hook is held rigidly, but there are a few where the hook is permitted to swing freely.

Pork Rind Strip Added

The action of a spoon may be enhanced by adding a strip of pork rind to the hook, with white being the preferred color. Some anglers add a tuft of feathers to the hook of the spoon, feeling that the shimmering of the feathers as the spoon works through the water makes it a little more attractive.

One spoon which I've found effective departs from the normal fish shape; it is shaped like an elongated diamond, with each of its sides bent upward.

A word of caution on purchasing spoons, or any lures for that matter. Stick with those made by major manufacturers, for they are likely to be well constructed. You can well imagine the shock that comes to a spoon when a 50-pound school bluefin tuna grabs hold of it. A good hook, screws that won't rust, heavy-gauge metal and quality plating, plus a heavy-duty split ring all add up to a lure that won't let you down.

Surgical Tubes Make a Hot Lure

One of the most unimpressive lures we've ever seen, let alone used, is one which is made of surgical tubing. It is, however, a great trolling lure. It is made of the same tubing used for a variety of purposes in hospitals. The basic surgical-tube lure, or tube lure as it is frequently called, is made by simply cutting a piece of surgical tubing from 4 to 18 inches in length from the spool on which it's dispensed. Taking the somewhat curved section of tubing, you use a

pair of scissors to make a tapered cut about two inches long at the
end of the tubing, cutting along the inside of the natural curve of
the tubing.

The next step is to attach an extra-long-shank 7/o or 8/o
O'Shaughnessy hook to either a nylon or stainless steel wire leader.
After the hook has been attached, slip the tubing onto the leader,
pulling it down over the hook and pulling the hook in firmly where
you made the tapered cut in the tail. This will bring the curve of
the hook in about two inches from the end point of the tubing.

When the tube lure is trolled through the water, water rushes
through the tubing, giving the lure an enticing action that gamefish
just can't seem to resist.

There are many variations of the basic surgical-tube lure which
we've just described. Some anglers rig the tubing on a Japanese
feather trolling head. Others add several brightly colored beads to
the leader just ahead of the tubing. We've observed anglers who
tied several feathers to the hook within the tubing, so that the feathers extended out beyond the tube, thus giving it an enticing action.

Most tubing is a natural amber color. But several manufacturers
have made it available in a variety of colors to accommodate fishermen, including jet black, gray, red and blue.

Tube lures usually work best when trolled at moderate speeds,
and they produce well on both the offshore and inshore trolling
grounds with a wide variety of gamefish.

Wobblers

There is a close similarity between spoons and wobblers; basically
they have the same action. For our purposes let us say that the
spoons have a single hook, which is usually rigid, while the wobblers
have a free-swinging single or treble hook which is attached to the
wobbler with a split ring.

Wobblers in general aren't used too much by the offshore troller,
but there is one model which produced many fine catches along
many sections of seacoast we've visited, so we'll mention it here. It
is approximately six inches in length and has the profile of a fish. Its
top is chrome plated, while its underside is covered with a strip of
plastic. Within the plastic are thousands of tiny sparklers in a wide
variety of colors and patterns. Gamefish go just wild about this
wobbler at times.

Cedar Jigs

The cedar jig is a vintage trolling lure which has changed little with the passage of time. It is constructed of a piece of either light or dark cedar which is turned on a lathe to an approximate diameter of three-quarters of an inch. A hole is drilled through the middle of the four-inch or five-inch piece of cedar and a lead head about an inch and a half long, tapering to a point at the top, is molded to it. Through the center of the lead head is a hole which meets the hole in the wood part of the lure.

The cedar jig is rigged by running a piece of leader material through the lure and attaching a hook to it. The hook is then drawn up into the hole through the center of the cedar jig. Because of the thickness of the lure, most anglers rig it with an 8/0 size O'Shaughnessy hook, as this permits the hook to extend well out from the jig where it can be in a good position to hook a gamefish.

Most trollers use the cedar jig in its natural finish, but boatmen have experimented with various colors, using one with a red head and white body and a solid yellow one. These bring good results, particularly on oceanic bonito, school bluefin tuna and Atlantic bonito.

Bone Squids

Originally bone squids may have been carved from a piece of bone, but today most of them are made from durable plastic. A bone squid closely resembles a spoon in shape and action. The size favored by most offshore trollers is about six inches long by an inch in width, with a depth of about a half inch. The bone squid resembles the hull of a boat, with an 8/0 O'Shaughnessy hook attached to it in a manner similar to that employed with a spoon, and an oversize split ring at its head for attaching your leader.

Most are white or ivory-colored and are used plain, although occasionally anglers add a strip of pork rind.

Jigs

Within the framework of the general-classification jigs we'll include those lures which for the most part are molded of lead and then chrome-plated or nickel-plated, although we must note that several companies now stamp them from stainless steel as well.

While most of the heavy-model jigs, such as the diamond jig, tri-sided jig and the butterfish jig, are not usually used for regular trolling, they do have an application once fish are hooked and are behind the boat in numbers. For while fighting a fish and continuing to troll very slowly, jigs of this type may be worked vigorously to bring strikes from fish which are still behind the boat or following the hooked fish.

There are, however, several models in lighter weights made of aluminum or thin stainless steel stock, which can be trolled with good results.

Some jigs have a rigid single or double hook which is molded right into them, such as the butterfish jig or the Belmar jig. Other models, among them the diamond jig and tri-sided jig, have a free-swinging 3/0 or 4/0 treble hook.

Plastic Lures

During the past few years great numbers of plastic baits have come onto the market. Some are skillfully engineered and work well, while others are a poor imitation of a fish and aren't worth the effort of trolling them.

Most of the better plastic baits are exact reproductions of natural baits on which offshore gamefish feed. You can get mullet, balao, eels, sardines, anchovies, squid and pilchards that look so true to life you'd think they were the real thing.

Some of these baits come with hooks molded right into them; all you have to do is fasten them to your leader. Others have to be rigged in much the same manner as a natural bait, which will soon be discussed.

The plastic baits have a place in the tackle kit of the serious troller. They will take almost all offshore gamefish, including billfish. We recall hooking, and subsequently losing, a beautiful white marlin the very first time we tried a plastic eel, while trolling off Chub Cay in the Bahamas. We do believe that if more anglers tried these fine baits they would make some great catches on them.

NATURAL BAITS

A gamefish will strike at almost any small fish it feels it can catch, including its own young at times. But we'll limit this discussion of

Most billfish are taken on natural baits rigged for trolling. The author landed this big striped marlin while trolling a rigged flying-fish bait off Mexico's Los Coronados Islands. Favored billfish baits on the East and Gulf coasts include balao, rigged eels and mullet.

natural baits to those forage species which gamefish normally feed on, plus the strip bait, which is a trolling bait used along all of our coasts with great success.

There are, of course, hundreds of different ways in which to rig baits for trolling. Each fisherman develops a way that suits his fancy or his particular area. What we'll do is discuss the fundamental methods of rigging natural bait.

Strip Bait Is Popular

A strip bait, the belly cut from a wide variety of fish, is one which you'll find in use no matter where you fish offshore, and inshore as well. Among the most popular are a strip of bonito or tuna, or any one of a variety of species which have a smooth, silvery belly. Many anglers use a strip of fresh squid, or even a large strip of pork rind, which makes a highly effective bait.

If you're trolling for big fish like dolphin, wahoo, sailfish, school tuna and other gamefish up to about 100 pounds, a strip of bait about eight or nine inches long by an inch and a half wide is perfect. Depending on the bait, it may be either an eighth of an inch thick in the case of squid or pork rind, or upwards of a quarter-inch thick if cut from the belly of a fish.

The bait is best cut out on a hardwood board, so that the cut is neat with no frayed edges. The most popular shape is that of a torpedo with a rather blunt head tapering to a point at the tail. Some anglers prefer to cut the bait to the shape of a fish, with a tail effect that will flutter. Both shapes are good.

For a bait of this size a 7/0 or 8/0 O'Shaughnessy forged hook is best. This should be honed needle sharp, so that it will quickly penetrate a fish's jaw. Most chartermen use a small file to sharpen their hooks, and sport fishermen would boat more fish if they did the same.

Attaching Leader

To attach the leader wire to the hook, pass about six inches of wire through the eye of the hook. Then take about four or five turns around the leader, finishing it off by twisting carefully and

This strip bait was cut from the belly of a bonito. It is cut to resemble the shape of a fish, and will flutter enticingly when trolled at moderate speed.

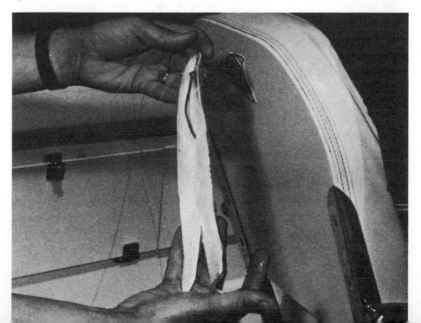

laying the final turns side by side, without overlapping them. This is easily accomplished by holding the wire in your fingers and turning it slowly. Make the final turn so that the remaining four or five inches of wire points upwards in line with the point of the hook.

Next, make a 45-degree bend in this remaining piece of wire about a quarter inch to a half inch from the leader, bending back toward the leader, not toward the hook. Where the wires cross each other you put a small half-turn loop in the short end, giving it a safety-pin effect. The remaining couple of inches of wire may then be cut off.

Next, lay the rig on top of the bait you've cut out. Use a small awl to puncture a hole in the bait right near the head of it. Back where the bend of the hook naturally lies in place on the bait, take your knife and cut a little slit for the hook. Now slide the hook through the slit, so that it lies flat on the rig, and open up the wire snap and slip it through the hole which you made with your awl. Once the bait is slipped onto the wire, slip the small loop around the leader again, and your strip-bait trolling rig is complete.

The strip bait should lie flat and not be bunched up on the hook. Some fishermen rig it so that there is a small ripple between the wire and the hook, but this should be minimal, for with too much flutter the bait will twist and not work properly.

A strip bait rigged in this manner may be used effectively as a skip bait—skipping on the surface—or as a subsurface bait taken deep with the aid of a trolling sinker or planer.

Rigging Baitfish

There are a number of fish which may be rigged for offshore trolling, each of which is often rigged in a somewhat different manner. One of the most popular fish used as a trolling bait is the mullet, and we'll discuss rigging this baitfish, for several other species may be rigged in much the same manner. In addition to the mullet, baits such as sardines, mackerel, flying fish and balao make excellent trolling baits.

One of the easiest ways to rig a mullet, and perhaps the best way for a beginner to start, is simply to run an awl through the mullet's mouth, and bring it out just about the middle of its white underbelly. Then slide the eye of the 7/0 or 8/0 O'Shaughnessy hook through the cavity made by the awl, and run it right up into the mullet's mouth.

Next, take the awl and run it through the mullet's lower jaw, through the eye of the hook inside the mullet's mouth and out the upper jaw. The leader wire is then run through the holes made by the awl and twisted around the standing part of the leader. A piece of soft copper wire is used to fasten the mullet's mouth closed, and the bait is ready to put behind the boat. Some trollers also tie the gills closed, using either dental floss or light line.

Sinkers Can Be Used Too

A variation of this manner of rigging is to place a small egg-shaped sinker onto the leader and to loop the wire outside of the sinker, so that the small quarter-ounce, half-ounce or one-ounce sinker rides against the lower jaw of the baitfish. This is particularly effective with rough water or where you want to keep the bait from skipping about too greatly. It also helps to stabilize the bait as it is trolled through the water.

Backbone Can Be Removed

When using baits measuring eight inches or longer many trollers like to take the backbone out of the mullet, making the bait limber and giving it a more lifelike action in the water. This is easily accomplished with a deboner made expressly for the purpose. The deboner is inserted in the mouth of the bait and slid back to the base of the spine, then it is forced up onto the spine and rotated and pushed down toward the tail, cutting right around the backbone as it is pushed. When you cover the desired amount of backbone you want removed—usually to back near the vent—you simply give a firm sideways push to the deboner, which breaks the backbone. You then slide the deboner out with the backbone right inside the deboner tube.

The bait may then be rigged in much the same manner as we discussed earlier. Some guides prefer to use a two-hook rig, simply fastening a second hook to the bend of the first hook, as discussed earlier under trolling lures. This results in one hook being up forward near the head of the bait, with the second or trailing hook near the tail. Rigging with two hooks is particularly effective with such species as king mackerel and barracuda, which are notorious for their habit of striking a bait short and chopping off the tail. The second hook usually gets them.

Remember that the bait should never ride on the hook, but

should always be held firmly at the head, so that it rides smoothly in the water. The easiest way to secure the bait firmly is with soft copper wire, which is easy to work with and inconspicuous. Some anglers use dental floss, which is very strong, employing a needle to sew the jaws closed and secure them firmly at the head.

Eels Are Good Too

Another extremely popular bait on the offshore scene is the common eel. These may be rigged in the same manner as a mullet, with just a single hook at the head, or it may be rigged with two hooks; one at the head, and a second trailing hook coming out near the vent of the eel. With the latter it is simply a matter of running a piece of heavy line through the eel with the aid of a rigging needle, securing the second hook to it, and tying the line to the eye of the head hook. Here, too, the eel must lie flat in the water to work properly.

Anglers often add a bit of attracter to all of these baits by placing a small Japanese trolling feather or a plastic skirt just ahead of the bait. The flash of color, whether fluorescent, red, orange, blue, green or yellow, is often just what it takes for a great gamefish to wallop it.

In any rigging of natural bait, the fisherman adds the personal touch that makes it work. Only through experience is it possible to rig baits and have them work as well as those rigged by the professional mate in the cockpit of a charter boat.

KITE FISHING PRODUCTIVE

Although most trollers employ dead natural baits, there are a number of top-notch skippers in the Florida Keys with whom we've fished who troll live baits with the aid of their outriggers, or preferably with the aid of a kite.

The technique is to obtain small live forage species such as pinfish, blue runners, grunts, snappers or any other small fish that will stay active. Preferable size is five to seven inches in length, although we've occasionally used larger baits. The smaller baits are preferred, however, as it is easier for medium-sized gamefish to mouth them.

A 7/o or 8/o O'Shaughnessy hook is attached to the end of either a monofilament or light stainless steel wire leader. The baitfish is hooked in the fleshy part of its back, just beneath the dorsal fin, so

From top to bottom are the rigged eel with Japanese feather head, mullet with an egg-shaped sinker, and balao with a plastic skirt on its head. All three are favorites of East and Gulf Coast trollers and will take a wide variety of gamefish when skipped across the surface.

that as you hold the leader the fish hangs horizontally in much the same position as it would swim.

Bait Swims on Top

If employing an outrigger with live bait, it is necessary to slip a swivel onto your line which runs free on the line. Instead of snapping the line into the outrigger, the swivel is snapped into the rigger, and then the outrigger line is run out to get the bait as far out to the side of the boat as possible. The angler then adjusts the amount of line he has out, lowering the baitfish into the water, so that as you troll along, the fish can swim quickly along with the boat. The bobbing and weaving action of the boat and outriggers will frequently cause the baitfish to leap into the air, after which it swims furiously upon re-entering the water.

Trolling a bait in this manner is extremely effective, but it takes patience to get baitfish, and then to develop the technique of presenting the bait and hooking the fish. Usually when a gamefish grabs the baitfish the line is snapped free of the outrigger by the strike, or the angler may simply free-spool line—remember that the line is held in the rigger with a swivel—until the gamefish gets the bait well into his mouth. When the fish is running well, a simple yank on the rod will drive the hook into its jaw, simultaneously pulling the swivel free of the outrigger.

Kite Gets Bait Way Out

The advantage of using a kite as an outrigger is that you can get your live baitfish well away from the boat. It's actually possible to fly a kite—the same type, incidentally, as your son would fly in the park—and get it up well ahead of the boat, or to the side.

This permits you to watch the bait from the flying bridge of a boat with no wake to distract you. Frequently you will see the baitfish jumping nervously into the air, and then see the shadow of a big gamefish approaching from the depths, slowly circling the bait to look it over. Often a hesitant gamefish can be coaxed into striking if you pull back on the line, causing the baitfish to hang suspended in the air for a second or two, which often drives the gamefish wild. When the fish strikes, your fishing line snaps free of a clothespin on the kite and you play your fish.

Trolling a live baitfish with the aid of a kite is more specialized than it appears at first. But along with trolling live baitfish from outriggers, it can prove extremely effective on the offshore grounds. We've landed many gamefish using this method, including dolphin, amberjack, barracuda, king mackerel, sailfish and little tuna, to name but a few that come to mind.

While some trollers simply use an ordinary kite purchased in a toy store, there are several manufacturers who produce kites designed expressly for gamefishing. These are made of plastic and hold up extremely well under prolonged use in offshore live-bait trolling. They are worth the small investment if you plan to pursue this type of fishing seriously.

TROLLING TECHNIQUES

While there are exceptions to the rule, by far the greatest amount of offshore trolling is done in what most boatmen refer to as blue water. You seldom find the deep-blue water of the ocean depths close to shore, so there are often long rides seaward before the lines are put over the stern.

Each section of seacoast varies. Boatmen sailing from San Diego often have to travel 60 miles or more to seaward to encounter the long-finned albacore, while trollers heading out of Chub Cay in the

Bahamas can be fishing in 1,000 fathoms of water within five minutes running time from the dock!

It would be a monumental task to attempt to list just how far from shore good blue-water fishing exists from the hundreds of coastal ports on our three coastlines. While one day the Gulf Stream off Florida may move within a few miles of land, a change in wind and tide can often push this fish-filled body of water many miles from shore, moving the fish along with it. From this you can well understand that nothing on the offshore scene remains constant.

Food Is a Factor

The availability of natural bait in an area is also a factor which determines where fish will be, as is water temperature. Lack of natural bait will often cause schools of gamefish to vacate an area, for they need a tremendous supply of food to satisfy their ravenous appetites.

Often winds play a role in the water-surface temperatures. Sustained strong winds can actually skim off warm surface water, causing cold water from the depths to rise to the surface. When this occurs, the gamefish will move with the warm water, along with the baitfish.

If you're fishing from a charter boat or a party packet, the skipper will often make a run directly to the offshore grounds that have been producing for him over the past several days; and private boatmen would do well to watch the professionals. However, always remember that the professional skipper's fishing is his livelihood, so never fish too close to him, or in any way interfere with his activities.

Put Lines in the Water

As you head seaward and the pale blues and greens of inshore water turn to an indescribable deep blue, it is time to put the lines in the water and start trolling.

Most pelagic species encountered on the offshore grounds are fast swimmers, and best results are obtained while trolling at a fair rate of speed. Many newcomers fail to realize this, and they idle their engines down as slowly as they will go, resulting in ineffectively trolled lures. If you advance the throttle, your boat will throw up a churning white wake, and the lures and baits will take on added action, skipping and dancing in the white water.

Proper trolling speed is something that each boatmen must learn by experience. There is no way we know to tell you the exact speed any given boat should troll, for boats are of different size and have different engines, gears and propellers; and all of these factors, among others, contribute to a boat's trolling characteristics.

A good basic technique is simply to throttle down to the same speed being employed by other trollers, and then to adjust your individual speed either faster or slower until strikes are received. While it does sound unusual, some boats have to troll faster than others in order to put up a good wake and get their lures to work properly.

Fish Four Lines

Occasionally a big charter boat may fish six or more lines, utilizing outriggers to keep the lures well spread out. But for most offshore fishing, four lines in the water is about normal for the average-sized boat.

Outriggers Are Helpful

Outriggers are a great help on a small boat, for they not only keep the lines well separated, but they give added action to the lures or baits fished from them. The constant weaving and trolling action of the boat causes the outriggers to rise and fall, which in turn imparts this action to the baits.

A good trolling pattern to start out with is to fish two lines straight back off the stern, one from each corner. These are commonly referred to as "flat lines" for they are fished flat off the stern, without the aid of outriggers. The second two lines, usually called "rigger lines," can then be fished from the outriggers.

Start with Variety

It is good to start out with a variety of lures, for you never know just what the offshore adversaries will be after. The selection of lures which you use will most often be determined by the species in residence. These will be covered in greater detail in the chapter devoted to each individual species and its habits.

As an illustration, let's say there are school bluefin tuna, oceanic bonito and Atlantic bonito in the area you plan to fish. For a starter, skip baits such as mullet and balao would be unwise, as these tend to be rather large for the school fish. So a good selection of lures would include a pair of trolling feathers, one on a flat line and the second on the rigger line. A cedar jig would be a good choice for the remaining rigger line, while a spoon held just under the surface with a small trolling sinker would be perfect for the other flat line.

Vary Distances Behind the Boat

Members of the tuna clan are by nature curious, and often you can see them darting through your wake, attracted by the churning white water of your propellers. This curiosity can often be their downfall, for the wise troller always makes it a point to fish at least one or two of his lures close to the stern where they'll be spotted by any roving band of gamefish.

A good pattern is to start off with one flat line eased out so that the lure is on top of the first wave of the wake being thrown up by your boat. If your boat is small, sometimes this wave will be extremely close; then you can ease the lure out to the crest of the second wave. However, tuna often will grab a lure within 25 feet of the stern, so don't put the flat lines out too far, or the lures may be in quiet water well back in the wake, where the cruising fish might not even notice them.

Use Longer Rigger Lines

The lines fished from the outriggers should be somewhat longer than the flat lines. For as the wake leaves the boat it spreads out behind it, and the rigger baits should be right on the crest of the waves and white water being churned up. Depending on the boat, this may require the lines to be anywhere from 100 to 125 feet long.

This pattern of fishing the lines can be employed with good results no matter where you fish. Of course, once you hook up and find that the fish are showing a marked preference for a specific lure fished at a specific distance behind the boat, then the best thing to do is switch all of the lines into the same pattern. We've seen times with school bluefin tuna where the rigger lines wouldn't get a strike at all, but just as soon as all four lines were dropped flat astern, all went down under smashing strikes simultaneously.

By the same token, we can vividly recall a couple of occasions when trolling for king mackerel in the Gulf of Mexico when the flat lines didn't bring a strike all day, regardless of whether we fished them short or long. The kings would only look at strip baits danced from the outriggers back around 125 to 150 feet from the boat.

So there you have it. You've got to be constantly alert, always trying different lures and different lengths of line until you find the combination the fish want.

Don't be complacent either. Because you score well one day with a certain combination, don't fall into the pattern of always using that combination. Fish frequently change their habits, steadfastly refusing an offering one day that just couldn't be kept in the water a day earlier because of repeated strikes.

Keep Alert

Once the land disappears over your stern you'll find that the ocean seems the same in practically every direction. But it isn't. There are many things happening on the ocean, and the alert troller can often parlay an almost casual observation into a good catch.

An important consideration is to change your trolling pattern periodically. Try a zig-zag pattern and figure eights. Each pattern will result in your baits acting differently in the water.

When you hook a fish try to remember just how you were going, and repeat the same general trolling pattern in the same area. Often you'll receive strike after strike, indicating that the fish are moving a certain way and will only strike a lure going in a particular direction.

We've frequently observed fish cruising on the surface, literally riding the crests of waves. When you hit them like this, you can often get strike after strike just by repeating your successful technique. Sometimes it will be trolling with the fish; other times it will be crossing in front of them or coming down on them.

Watch for Fish on Top

When you keep watching the water, you'll frequently spot baitfish nervously working near the surface. This is a good sign, for when the bait is on top, gamefish are usually the ones that put them there. If the bait is just flittering and nervous, it often indicates bigger fish have recently worked them over. If the baitfish are leaping clear of the water, often several dozen at a time, it can only mean that big fish are after them from below. Often from a boat you actually watch dolphin, king mackerel, yellowtail, the tunas and bonitos giving the forage species a mean cut. It is times like this that trollers wait for with a passion, for gamefish are often in such a feeding frenzy that they are easy to catch.

Approach with Caution

You must approach the feeding fish with caution, however. For the quickest way to startle the fish and disperse them is to troll right through the mass of feeding fish.

Instead, approach slowly and circle the school, making turns out from the school so that your arc will carry your lures right in along the edge of the feeding fish. Often your lures only have to get within 20 or 30 feet of the commotion before they'll be quickly grabbed by the feeding fish.

You've always got to be alert for signs of fish on the surface when trolling offshore. Here George Seemann, Herb Schoenberg and the author watch for signs of feeding fish as they work the offshore grounds off Joulters Cays in the Bahamas.

If you're careful to use a pattern that keeps your boat from running down the fish, you can often pick fish after fish out of the school without disturbing the feeding of the fish whatsoever. But just run through them once, and it will often be the finish of your sport.

Fish Often Just Cruise

One of the most frustrating experiences encountered by offshore trollers is seeing huge schools of fish right on the top which absolutely refuse to take any lure you put before them, no matter what the approach. Careful investigation of these fish will often indicate that they're just cruising, and not chasing baitfish. At such times even the most skillfully presented lures go unnoticed.

Here a change of technique is required. Instead of staying clear of the school and skirting the edges of the fish, it sometimes pays to determine which direction they're moving in, and with your lines still in trolling position, to race up on the fish from behind, deliberately putting them down.

As soon as you feel you're directly above the startled fish, quickly ease your throttles back to trolling speed; often the fish will move back to the surface, frequently right in the middle of your baits. All it takes is one curious individual to swat a bait, and often bedlam breaks loose as the school goes on a feeding frenzy.

Watch for Slicks

There are times when the ocean takes on a glassy, smooth appearance, and you'd swear there wasn't a fish in it. When this happens, look for a slight oil slick on the surface of the water. Occasionally the slick may be as small as your boat, or once in a while it will cover half an acre or more. The slick often is the oily aftermath of gamefish feeding in the depths. When a fish bites a small oily forage species such as mackerel, menhaden, herring, anchovy and the host of other baitfish, there is often an oily seepage from the fish which drifts to the surface, leaving a very pronounced slick.

Often by trolling through the slicks you can excite the interest of the feeding gamefish, drawing them to the surface and to your baits dancing along in the wake.

Watch for Gulls

The many different species of sea gulls, terns and other seabirds often disclose the presence of feeding fish while you're still far from the scene of action. Constantly be alert for diving and tightly circling gulls. This usually indicates activity below. For the gulls know that when fish are feeding they can come by an easy meal by picking up the scraps of mutilated baitfish or of those which are fluttering on the surface, having been wounded by a slashing gamefish.

Floating Debris

Flotsam has a habit of collecting and drifting about together in the ocean. Occasionally it may be nothing more than a couple of timbers or a few crates. At other times there may be a huge raft of the floating debris stretching for a quarter mile or more.

Taking up residence around almost any floating object found well out in the ocean will be many baitfish. They find sanctuary, for what little it is worth, among boards, boxes and cans which drift across the broad expanse of water. Gamefish know that baitfish seek the shelter of the flotsam, and dolphin, king mackerel, oceanic bonito, members of the jack family, the tunas and a host of other species often congregate below to enjoy a leisurely meal.

So whenever you see anything floating on the ocean, make certain to investigate it and troll by. Even a single big plank or box may produce fantastic fishing.

From the vantage point of the flying bridge we've frequently eased up to floating debris and made a visual inspection when the water was clear, particularly in the tropics. If we spotted the flashes of fish below we spent some time trolling through the area. If not, we just proceeded until we found some flotsam that held hungry gamefish.

Weed Line Produces Too

Many newcomers might shy away from huge rafts of weed floating on the surface, for fear that their lures or baits would become entangled in it. Actually, when you see the big weed lines that form on the ocean you should make an attempt to troll as close as you possibly can without getting fouled in the weed. For as with flotsam, baitfish seek sanctuary within weed lines, and the bigger fish know this and often take up residence below.

High Bottoms Are Good

A check of a Coast and Geodetic Survey chart of the area you plan to fish will often indicate underwater canyons, gullies or patches

The oceanic bonito is a world traveler that cooperates with trollers, chummers and offshore casters alike. It has a very weak mouth and must be played carefully. It usually averages 5 to 10 pounds, although fish of 20 pounds are not uncommon in southern waters.

of high bottom. All of these spots are worth trolling over, for they cause rips and currents that hold baitfish, even though the bottom itself may be many fathoms below.

Where the bottom is shallow and strewn with rocks, coral or other underwater debris, there is almost certainly an abundance of natural baitfish, and invariably substantial numbers of gamefish too.

Look for spots that drop off from moderate depth to extreme depth, and make it a point to troll along them. Often gamefish congregate along the drop-off.

However, don't sell extremely deep water short either. We've enjoyed fantastic sport while trolling in water over 1,000 fathoms deep off Bermuda, and in approximately the same depth at the tip of the Tongue of the Ocean in the Bahamas. In both instances the bait was plentiful, which in turn held the gamefish in some of the deepest water in the world.

Look for Commercial Draggers

Off many of our coasts there are deep-water draggers, hauling their drags across the bottom to collect clams, scallops, lobsters and fish. When you observe one of these working in the area you are fishing, it certainly pays to investigate the water immediately in the wake of the commercial men. For as they haul up their catch and dump it onto their decks, they often discard huge quantities of trash fish, and unsaleable clams, scallops and the like. The gamefish often follow boats like this for days on end, feeding on everything that is thrown overboard.

We've enjoyed some fine fishing by just trolling back and forth across the wake of such a boat—keeping our distance of course—catching dolphin, oceanic bonito and little tuna until arm-weary.

In the case of scallopers, they often shuck the bivalves immediately upon dumping them onto deck, tossing the broken shells and smashed scallops overboard, where the fish have a feast just swimming along with the boat enjoying the free handout.

Work Lures When Fish Are Hooked

One of the best pieces of advice we can offer the offshore troller is to alert the anglers in the cockpit to work their lures vigorously once a fish is hooked. This is extremely important. For if you hook a fish and simply ease the boat out of gear, your lures will then hang listlessly in the water, and you will seldom receive additional strikes.

But if you ease off on your throttles, keeping the boat moving forward slowly, and your anglers work their rod tips with a jigging action, you can often coax strikes to two or three or even all four lines.

Sometimes, in the case of king mackerel, school bluefin tuna, albacore, bonito and dolphin you can keep one or two fish in the water at all times, not landing them until another fish has been hooked. The hooked fish keeps the school close by, and anglers who quickly get their lures back out, quickly receive strikes while the excited gamefish mill about.

Inshore Trolling

Inshore trolling varies considerably from offshore trolling. The conditions are different, and different species inhabit the waters. On the inshore trolling grounds the water is most often quite shallow, for these grounds encompass the ocean waters close to shore, bays, sounds, rivers and estuaries.

The inshore species which are the targets of trollers vary considerably in size. The tarpon frequently weigh upwards of 50 pounds. On the other hand, Pacific barracuda, shad and Spanish mackerel—all inshore species—usually weigh only a few pounds.

MEDIUM AND LIGHT TACKLE IS BEST

Occasionally regulation-class tackle is employed while trolling for tarpon and other big inshore species, including the king salmon, and even striped bass and pollock. But tackle of this type isn't really necessary, as the waters are seldom extremely deep, which means you can use lighter tackle and enjoy fine sport.

Offshore trolling is a waiting game. You never know just what to expect, for the ocean depths yield a great variety of gamefish. This foursome is trying their luck aboard a charter boat out of Miami Beach, Florida.

We've found that while trolling for big tarpon, bluefish, snook, channel bass, striped bass, yellowtail and big pollock the basic boat outfit described under general-purpose tackle is ideal.

A light bay or popping outfit is a perfect combination even for these heavyweights if you're trolling protected waters where strong currents aren't a factor. It's also best for the host of smaller species which will take a trolled lure, including jack crevalle, ladyfish, common mackerel, blue runner and the smaller fish mentioned earlier.

Rigging Is Essentially the Same

Much of the terminal rigging employed for inshore trolling is akin to that used offshore, with the exception that the size is somewhat scaled down.

The basic manner of preparing your double line and attaching a ball-bearing swivel with coastlock snap remains the same. The only exception is that many inshore trollers use only a five-foot to six-foot length of double line. Some don't even use a double line and just tie their line directly to the swivel.

LEADERS

Leaders should be scaled down too. Number 6 or 7 stainless steel wire, having a diameter of .016 and .018 of an inch and testing at 58 and 69 pounds, respectively, is more than ample for most of the species you encounter. Its fine diameter is a must when trolling in clear, shallow waters.

When inshore trolling for big fish, use a leader measuring six to eight feet long; you may scale the leader down to three or four feet while trolling for small fish.

Nylon Is Superior

Many trollers prefer wire leaders where they're apt to encounter toothy adversaries like bluefish and barracuda. But for best results on the inshore grounds you should use nylon monofilament leaders which test in the range of 20 to 40 pounds.

The information given earlier on snaps, clips and trolling sinkers applies for inshore trolling situations too. Seldom will you be trolling in extreme depths, so you will find little use for deep-trolling devices such as planers and underwater outriggers.

TROLLING NATURAL BAITS

Many of the trolling baits used offshore have little application for inshore trolling. This is particularly true of mullet, balao and other whole fish rigged as skip baits. Strip baits, however, often account for the capture of many fish on the inshore trolling grounds. Natural baits used by the inshore troller are seldom fished on the surface, but at intermediate levels and along the bottom.

Rigged Baits Produce

There are several natural baits which the inshore troller can put to good use. In addition to strip baits, two of the finest we've used are the common eel and the needlefish. Both are long, thin baits which adapt themselves well to inshore trolling; and because they're a major factor in the diet of several gamefish, they're a lure which is worth the few minutes' effort it takes to rig them.

Eel Must Be Rigged

There are many different ways of rigging an eel. In fact, some trollers don't even rig the eel, but simply remove its skin, slip the skin over an eel-skin rig, and troll it. However, an eel which is properly rigged is a potent trolling lure for striped bass, snook and bluefish. We recommend it over the eelskin rig, as the rigged eel can be used for boat casting as well as trolling.

The best size for trolling are eels which measure anywhere from 8 to 18 inches. The smaller eels are fine for fish up to ten pounds, while the big eels are brought into play for lunker stripers and snook.

You'll need a rigging needle with which to run a doubled length of 36-pound-test line through the eel. This is best accomplished by slipping a loop of line onto the needle and then running it through the eel and bringing it out in the vicinity of the eel's vent.

Next, slip an O'Shaughnessy hook, size 6/0, 7/0 or 8/0, onto the line and draw the line back into the eel.

Then a small block tin squid is brought into play; its hook is slipped into the lower jaw of the eel and out the upper jaw. Some anglers vary this a bit by running the hook through the head instead. Either way works well. Next, the line is tied to an eye which extends out of the top of the block tin squid. The eel's mouth is tied shut and a harness of light line or dental floss is tied around the eel's head where the hook protrudes so that it doesn't rip apart. The lure is ready for trolling or casting.

Bear in mind that the tail hook must not be drawn up tight, but should lie flat so that the eel will not spin when trolled through the water. The block tin squid at the head of the eel will give it action.

Needlefish Good Too

Along the Gulf Coast, we've enjoyed fine results with snook, red-fish and king mackerel while using needlefish rigged on a bucktail jig. It is a very easy bait to rig.

All you need do is tie a 7/0 or 8/0 size lead-head bucktail jig to your leader. Then take the needlefish and work the hook of the bucktail jig through the head of the needlefish. Secure the snout of the needlefish to the body of the bucktail jig with soft copper wire, and it's ready for trolling.

You don't necessarily need a big boat to catch big fish. Howard Beyer landed this bull striped bass while trolling a plastic rigged eel from a rented outboard skiff at Sandy Hook, New Jersey.

Guide Leldon Thompson just swung aboard this nice snook for Linda Rosko. She hooked it while trolling a needlefish rigged on a bucktail jig in the waters off Marco Island on the Gulf of Mexico. When trolled on a light popping outfit snook of this size provide superb sport.

Some anglers go a step further and use a second hook in the tail, much as you would rig an eel, but this is seldom necessary if the fish are in a feeding mood. For big snook we've often used foot-long needlefish, while smaller baits were employed when smaller fish were in residence. Keep in mind that it's always best to use a bucktail jig with a big hook, so that it extends out of the needlefish's head sufficiently for you to hook a gamefish.

You can often improve the fish-catching effectiveness of a needlefish rigged in this manner by working your rod tip, causing the needlefish to dart ahead and then falter as you slowly troll it.

PLUGS

Most of the lures used by the offshore troller produce well inshore too. But there are other lure types as well.

A plug is a lure which is most often made of wood or plastic, painted to resemble a fish, with several sets of treble hooks on it. There are literally hundreds of different models of plugs, but we can narrow them down to several basic types.

Two of the finest types of plugs used by trollers and casters are the swimming plugs—surface swimmers and subsurface swimmers.

Those made to work on the surface float at rest, and when trolled very slowly they work back and forth with a lazy swimming motion. They are particularly effective in bays and rivers and when ocean waters are relatively calm. Most surface swimmers have either a metal or plastic wobble plate which cannot be adjusted.

The action of the swimming plugs can often be enhanced by adding a few feathers or bucktail to the tail hook of the plug. But don't add too much of a skirt, as action will be retarded.

Subsurface swimmers are made to work at intermediate levels, or in some cases near the bottom. Their lip is designed somewhat differently from a surface swimmer, in that you can bend the lower spoon of the lip and thus alter the action of the plug, making it work either near the surface or in the depths. This is accomplished by bending the lip. If you want the plug to work near the surface, bend the lip down. If you want it to work very deep, bend the lip up until its spoon is almost horizontal.

With all swimmers a slow, lazy troll or retrieve is best.

Other Plugs

Mirror-type plugs catch a lot of fish while trolling too. They come in surface, medium-depth and deep-diving models. They are de-

Pictured here are some of the lures favored by inshore trollers. Included are, from left to right, surgical tube lure, subsurface swimming plug, bucktail jig, plastic rigged eel and surface swimming plug. These lures will take a wide variety of species, including striped bass, bluefish, snook and channel bass.

signed to resemble a fish closely, and most models have no lip to give them action. They have an eye located on the upper part of their head to which your leader is attached. When trolled they have a sliding action, pulling from side to side as they glide through the water. Their action is enhanced considerably when trolling by vigorously working your rod tip.

The propeller plug is another type of plug which finds favor among trollers, particularly those who troll quiet, sheltered waterways for snook, stripers and blues. It has small metal propellers mounted fore and aft which spin when the plug is either trolled or retrieved. The propellers cause a surface disturbance and leave a "V" wake similar to that of a mullet swimming near the surface. When mullet or other surface-swimming baitfish are in the area, this plug is a real killer.

Popping plugs are made with a scooped or concave head. The head pushes water ahead of the plug, making a gurgling commotion at the surface. Some popping plugs are balanced to weave and bob in the water, others to lie flat on the surface. While trolling popping plugs you add to their action by a steady working of the rod tip, so that they chug through the water throwing spray before them. You can impart short pops to the plug by working the tip in quick short movements or drawing the plug back three or four feet at a time with the rod tip before letting it come to rest, repeating the motion as you slowly troll along.

The reason plugs are seldom used by offshore trollers is that they work best when trolled at slow speeds. When trolled fast they do not work properly, often spinning or gliding along the surface with no action whatsoever. Although they are most favored by the caster, they do work very effectively when trolled slowly and given an added bit of action by working the rod tip.

Many Sizes and Finishes

Plugs of all types come in literally dozens of finishes, made to resemble most natural baitfish found in salt water. They also come in many sizes, ranging from tiny models that resemble a small mullet to plugs measuring a foot or more in length, which are designed to look like a menhaden, mackerel or herring.

The important thing to remember in selecting a plug is to pur-

The subsurface swimming plug has an enticing side-to-side swimming movement as it is either trolled or retrieved. By adjusting the wobble plate you can cause the plug to work either deep or shallow. When gamefish are feeding on small baitfish this lure produces excellent results.

At rest the surface swimming plug floats on the surface. When trolled or retrieved it has a lazy side-to-side swimming motion, causing a substantial amount of surface disturbance which drives gamefish into taking it.

The mirror-type plug doesn't have much action when trolled or retrieved steadily. It's action must be brought out by working the rod tip, causing the plug to dart ahead and falter, much like a wounded baitfish. It is made in surface, subsurface and deep-running models.

The propeller plug comes in surface and deep-running models. Its major attraction is its twirling propellers, which brings strikes from a wide variety of gamefish as it sputters through the water.

chase a size and finish which closely approximates the natural bait-fish in residence where you plan to fish.

BUCKTAIL JIGS

At first glance many bucktail jigs closely resemble Japanese trolling feathers. There is a difference, however. In a bucktail jig the hook is molded into the head of the jig, and there is an eye on which to attach your snap or leader directly on the top of its head.

This lure is usually called a bucktail. However, depending on where you fish, you may hear it called a doodlebug, bug eye or any one of many trade names.

It comes in two basic types: one has a torpedo-shaped head usually adorned with glass or bead eyes; the other has a flat shape somewhat like a lima bean.

Both types of bucktails come in a number of sizes, ranging from tiny 1/o models weighing only a fraction of an ounce on up to 8/o bucktail jigs that weigh a full three ounces.

On the average, the boatman who employs bucktails for trolling will find the lightweight models best for creeks and estuaries; the heavy jigs are used to probe the depths of rips found just offshore and the deep water of passes and inlets.

A jig's action may be enhanced by the addition of a strip of pork rind. Many trollers favor tail-hook pork rind, which has a small hook affixed to the rear part of the pork strip and frequently hooks fish that strike short.

The lima-bean-shaped bucktail jig has long been a favorite of trollers and casters alike. It is an extremely versatile lure that is made in many sizes and will account for almost any fish that swims.

METAL SQUIDS

Old timers still speak of metal squids as block tin squids, for years ago almost all metal squids were molded of pure block tin. The soft metal was easy to mold and had a soft luster which proved the downfall of many striped bass, bluefish, weakfish and other inshore gamefish.

Metal squids are a molded lure having a keel, with considerable depth to the lure. As with many vintage lures, they come in hundreds of models, made to resemble every type of baitfish you can think of.

Today they are molded of a variety of metals. Some are of block tin, but they are more often made of lead which is chrome or nickel plated. Some are painted in solid colors, and many have bright red heads.

Most metal squids have a single hook which is either molded into the squid and rides upright or is attached with a swiveling pin which permits the hook to move back and forth. Favored hook sizes range from 5/0 through 7/0.

Many metal squids are dressed with a feather or bucktail skirt. If plain, it may be made more attractive to gamefish by adding a strip of pork rind to the hook.

MEASURE LINES

As a great deal of inshore trolling is done with the lures working out of sight well beneath the surface, it is wise to measure your lines before leaving dockside. We measure and mark our lines at 100 and 125 foot levels, for we find these two lengths very suitable for a wide variety of inshore trolling situations. It is important that the lines be marked, for in this way you can immediately let the line right back out to the same level where a fish was hooked. With lines that aren't marked it is virtually impossible to know just how far behind the boat they are.

Generally speaking, most inshore trolling is done from boats considerably smaller than those used for blue-water trolling. In fact a great deal of inshore trolling is done from outboard-powered boats, which because of their smaller size, prevent you from trolling as many lines as offshore.

Fish at Different Levels

It is difficult to prescribe an exact trolling pattern for inshore fishing. Offshore trolling is pretty much standardized, but inshore you've got many more factors determining which lures you'll use and which patterns to troll.

We'll begin by giving a basic inshore trolling pattern. Using three lines it is wise to fish them at two different lengths, one at 100 feet and two at 125 feet. In this way you have lures at two levels.

Depending on the depth of the water, you can either fish the lines straight back without the aid of trolling sinkers or add torpedo-shaped trolling sinkers to take the lures deep.

Whatever the case, make certain the lines are staggered so that they do not hang on each other as you make a turn. The lines sent deep with trolling sinkers should be held shorter that those lines which stream back without them, so that as you turn, one line and its lure goes over or under the other line.

The types of lures you use will depend in large part on the natural baitfish in residence. If Spanish mackerel are feeding on fingerling pilchards, then small spoons, bucktails or Japanese trolling feathers are in order. For tarpon chasing pinfish and squirrel fish, most certainly a seven-inch or eight-inch swimming plug or spoon would be more appropriate than a small lure.

We've used a three-line trolling pattern, using big spoons, with two lines deep with trolling sinkers and one high, and succeeded in catching bluefish off Rhode Island, stripers off New Jersey, channel bass off North Carolina and giant tarpon in the passes of the Gulf Coast of Florida. This was fishing in open water, with depths that averaged 15 to 25 feet. In each case the big fish would move with the tide, working along channel edges or in tide rips formed just outside inlets and passes or around points of land.

The technique used was remarkably simple in every case, and it just points out that a technique which works in one place will work equally well with other gamefish at a spot far removed.

SLOW TROLL

Once the lines are out you can watch the rod tips and usually know if the lures are working right. With spoons, metal squids,

rigged eels and swimming plugs the action of the lures causes the
rop tips to pulsate with a steady rhythm.

Most inshore species like a lure working at just about half the
speed you'd use on blue water, so make certain to idle back on
your throttles.

As we've said, trolling isn't just towing a lure, and this applies
inshore as well. Fish congregate in rips and eddies, which are most
often found near points of land, where there is an inlet or pass, or
where several currents clash—all places where baitfish are concen-
trated.

But it takes skill to fish such locations; there's a lot more to it
than just riding around with your lures out behind the boat. In many
tide rips your boat is almost motionless when idling against the
current. While a current such as this acts as a brake, it can prove
advantageous, too, if you know how to weave back and forth, making little headway, but with your lures working well.

In moving down with a strong current you've got to speed up in
order for your lures to work. Too slow a speed will result in the boat
and lures being pushed along by the current, and the lures will just
drag behind. This is readily apparent when you watch your rod tips
pulsate. They just won't be working until you advance the throttle.

At different stages of the tide you'll have to adjust your speed
accordingly. The main thing is to keep the lures working, for if
they're not, the fish just won't hit them.

Get Lures Deep

In some rips and inlets where the currents have cut the bottom
out and the water is very deep, you may have to resort to either
wire line or lead-core line in order to get your lures down deep to
where the fish are feeding.

Occasionally fish will be feeding so close to the sea floor that
in order to get strikes your lures will actually have to touch bottom
occasionally. This is accomplished by letting out your line until you
feel the lure bouncing along. Then you simply take several turns of
the reel handle, bring the lure in several feet, and thus lift it up off
the bottom.

When trolling in shallow water you may find that 75 feet of line
will be ample to get lures deep, whereas in depths of 25 or 30 feet,

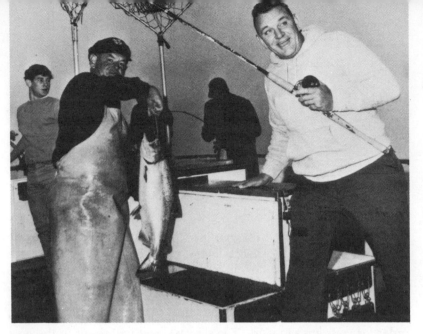

This king salmon was cruising thirty-five feet below the surface when it struck an anchovy bait trolled at that depth with the aid of a three-pound cast-iron sinker. San Francisco anglers frequently employ heavy sinkers attached to their line with a sinker release mechanism that causes the sinker to fall free when a fish is hooked.

a full 300 feet or more of wire line trailing behind the boat may be necessary to get down to where the fish are feeding.

Keep Alert for Baitfish

You should always keep alert, watching for signs of feeding fish. Much the same as offshore, schools of nervous baitfish will often disclose gamefish close by, as will sea gull activity.

Inshore gamefish, especially when feeding on the surface, are often extremely boat shy, so you must always approach with caution, being careful to skirt the edges of a feeding school so as not to disturb them.

Circling or running a wide "S" curve along the edge of the school is usually most productive. As you skirt a school and make a turn away from the fish your lures will often be struck. For the fish frequently observe the lures—which they feel are baitfish—making a break from the main school, and strike them as they attempt to get away.

Many More Down Deep

When you see several dozen gamefish feeding on the surface, there may be ten times that number down deep. We've frequently spoken with anglers who when they saw fish feeding on top and tried several surface lures without success, just gave up in disgust. They were wrong!

Always put several deep-working lures out even when the fish are on top. Often the deep-feeding fish are easier to fool than the excited gamefish which are feeding on the surface.

Alter Speed

If it is evident that fish are in an area and you aren't getting strikes, try changing your trolling speed. Some times just a little more speed, or less, may be all that's needed to coax gamefish to strike your lures.

Remember that even in the ocean there are currents, and although the water seems to be motionless, it might well be moving at a speed of several knots. This means that when you're heading in one direction you're bucking the current, while in the other direction you're running with it.

Wind has much the same effect on a boat. If there's a strong wind blowing it will slow your boat speed down considerably when you're trolling into it. The reverse will be true when you're trolling with the wind. You will, of course, have to compensate with an adjustment of your throttle. A rough ocean or bay will hold down your trolling speed somewhat too.

Look for Reefs

As most inshore trolling is done in relatively shallow water, bottom conformation is important. Fish are far more likely to congregate over an underwater plateau strewn with rocks and other debris than over a smooth sand bottom with nothing to hold or give protection to baitfish and other food.

A Coast and Geodetic Survey chart is a useful aid in locating good bottom. In fact, you'll note almost every major inshore fishing hotspot clearly marked on these charts.

Watch Tides

The inshore troller who fishes rivers and bays must pay particular attention to tide conditions. In many areas the rise and fall of the tide is four feet or more, which results in a marked change of trolling water and conditions.

On a flooding tide gamefish will often move out of the deep water of channels to feed on the shallow flats, returning to the deep-water channels when the tide is low. Often great schools of striped bass, channel bass, snook and other fine gamefish can be trolled in very shallow water if the boatman is careful and quiet.

Because fish move about a great deal in search of food,, it is wise not to spend too much time in one area. After giving a spot a reasonable try with good conditions, move on to another spot and keep nosing about until you locate fish. You can, of course, overdo this by spending a lot of time running from spot to spot, with little time left for fishing. But the wise troller plans his day's strategy so he can cover several spots that produce well and simply moves from spot to spot until a feeding school of fish is located.

Troll Around Breakwaters

Scattered along the coast are thousands of rock jetties and breakwaters which extend seaward to hold back the ravages of the ocean. These piles of rocks provide sanctuary for many forms of bait and crustaceans. As a result, gamefish frequently congregate in such spots to enjoy a meal. This is also true around jetties built at passes and inlets, for on a dropping tide there is an abundant amount of food carried along with the current.

The troller improves his score considerably if he visits spots such

Inshore trollers prefer small open boats. Here Mark and Susan Sosin probe a tidal estuary as they search for feeding gamefish.

A salt-water killie or minnow makes a fine trolling bait and is particularly effective when trolled along the bottom for summer flounders. It should be hooked through the lips so that it can swim freely and won't spin as it is being trolled.

as this at low tide, in order to get a thorough picture of how the rocks and pilings lie. For when the tide is high many of the rocks and pilings are submerged, and they could be a potential hazard to a troller.

Trolling either parallel with the breakwaters, or skirting along the seaward points of rock jetties often produces strikes from stripers, blues, snook, tarpon and a host of other species which come in search of a meal.

Drift-Trolling Effective

Much of what we have discussed in this section on inshore trolling has dealt with trolling either rigged natural baits or lures. But there is a type of fishing called drift-trolling. It is a very effective method which combines trolling, bottom fishing and drifting.

Drift-trolling is a technique employing a single-hook bottom rig such as those discussed in our bottom-fishing chapter. Once the rig is permitted to settle to the bottom, the boat is brought into play by slowly trolling the rig, periodically taking the boat out of gear to drift a while, and then placing it in gear to move ahead and troll again.

This technique works extremely well when using seaworm baits for striped bass, when baiting with live killies for summer flounders, and even when fishing for 100-pound-plus tarpon in spots such as Boca Grande Pass on Florida's Gulf Coast. Drift-trolling permits

The author unhooks a southern flounder for his son, Bobby, which was landed as they trolled along the edge of a channel while using live killies. A drift-troll technique was used, alternately drifting and trolling until feeding fish were located.

Charles "Doc" Hamaker landed this beautiful shad while trolling a shad dart in the roiled and muddied waters of the Susquehanna River where it meets Chesapeake Bay. By probing all of the spots of the river he found where the fish were feeding and enjoyed fine sport trolling the small darts along the bottom.

you to cover a lot of area and to present bottom bait in a lifelike manner. The results enjoyed with this technique can be most gratifying, especially when other accepted fishing methods fail to produce.

Inshore trolling will produce gamefish almost anywhere they reside. Never pass a spot by because it looks like it could hardly hold a population of fish. We've enjoyed fantastic trolling for harbor pollock in Maine rivers that you might hardly give a second glance to, blitzed snook in rivers which looked so murky that you felt a fish could hardly see the lure, and walloped shad on darts trolled in waters flooding the banks because of a rain storm. The secret of success in inshore trolling is to keep searching and continue trolling good lures in waters frequented by the gamefish you're after. Determination has a way of paying off, especially to the boatman who has a yen for experimentation and the perseverance to stick with it.

Solid monel wire line has its place in inshore trolling, especially when you want to get lures deep in swift tide rips. Bob Rosko hooked the 36½-pound striper held by his dad while trolling a subsurface swimming plug at Sandy Hook, New Jersey.

4 Chumming

MOST of our readers have, no doubt, observed the feeding of tropical fish in a home aquarium. Fish which are busy swimming about the tank suddenly swarm to the surface when food is dropped into the water. They stay near the surface until all of the food which is floating and drifting about is gone. Then they retire to the bottom, to continue hunting for scraps which have settled.

Chumming in salt water is much the same as feeding tropical fish, only on a grand scale. We sincerely doubt that there is a fish in salt water which won't respond to chumming techniques, for all fish spend a good deal of their time hunting for a meal. While looking for something to eat—which may be difficult to find at times—they quickly move toward any pieces of food which drift by. Unknowingly they are being drawn to the baited hook of salt-water anglers who are chumming. As you may have gathered, chumming is actually nothing more than dropping food into the water, to be carried to the fish by the tide or current.

Chum can be any type of food which will attract fish. There are so many different kinds of chum, which are presented in such a wide variety of ways, that we will only attempt to discuss the major techniques which are used along the seacoast.

Offshore Chumming

It stands to reason that you could chum for hours on end where there are no fish, and wind up catching nothing. So an important consideration before dropping any chum into the water is to select a location for your chumming activity that is frequented by the species you're after.

This isn't too difficult to do, for there is often a great deal of latitude—your chum will attract the fish to your boat, providing the tide or current carries the chum to the general area being frequented by feeding fish. We say feeding fish, because it is important to note that fish which are off their feeding schedule because of changes in barometric pressure, a decline in water temperature or various other factors will often not respond to chumming techniques, or any other sport-fishing techniques for that matter.

TROLL TO LOCATE FISH

With such species as school bluefin tuna, albacore, bluefish and king mackerel a favorite technique is to troll for them, employing the same tactics and equipment discussed in our trolling chapter.

As soon as a double or triple hookup is received while trolling, the boat's engines are shut down and chum is tossed overboard, hopefully attracting the school of fish close to the boat, within range of the baited hooks of the angler.

Initially many may wonder why not just troll? On party boats this would mean only a limited number could fish, and even on a private boat it means that someone always has to be running the boat and consequently cannot fish.

By shutting down the engines and chumming, everybody including the chummer can fish, and more anglers can fish from the boat at once.

LIVE BAITFISH AS CHUM ON WEST COAST

On the West Coast live sardines and anchovies are popular both as chum and hook baits. Boats sailing to the fishing grounds take on huge quantities of the fingerling baitfish, which are kept alive and frisky in huge bait wells.

While the boats troll on the West Coast the chummer always stands at the well, immediately ready to toss several small netfuls of live chum into the water as soon as a hookup is received.

Should the first chumming activity result in albacore or other

Captain Ernie Ruiz gaffed this big Pacific bonito for Bobby Rosko, who landed it while using an anchovy bait and chumming at the Todos Santos Islands off Ensenada, Mexico. The Pacific bonito is a game fighter, often growing to ten pounds in Mexican waters, where it provides party-boat anglers with fine sport on light tackle.

The author landed the husky albacore just gaffed by Gene Grimes while chumming and baiting with live anchovies off the coast of Baja California.

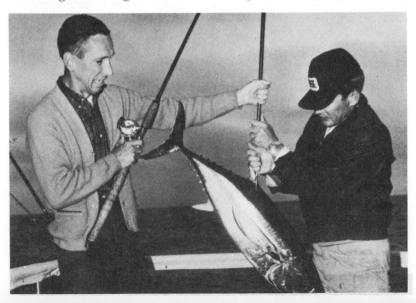

Captain Dick Gaydosh passes a scoop of live anchovies to a deckhand on his party boat New Lo-An prior to departing for the fishing grounds off San Diego, California. The anchovies are kept alive in live tanks and used as chum and hook baits when the fishing grounds are reached.

This is the way most live-bait fishermen hook their anchovies on the West Coast. The anchovy is hooked just under the collar of its gill plate so that it can swim freely.

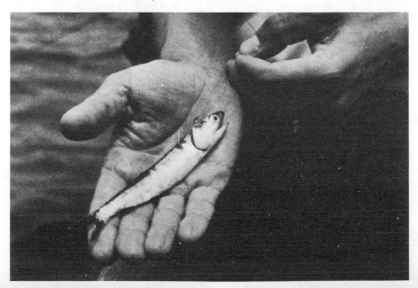

gamefish swarming around the boat, the chumming continues and anglers all switch from trolling tackle, usually regulation-class tackle, to lighter general-purpose tackle such as a basic boat outfit to enjoy maximum sport.

CHUNKS POPULAR ALONG GULF

Along the Gulf Coast boatmen frequently troll for king mackerel until a sizeable school is located, whereupon they hold schools of the fish close to the boat by chumming with small pieces of mullet. The mullet is a popular baitfish along the Gulf of Mexico, and it is diced into pieces about the size of a dime, which the kings find to their liking, swarming all around the boat, darting through the chum and picking up the pieces as quickly as they can, often to their amazement finding a hook in a piece of chum!

GROUND MENHADEN TOPS ON EAST COAST

Offshore trollers with their sights set on bluefin tuna find that schools of the husky bluefins can be held close to the boat by chum-

Here's Frank Ray, Jr., tossing out a tempting chum while fishing at the Three Sisters Reef off Bermuda. He mixes hogmouth fry with sand, mashing it together and then throwing it overboard. As it settles the huge schools of fish which live on the reef move right up to the boat, providing anglers with fast and furious fishing for a great number of reef species.

ming with finely ground menhaden (popularly called mossbunker or
bunker) once several tuna are hooked on the trolled lines. The
chum just whets the appetites of the tuna, which boil around the
boat picking up the tiny pieces as they settle in the water. The
anglers then slip hooks baited with butterfish or chunks of menhaden into the water and the fun begins.

Just An Illustration of Variety

These three illustrations point out the wide contrast of chumming techniques employed by trollers who first hook into fish and
then start chumming. So you can well understand the almost limit-
less techniques which can be employed while using some form of
chum to attract and hold gamefish close to your boat.

FIRST RIG TERMINAL TACKLE

Terminal tackle for chumming, regardless of what kind you do,
is extremely limited. One might say that all you do is tie a hook on
your line, bait up, and start fishing! It is, however, a little more involved than that.

As mentioned earlier, the basic boat outfit is most popular for
chumming, although regulation-class tackle is often used on heavy
fish, as is medium-weight spinning tackle when casting a live bait
into the chum line becomes necessary.

Regardless of the tackle, only monofilament lines should be employed. When chumming, the fish are usually attracted to the surface, and they sometimes take a bait right within view of the angler,
so having the line as inconspicuous as possible is important.

Variety of Hooks Used

Hook sizes will vary from one species to another, and also vary
according to the bait you're using. The thing to remember is that
hooks used for chumming generally run smaller in size for a given
species than those used for trolling.

While chumming, the bait must conceal the hook, which would
be rather difficult were the hook bulky or large. Because of the
importance of concealing the hook in a small bait, many anglers
employ small but extremely strong hooks designed expressly for
chumming. These are called tuna and albacore hooks and come in a
short-shanked beak style having an offset point.

*The author landed this big blackfin tuna while fishing with Captain
Russel Young aboard the* Sea Wolfe *out of Somerset, Bermuda. The
tuna was attracted to a live ocean robin bait fished in a chum line of
hogmouth fry mixed with sand. The blackfin is a great fighter, especially
when taken on light tackle.*

The hook sizes favored by chummers range all the way from
number 4 on up to the 7/o size. The size of the hook depends on the
size of the bait you'll be using. We vividly recall using number 4
hooks while baiting with hogmouth fry and fishing for blackfin tuna
off Bermuda, while just a short while later we switched over to 7/o
hooks because we were using live ocean robins while chumming for
giant amberjack.

Always keep in mind that you've got to tailor the hook to
the bait you're using, while taking into consideration the size of the
fish you're going for as well as the size of their mouths.

As an example, while fishing for albacore with a small anchovy
bait, a number 2 or 3 short-shanked hook is ideal, whereas while
after bluefish of the same size, say 10 to 15 pounds, a long-shanked
7/o hook would be ideal when used with half a butterfish as bait.

With species such as oceanic bonito, school bluefin tuna, blackfin tuna, yellowfin tuna, albacore, little tuna, amberjack, yellowtail
and dolphin, to name but a few, it is possible to tie the hook
directly to the end of your line, for the chance of the fish biting
through the monofilament is minimal.

Wire Essential at Times

With species having a set of sharp teeth, such as bluefish, king mackerel, barracuda, wahoo, sharks and other toothy individuals, a short wire leader is a must. A two-foot to three-foot length of number 8 wire is usually quite satisfactory, except with sharks, which have a tough sandpaper skin. With them you'll need an eight-foot to ten-foot leader to keep their skin from fraying the line badly.

The connection between line and leader can be a small barrel swivel. A number 5 or number 7 swivel is fine, for while they are small, they test many times the strength of the line you're using.

Clinch-On Sinkers Are Helpful

Most of the time all you have to do is bait up, and either cast or drift the bait back to your chum spread. But there may be times when a fast drift or strong current will keep your bait too near the surface to be effective. To overcome this and get the bait to intermediate levels, most chummers employ small clinch-on sinkers.

A number 6 clinch-on sinker weighs a half-ounce and a number 9 weighs seven eighths of an ounce. Having several of each size on hand will accommodate most situations you're apt to encounter.

Rubber-Cored Sinkers Ideal

While the clinch-on sinker finds great use, a newer type rubber-cored sinker proves far more effective for adding just a bit of weight while chumming. They come in many sizes, and have a core of rubber within the sinker. The line is slipped into a slot which runs the length of the sinker, and then a small piece of rubber is turned one half turn around each end of the line. This secures the sinker to the line, but leaves no chance of nicking the line, which is often the case with clinch-on types. The rubber-cored sinkers prove much easier to use too, for one can change them quickly.

Plastic Floats Are Necessary Too

Sometimes conditions are such that there is little wind or current, with the end result that your bait sinks directly to the bottom, whereas your chum is carried away from the boat. The only way to overcome such a situation is to employ a small plastic float on your line, attaching the float so that your bait will drift back in the chum at the level you desire.

We've tried a number of different types of floats, ranging from small pieces of specie cork slipped onto the line to wooden floats, but have found that the best floats of all are the economical plastic floats which are so popular with fresh-water anglers.

The plastic floats are usually half red and half white. They have a spring-operated push-button mechanism which permits you to snap them quickly and conveniently onto your line at any level.

The best sizes for salt-water use while chumming are those which measure one and a half, one and three-quarter or two inches in diameter. Remember that you're occasionally using a large, live baitfish, which requires a sizeable float to keep from being pulled under.

A clinch-on sinker such as this proves helpful in taking your line deep when currents are strong and the line is swept away from the boat.

A rubber-cored sinker has a core of rubber and it may be attached to a light line without fear of damaging the line. This type of sinker is very popular on the West Coast, but has not caught on elsewhere, although it is extremely useful for chummers everywhere.

When a dead calm or slow current causes your bait to sink into the depths too quickly a plastic float such as this should be attached to your line to keep the bait at the desired level.

When you're starting a chum line, don't disperse an excessive amount of chum into the ocean. Do it sparingly, otherwise you'll overfeed the fish and they'll often stay well away from the boat, just feeding on the chum as it drifts by. If you're using ground menhaden, herring or other such oily fish, use a soup ladle and mix some sea water with the ground chum to form a heavy soup which is easily ladled overboard.

As you toss out several ladles full of chum, watch to see how it disperses in the water. A good pattern to develop is to wait until one ladle-full drifts 50 feet or more from the boat, and then toss out another ladle-full.

When you chum by dribbling overboard pieces of fish, ground fish or live fish, you create what is commonly referred to as a chum line, chum spread or chum slick. These are terms used to refer to the long, unbroken line of chum that is steadily drifting away from your boat. The term slick finds popular usage because when using ground fish as chum there is a slight oily slick which forms on the surface of the water. On a calm day you can often see this oily chum slick extending a mile or more down-current from your boat.

As you are getting a chum slick going, bait up and ease a bait out in the chum line. If baiting with live baitfish such as tinker mackerel, pilchards, anchovies or sardines, hook them lightly in the heavy fleshy part of their back, so they can swim freely. Some anglers also enjoy good results by hooking them lightly through the lips.

In the case of dead bait, such as hogmouth fry, spearing, sand launce, butterfish or pieces of menhaden or mullet, place the bait on the hook so that it conceals the hook, but leave the point and barb in a position where it is not imbedded deeply in the bait, so that it can penetrate fast when a fish sucks it into its mouth.

KEEP BAIT MOVING

To present your bait in a chum line as effectively as possible, it must look natural and lifelike. Remember that the chum is constantly moving with the current, and in order to be effective your bait should be moving too.

A good practice with live bait is to cast it a short distance from the boat, and while keeping the reel in free spool, permitting the bait to swim about freely. Sometimes the baitfish will stubbornly stay near or under the boat, but more often it will swim out, often swimming 100 feet or more from the boat. Care should be exercised, of course, to watch which way your line is going at all times, in order to avoid tangles with other lines.

In the case of dead or chunk bait, make certain to keep the reel in free spool, permitting the bait to drift out at the speed of the current. Once your bait has drifted 100 feet or more from the boat, it is wise to reel it in again and start all over, so that the bait is constantly drifting along with the chum.

Never let the bait hang in the current, for in doing so it will invariably spin, and while it may be grabbed by a careless gamefish, on those days when the fish are being selective you'll find your score suffering because your bait isn't moving.

WATCH FOR FISH IN SLICK

It is wise always to keep alert for fish moving in the chum slick. When the water is clear, as it most often is offshore, you can often see the gamefish cruising through the slick, picking up pieces of chum.

Unfortunately, there are times when you'll spot the fish in the chum slick, but they won't take a bait.

A trick which we've used in Bermuda is to take several small baitfish and mash them into a meal chum. Using corn meal to hold the chum together, mold the mashed fish (fry of some forage species) into a flat patty much like a hamburger.

Then place a single small baitfish on the hook, and carefully work it into the flattened mass of corn meal and mashed fish, folding it over and rolling it into a ball, so as to conceal the single small baitfish inside.

Carefully stripping line from your reel, toss the "meatball" out away from the boat. As it settles in the tide it will start to disintegrate. Drifting away from the ball will be pieces of fish which cruising gamefish will quickly pick up. Often they'll vie for the ball of small fish, and most certainly for the single remaining whole

fish as it drifts down into the depths. This system works when the
fish absolutely refuse to take a single baitfish being drifted out alone.

CHUM BALL IN HAIRNET

Another successful chumming technique when the fish are being
selective is to take a handful of chum and deposit it in a small bag
made from a lady's hairnet. The ball of chum should be about
one and a half to two inches in diameter. After filling the net to this
size, carefully tie it closed around the hook.

Once the chum bag has been prepared, take half a ladle of chum,
place the chum bag in the ladle, and toss both the chum and the
chum bag out together.

Keep the reel in free spool so that the chum bag drifts back with
the chum. As the cruising gamefish move through the slick to pick
up the chum, they'll quickly take the chum bag, which appears as
a ball of chum drifting along with the current.

KEEP BAIT ALONG EDGE OF KELP

A great deal of the chumming off the California coast is done
close to the kelp beds, which harbor great numbers of fish. Even on
the East Coast fine fishing is often encountered where there is an
abundance of heavy green seaweed or the pale brown type of weed
which floats on the surface.

The secret here is to keep your bait as close to the kelp or seaweed as possible, and to have the fish come out of the kelp to get
your bait. However, when a fish is hooked in a heavy kelp or weed
growth there is often a problem getting it out, so it is extremely important that you try to work your fish out into open water as
quickly as possible. This often calls for horsing tactics—trying to
reel the fish in quickly—when the fish is first hooked. Once you
get the fish out into open water then you can let him have his
head and let him wear himself down where he won't get your line
loaded up with many pounds of the heavy kelp or weed.

SAND IN CHUM HELPFUL

While chumming on Challenger Banks off Bermuda we noticed
that many of the local guides use common sand as a supplement to

Anchovies are favored as chum aboard West Coast boats. They are kept alive in live tanks such as this, through which water is constantly pumped, thus providing the needed oxygen to keep the anchovies in perfect condition. A small net or scoop is used to remove the anchovies from the live tank.

John Mason, deckhand on the sportfisherman Angela out of Los Angeles, tosses out a netful of live anchovies as he starts a chum line. Inshore fishermen attract Pacific barracuda, Pacific bonito, halibut, kelp bass, sand bass, yellowtail and white sea bass to the chum of lively anchovies.

the chum. They add a pail of ordinary sand to each pail of hog-mouth fry which they use as chum, often squashing the fry to cause the juices of the small forage species to mix with the sand. As it settles into the depths the sand sparkles and sinks quickly, helping to attract gamefish.

Although this is the only spot we've observed sand being used as a supplement to chum, it would seem to us that it would work equally well while chumming anywhere. In fact, it might even improve results. Bermudians swear by it!

JIGS BRING STRIKES WHILE CHUMMING

While most anglers employ natural baits in a chum slick, there are many fishermen who turn to artificials and enjoy fine results. Almost all the members of the mackerel clan, including the Atlantic mackerel, Spanish mackerel and the princely king mackerel respond to lures worked through a chum line. So do bonito, yellowtail and little tuna, as well as the albacore.

This happy angler landed a beautiful yellowtail while drifting an anchovy bait off the kelp beds at the Todos Santos Islands off Mexico's Baja Peninsula. He used a general-purpose boat outfit and light monofilament line to present the anchovy to the hungry gamefish.

Diamond and tri-sided jigs, hammered stainless steel jigs, and deep-diving jigs all produce well. The technique varies, with West Coast anglers usually casting their lure away from the boat and retrieving erratically, alternately jigging with their rod tip. East Coast fishermen usually let their jig settle into the depths and then work it back with a vigorous jigging of their rod tip.

The bucktail jig, with bucktail skirt and lead head, is a very effective lure when worked through a chum line, accounting for many varieties of fish.

FISH IN KNOWN HAUNTS

As we mentioned earlier, it's important that you chum in areas frequented by gamefish. Fishing grounds worked by the charter and party boats are good locations. But if you must make your own decisions on where to fish, look at a Coast and Geodetic Survey chart of the area you plan to fish. Most gamefish frequent areas where baitfish are plentiful. So look for broken and irregular bottom, shallow underwater plateaus, or lumps of bottom. Look for a confluence of currents where bay and ocean meet, or a peninsula where a tide rip forms and gamefish feed. Spots like this are more apt to hold gamefish than flat, unbroken bottom.

Sixth Sense Useful in Striking

While a great deal has been written about striking fish, we are duty bound to admit that it takes a bit of sixth sense in order to know just when to strike when a gamefish mouths your bait in a chum line.

Usually you can feel even the lightest pickup, because your line is running free. Sometimes you can even feel your baitfish swimming about nervously at the approach of a big gamefish.

As a rule you have to hesitate a moment and let a gamefish move off with a live baitfish, because the baitfish is usually larger and more active than dead bait, resulting in the fish first taking it into its mouth, and then pausing for a moment before swallowing it.

With dead bait drifted through a chum line, or with meatball-type baits and hairnet bait it is usually best to strike immediately when you feel the fish, for invariably the fish just swims up and takes the bait in one movement.

Chumming Inshore and for Bottom Species

While chummnig produces fine results with pelagic species, the boatmen can enjoy equally good results with species that frequent inshore areas, as well as bottom feeders. In fact, the fishing can get so fast and furious on the inshore grounds that it can actually become tiresome!

Techniques vary considerably more inshore than they do offshore, in that the systems employed are most often geared to a specific species. It should be noted, however, that many of the chumming tricks used for one species will work equally well with others.

SPOT IS IMPORTANT

As with offshore, you've got to fish a spot known to hold fish. This isn't as difficult to do inshore, for there are bays, rivers and estuaries that are always loaded with fish, as are the spots where ocean and bay waters meet or where passes and inlets empty into the ocean.

Striped bass are one of the most popular of the inshore fish which readily respond to a chum line. Anglers in the Chesapeake Bay area have for many years been taking substantial catches of "rock," as they are called in that area, while chumming with grass shrimp, pieces of blue crab and crushed soft clams.

The favored techniques employed are much the same as for offshore fishing, with the exception that lighter tackle is used. The best suited type of tackle are the popping outfit or a light salt-water bay outfit.

Anchoring is usually done in a tideway where the current is strong enough to carry the chum a considerable distance, which attracts the roving schools of stripers.

Naturally, hook sizes are smaller than for offshore species, with Eagle Claw and Beak styles favored.

Much the same as with offshore fishing, clinch-on sinkers are used to take the bait deep when the current is strong, and plastic floats are brought into play when the current is slow and the bait must be kept from settling to the bottom.

Anchor Off Jetties

Many small-boat men enjoy fine chumming while anchoring off coastal jetties or breakwaters. Using a chum of grass shrimp, ground clams, clam stomachs, mussels, diced squid or almost any other food, they let the chum line drift in toward the submerged rocks and attract any fish which live around them.

This technique works extremely well with striped bass, weakfish, tautog, sheepshead, mangrove snappers, yellowtail snappers, kelp bass and a host of other bottom feeders. They readily come away from the reefs, mangroves or rocks which they call home to enjoy the offering of chum.

Crushed Clams Are Good

For such bottom feeders as porgies, sea bass, codfish and pollock, many anglers crush whole sea clams with a hammer and then drop the clams overboard. The smashed clams immediately settle to the bottom with pieces drifting off, bringing the bottom feeders to the area, where regular bottom-fishing techniques are brought into play.

Still another way of attracting these bottom feeders, as well as groupers, snappers and a host of tropical species, is to find a good patch of bottom and to use several cans of dog or cat food in place of regular chum. We've employed this system in the Bahamas and caught fish until arm-weary.

Simply take the top off the can, then puncture a couple of holes in the bottom and throw the whole can overboard. When the can settles on the bottom, the finely ground food will disperse, attracting many bottom feeders.

Use Chum Pot

Still another way of attracting bottom feeders to your hook is to use chum which is placed in a chum pot. The chum pot is nothing more than a wire basket made of quarter-inch galvanized wire mesh which is approximately the size of a round oatmeal box. It has a lead bottom, which takes it deep and holds it on the bottom. The top is removable so that chum may be inserted, and it is attached to a line in order to be raised and lowered with ease.

There are a great many ingredients which can go into the chum pot. The most frequently used chum is ground menhaden which is put into the pot in a frozen log. When resting on the bottom, the chum thaws and gradually oozes from the chum pot, attracting bottom feeders from great distances.

Many anglers along the middle and north Atlantic Coast put black mussels through a meat grinder, which work very well in a chum pot. We've also employed dog and cat food in the chum pot, cooked rice, and even whole-kernel corn! While fish don't have corn included in their regular diet, it does seem to attract them.

Bread Attracts Them Too

In Bermuda we learned of an unusual technique which is employed to take pompano along the island beaches. Anglers take a loaf of white bread and cut off several corners of the bread, which are set aside for bait. The remainder of the bread is broken up into pieces the size of a nickel. Then the angler takes two or three cans of sardines, pours the oil over the broken-up bread and shreds the sardines. When the whole mess is mixed together, chumming commences. Soon the pompano move into the oily slick, at which time the corner pieces of bread are placed on the hook and eased towards the pompano feeding on the chum. As soon as they spot the piece of bread on the hook, they're onto it in a flash!

CHUM ON SHOALS

One of the most effective methods we've ever employed to take big channel bass from the shoals of the Outer Banks of North Carolina is to anchor right in the turbulent water and to employ ground menhaden as chum. The favorite method is to freeze a gallon can full of the ground bunker, and then as soon as it thaws enough, to slip the whole slug out of the can, and put it in an onion sack. The onion sack with its frozen block of bunker is lowered to the bottom —actually the water is only four to six feet deep—with best results occurring late in the day and especially after sundown.

As the bunker thaws, the tide carries it from the onion sack and the big channel bass move in, at which time you fish for them with a conventional bottom rig, using a big chunk of mullet or menhaden as bait. Half a spot is also a good bait, as these small fish are plentiful in the area and constitute a major portion of the channel bass's diet.

Sand Fleas Are Good Chum

Years ago we read that millionaires chummed for giant stripers in New England employing lobsters as chum. Well, we'd much rather enjoy the lobsters than use them as chum! But most fish will respond to a chum line of crustaceans. The plentiful little sand fleas which are found along the surf are excellent bait for such species as black-fish, sheepshead and pompano. The sand fleas make fine chum. They should first be crushed, however, so that they are immobilized and cannot bury themselves in the sand should they reach bottom.

NIGHT CHUMMING IS GREAT SPORT

During the last decade, chumming at night has grown in popularity wherever gamefish abound. While many small-boat men don't care to venture forth at night to chum for their favorite gamefish, many step aboard party packets to enjoy fine sport.

Many of the boats sail an hour or two before dark, in order to reach the chumming grounds before darkness sets in. Chumming commences and continues on into the night. The boats are illuminated with batteries of floodlights, which makes it just as easy to see at night as during the day.

Night chumming is often far better than daytime fishing, particularly with bluefish, bonito, white sea bass and other gamesters. Often the bigger fish aren't as wary at night and respond quickly to a chum spread.

Often nighttime chummers attract huge schools of baitfish under the lights of their boats, which in turn attracts more gamefish. It's a sight to behold, for often three or four species of fish move in under the lights and can be seen darting through the chum line, picking up small baitfish, pieces of chum, and the baited hooks as well.

It's not uncommon on the West Coast to land half a dozen or more species in an evening's chumming. Much the same is true on the East Coast, where chummers often dock with bluefish, bonito, small dolphin, fluke and porgies, all of which move into a nighttime chum spread. Sharks frequently move in at night too, providing fine light-tackle sport when taken from a chum line.

EXPERIMENTATION PAYS OFF

It certainly pays to experiment with chumming techniques, for you never know whether or not fish will respond to chum unless you

Harold Whitmeyer sailed offshore on a New Jersey party boat one evening to land this nice bluefish while chumming. He used a long shanked Carlisle hook and baited with a chunk of menhaden, which was drifted out in a chumline of ground menhaden, popularly called mossbunker along much of the Atlantic Coast.

June Rosko just swung aboard this Pacific barracuda landed by her daughter Linda while they were out on a twilight party-boat trip out of Oceanside, California. Twilight chumming trips are popular with family groups on the West Coast, with the boats sailing just after dinner and returning shortly after dark. Often each angler aboard has several species in his bag.

try. We know a striped bass guide who for many years anchored just beyond the reach of the breakers in the surf and fished with sandworm baits on the bottom for bass. He enjoyed average success until he started chumming with small pieces of sandworm. Then his catches soared.

The stripers simply moved along the surf, picking up pieces of seaworm which came drifting by; and eventually they moved right up to his boat, where they got hooked. Often other boats anchored nearby had trouble getting strikes, while the guide—thanks to his experimenting with chum—made many fine catches.

On the West Coast we know of a party-boat skipper who won't grind his chum from dead baitfish. He actually puts live anchovies through his grinder when chumming for kelp bass, yellowtail and other gamefish, because the live baitfish when ground make a bloody chum, which brings him far better results and a finer slick than were he grinding chum with baitfish that had been dead for some time.

Effectiveness Can Be Proved

Occasionally skeptics have asked why we bothered with chumming, for they felt they'd catch just as many fish while not using chum. Such is seldom the case, however. A simple way to prove to yourself that the chum is what's attracting the fish is to examine the stomach contents of the fish you catch. We've done it often, and found every type of chum imagineable in their stomachs, including ground menhaden, clam stomachs, grass shrimp, dog and cat food, and even that whole-kernel corn we mentioned earlier! Naturally, in the cases where we used live baitfish it was difficult to tell, except when we saw the gamesters were streaking through the chum line to pick up every baitfish we tossed overboard!

Easy to Obtain

Almost all of the different natural foods we've mentioned as used for chum are readily obtainable at most coastal ports. On the West Coast the obtaining of live bait is big business, and practically every harbor has a bait barge which is loaded with live baitfish.

Along the East Coast ground menhaden is frozen in five-gallon tins, or put up in plastic bags and then packed in cardboard containers for ease in handling. You can even buy fresh menhaden and grind them yourself if you so desire.

Grass shrimp are available in some areas, as are clam stomachs and most other kinds of popular chum. Some boatmen of our acquaintance always have a case of fish-base cat food on board, so they're never without chum!

CHUMMING IS RELAXING

The increased popularity of chumming among boatmen in recent years can be attributed to several things. First of all, there's no question that when you get a good chum slick going you can often catch more fish than by other methods. Second, it's a relaxing type of fishing. A fellow who goes out on his own boat with two or three friends can fish with ease while handling the chum bucket. Additionally, it's a great type of fishing when you're taking some friends or youngsters along who aren't expert anglers. Often when the fish move into the chum line it's simply a matter of letting the bait out to where the feeding fish are. The fish frequently take the baits quickly.

Many gamefish and bottom feeders take up residence around offshore oil rigs in the Gulf of Mexico. Boatmen often tie up to the platforms and coax fish to the surface by employing crabs, small fish, shrimp and squid as chum.

5 Bottom Fishing

OF the many forms of salt-water fishing available to the boatman, bottom fishing is without a doubt the most relaxing and fun-filled. It's a grab-bag type of sport, for you never know what species will take your bait. Most anglers really don't care either, for they're out in the sun enjoying the broad expanse of water around them, and whatever scrappers decide to take their bait just add to the enjoyment of the day.

It's doubtful if anyone ever took a count, but there must be at least several hundred species which take up residence on the bottom of the Atlantic and Pacific Oceans, as well as the broad expanse of the Gulf of Mexico. Even the many bays, rivers and estuaries which empty into these bodies of water are crowded with bottom feeders, which are always looking for a meal. We will, however, limit our discussion of bottom feeders to those which are most plentiful and provide maximum enjoyment for boatmen who send their baits down to the bottom.

Broadly speaking, bottom feeders are those salt-water species which are not classified as gamefish and which spend most of their time cruising at intermediate levels or along the bottom as they search for a meal. In the main they're not great fighters, but when caught on reasonably light tackle they offer stubborn resistance that can be lots of fun.

Techniques which are used to catch them vary along each section of coast, but the basic outfits used by boatmen are quite standard. An angler would find that the basic boat outfit he used for pollock off Long Island would work extremely well for grouper fishing off Louisiana or hauling in ling cod off the Oregon coast. Here it is important to remember that the only major variation in the selection of a fishing outfit would depend on whether you did your fishing in the open reaches of the ocean or the confines of bays, rivers and estuaries.

Generally speaking, ocean fishing produces bigger fish. The water is usually deeper and often the currents are swifter, which necessitates heavier tackle. Fishing in protected waters, where the currents are slower and the water shallow, permits you to scale down your fishing outfit considerably.

One of Two Outfits Ideal

Over the years we've fished with many different types of fishing outfits, and have found the two which are discussed under general-purpose tackle ideally suited to bottom fishing. We use the basic boat outfit for all ocean fishing and party-boat fishing, while the bay or popping outfit is brought into play in bays, rivers and estuaries while fishing from small boats.

An angler equipped with these basic outfits can fish on any of our coasts and enjoy fine sport. While anglers' favorites differ on each section of coastline, the degree of variation from these fundamentally sound outfits is minimal.

MULTIPLYING REEL BEST FOR BOTTOM FISHING

While occasionally bottom fishing may require a slight degree of casting, in the main it is simply a matter of permitting your rig to settle to the bottom and retrieving it when a strike is received or to check your bait. Because of this the multiplying reel is superior to a spinning reel. While in many areas anglers bottom fish with spinning tackle, it is not to be recommended. As mentioned earlier, spinning tackle is designed for casting and should be used as such. In our judgment the spinning outfit used for bottom fishing is a poor substitute for a conventional bottom-fishing outfit.

TERMINAL RIGS VARY

To give you as broad an outlook as possible we will discuss the many different styles of terminal rigs found to be popular along

Bottom fishing is perhaps more relaxing than any type of salt-water fishing. It's full of fun too, for you never know which of the many bottom feeders will take your bait as you drift along.

The grouper family are popular bottom feeders with Bahamas, Florida and Gulf Coast anglers. Fish like this husky Nassau grouper, landed from a reef off New Providence Island in the Bahamas, make an excellent chowder. They'll test your tackle to the utmost as you pump them from the depths.

various sections of coastline, along with the natural baits and techniques employed while using the rigs.

Before proceeding, we would like to point out that we've often tried many of these rigs in areas other than where they enjoy peak popularity. In most instances we've enjoyed fine fishing, which points up the fact that you're not bound by local tradition and habits in the type of bottom rig you use.

Single-Hook Rig Is Popular

Along the Gulf Coast a single-hook bottom rig is most popular. In fact, you can fish for days on end and seldom see anglers employing anything other than the rig we're about to discuss.

It's a very simple rig to make up. First an egg-shaped sinker is slipped onto the line. A sinker of this type has a hole right through the middle of it, which permits it to slide on the line as the rig rolls along the bottom or as a fish takes the bait.

After the sinker is slipped on, a small barrel swivel is tied to the end of the line, which prevents the sinker from sliding off. Then a 24-inch to 36-inch piece of nylon leader material is tied to the swivel.

The final step is to tie a hook to the leader, and you're all ready to go down to the bottom for variety galore.

As this rig rests on the bottom, it can roll with the current very easily. When a bottom feeder takes the bait, it can pull and tug without feeling the weight of the sinker. Without the weight of the sinker interfering, the angler can also feel even the lightest nibble.

Components Vary

The various components used to make up the rig will vary, of course, because of the local conditions you encounter, the species being sought and the baits being used.

Inasmuch as most southern species have big mouths and lots of sharp teeth, most anglers use leader material that tests at least 20 pounds, although 30-pound and 40-pound test is by far the most popular, as it is less apt to fray or be bitten through by a big fish.

As to the sinkers, it is good to carry a selection with you ranging in weight from a quarter-ounce to four ounces. In the main, the small sizes will be put to use in the protected reaches of sounds and rivers, while the heavier weights will be brought into play while fishing well out in the depths of the Gulf or in the swift passes which empty into it.

Colonel Dick Crawford landed this husky sheepshead while fishing with a live shrimp in a mangrove-lined creek that empties into the Gulf of Mexico in Florida. The sheepshead takes a bait very fast and can empty your hook in an instant. To hook them you've got to strike the instant they take the bait.

A bottom rig such as this is very easy to make up. It is in most popular use along the Gulf of Mexico but can be used with good results on almost any inshore bottom feeders. Shrimp is one of the favorite Gulf Coast baits.

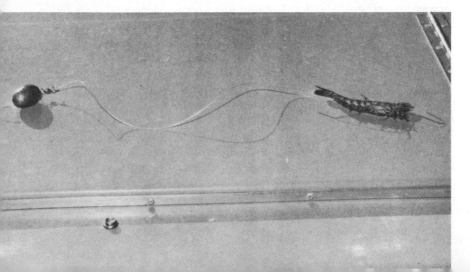

The big red snapper just swung aboard by George Seemann took a whole balao bait fished on the bottom by June Rosko while fishing above a reef off Chub Cay in the Bahamas. The red snapper, in addition to being a fine table fish, gives a good account of itself when taken on medium-weight tackle. It is a favorite of Bahamas, Florida and Gulf Coast anglers.

Claw-Style Hook Is Best

You'll see practically every hook style imagineable in use with the rig we've just described. But over a period of years, having tried many styles, we've settled on the Eagle-Claw or Beak style hook as best. Hooks of this style are made of fine wire which lends itself well to natural baits. They have offset points which are needle sharp and penetrate fast. Hooks of this style are made with bait-holder shanks too, which are helpful when using chunks of bait, as the barbs on the shank of the hook hold the bait secure.

As to hook sizes, it is wise to carry a wide selection with you at all times, to be prepared for whatever fish you may encounter. Sizes number 2 and 3 are often useful when using tiny shrimp or small pieces of mullet as bait for such bottom feeders as croaker, mangrove snapper, whiting and small grey trout. When big fish are in residence, such as Nassau and yellowfin grouper, or even such gamefish as snook and redfish, it is necessary to employ a large hook with live pinfish bait, at which times a 6/0 or 7/0 size is appropriate.

Large Variety of Baits

With a rig such as we've just described, there are a wide variety of baits which may be used to catch an almost unbelievable variety of both bottom and game species which roam the floor of the Gulf and its tributaries for a meal.

The shrimp is without a doubt the most popular bait of the Gulf Coast angler. It is usually in plentiful supply, kept alive in the aerated holding tanks of bait dealers, who sell them by the dozen or the hundred, whatever you wish.

As we flip through several vintage log books we find we've caught many species on this rig while using shrimp baits fished directly on the bottom. Included were such gamefish as snook, redfish, tarpon, bonefish and amberjack. Among the bottom feeders and semi-game species were the jack crevalle, ladyfish, many varieties of groupers and snappers, gafftopsail catfish, croaker, Spanish mackerel, pompano and seatrout. There may have been more, but this will give you an idea of the great fondness Gulf residents have for live or dead shrimp fished on the bottom.

Next on the list of popular baits is the mullet. This baitfish is also in plentiful supply and brings in many bottom feeders.

There are two popular ways of preparing a mullet to be used as a bottom bait. First the mullet is filleted, so that there is one slab of bone-free meat from each side of the fish. If you're after small bottom feeders, such as mangrove snapper, ladyfish, croaker, and sea-

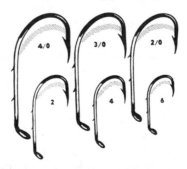

Eagle-Claw or Beak style hooks are ideally suited to bottom fishing with natural baits. Their fine wire construction, sharp points and offset point lend themselves well to using small pieces of soft bait that would fall apart on a bulky hook. The bait-holder shank keeps the bait from bunching up on the curve of the hook.

trout, you can cut the mullet fillet in small chunks, measuring about half an inch in width by an inch to an inch and a half in length.

If king mackerel, Spanish mackerel, jacks or other husky fish are your target, then a strip bait of mullet is best. This should be cut in a torpedo shape, tapered to a point at the tail so it flutters in the water. Size will depend on the fish being sought, with the most popular baits measuring from four to six inches in length by three-quarters of an inch in width.

You needn't use only mullet for small chunks or as strip baits for bottom fishing. When we've run out of mullet we've frequently cut baits from whatever species we had aboard, including mackerel, snapper and croaker, which worked equally well.

LIVE BAITS ARE GOOD TOO

With some husky bottom feeders a live baitfish is best. One of the most popular baitfish found along the Gulf Coast is the pinfish, although squirrel fish, grunts and almost any fish in the four-inch to six-inch range will work out quite well.

These big baitfish are employed with the same rig, hooked gently either through the lips or the fleshy part of their backs, and worked down on the bottom for big grouper, the giant jewfish grouper, snook, redfish and big tarpon. The last three species mentioned are among our finest gamefish, but they'll readily take a live bait fished on the bottom, particularly when fished in the many passes emptying into the Gulf of Mexico.

Use Plastic Float to Keep Bait Up

Pilchards are also a fine baitfish, particularly popular with anglers who fish for Spanish and king mackerel. Occasionally these two species, as well as grey weakfish and seatrout, frequent intermediate levels and do not require that the bait be fished directly on the bottom. At such times many bottom fishermen simply employ a small egg-shaped sinker and use a plastic float to suspend the bait at intermediate levels.

Marked Difference on West Coast

Quite a bit of the bottom fishing which is done offshore on the West Coast is done in extremely deep water. It is not uncommon to bottom fish in waters with depths of from 200 to 500 feet and more. To do so requires specialized rigging which differs markedly from that which is employed on the East and Gulf Coasts.

The basic bottom rig for rockfishing, for example, is called a ganion rig. Because the great depth of water makes the process of reeling in tiresome, most anglers prefer to use a multi-hook rig, which enables them to reel in less frequently and to bring in several fish at a time. The ganion rig is designed with this purpose in mind.

Included under the general term of rockfishing are such species whose local names include cow cod, rock cod, ling cod, grey grouper and many other varieties of bottom fish.

The ganion rig is best employed with either solid monel line, lead-core line or Dacron line. These lines do not stretch and can be worked more vertically from boat to bottom. Monofilament tends to have too much stretch, and braided nylon tends to be dragged by the current away from the boat, instead of going straight to the bottom.

MAKING UP A GANION RIG

Onto the end of the line most West Coast anglers tie a ball-bearing swivel with coastlock snap. This insures smooth swiveling of the ganion rig which is attached to it, and keeps the line from twisting and tangling in the extreme depths.

Onto the coastlock snap a six-foot to eight-foot piece of 50-pound or 60-pound-test line is attached. Into this section of line the angler ties anywhere from four to six loops. Onto these loops are later fastened snelled hooks, which are hooks with leaders already attached.

To the end of the long piece of line a sturdily constructed snap swivel is tied, onto which your sinker is attached. And here's the rub: you use sinkers that weigh anywhere from 10 to 24 ounces! One can well understand that with a rig like this you need a sturdy rod, and many anglers even use 50-pound-class regulation rods, or stiff-action rods of the general-purpose type.

Big Hooks Best

As most of the bottom feeders you encounter have big mouths, some big enough to accomodate your fist, most anglers stick with big hooks on all four to six loops of the ganion. Sizes 6/o through

8/o hooks are favored and these are usually snelled to 40-pound or 50-pound-test nylon or nylon-covered stainless steel cable leader material.

The accepted technique used with a rig of this type is to drift across the deep holes, keeping the rig just off the bottom so that it does not snag. This is accomplished by letting the rig settle directly to the bottom, and then reeling it up several feet.

MANY BAITS PRODUCE

A wide variety of baits may be used successfully while rockfishing. Actually, the bottom feeders will readily take most anything that looks like food. Favored baits include chunks of squid, sardines, anchovies, mackerel, or any other type of fish which is available. Many anglers will take a small live rockfish that they catch and bait up with that, finding that a small live bait will often entice a lunker rockfish.

As one drifts along with this rig and receives a strike, the hook is immediately set but the angler does not reel in. You simply continue to drift along, waiting for strikes and lifting back to set the hook firmly. Once you feel extremely heavy weight dragging the rod, you know that several of your hooks have fish on them, and you proceed to reel them in.

Some anglers employ up to a dozen hooks on the rig, using extremely heavy tackle, but with a rig such as this it becomes more work than sport. Accordingly, we recommend sticking with a ganion made up of only four to six hooks.

BONUS OF BIG SEA BASS

The California counterpart of the Gulf Coast angler's jewfish grouper is the black sea bass, which often weighs upwards of 500 pounds. The big black sea bass are hooked while bottom fishing with small fish as bait; they call upon all the skills an angler can muster to pump them from the bottom to within gaffing range.

Another prize of the California, Oregon and Washington bottom bouncer is the halibut. Most halibut weigh from three to ten pounds, but there are many taken during the course of a season that pull the scale down to 40 pounds and more. A small live baitfish fished a foot or two off the bottom works best.

Rockfish are a favorite of West Coast bottom fishermen. Emil Adams landed this average-size rockfish—of which there are approximately 50 species—while bottom fishing with a live anchovy bait. It was but one of several he landed in a morning's fast fishing just outside the Golden Gate Bridge.

MODIFIED IN SHALLOW WATERS

Where the depths are more reasonable, West Coast anglers modify their ganion rigs, including only two or three hooks and using sinkers of considerably less weight. Rods, reels and lines are scaled down too, for fishing in shallow water doesn't require the sturdy gear of the offshore depths. The West Coast bottom fisherman finds that variety is a keynote of his fishing.

This is also true of bottom fishing on other coastlines. In addition to the species already mentioned, bottom fishermen often score well with white sea bass, barracuda and deep-traveling bonito. With these species, however, smaller baits are preferred, with hooks in the 1/0 or 2/0 size being ample.

High-Low Rig East Coast Favorite

The most popular rig employed for bottom fishing along the middle and north Atlantic Coast is the high-low rig. As its name implies, the rig enables the angler to fish with one high hook and one low hook.

The high-low rig is a ready-made rig which is available in most coastal tackle shops. It comes in a wide selection of types.

It is made of heavy nylon leader material and measures about 18 to 24 inches in length. At the top of the rig there is a snap to which you tie your line. Immediately below the snap there is a swivel arm, to which you tie a snelled hook.

At the bottom end of the rig there is still another swivel arm, to which you attach your second snelled hook. Just below the swivel is a couple of inches of leader material on the end of which is a snap onto which your sinker is attached. With this rig, one hook is fished directly on the bottom, while the second is about two feet up from the bottom.

As with fishing everywhere, proper sinker weight is dependent upon depth of water and current. A bank-style sinker is favored by most East Coast anglers, who use weights ranging from one ounce to more than 12 ounces. The bank style is a six-sided, elongated sinker which is well suited to sandy as well as rocky or irregular bottoms, as its shape does not foul on obstructions easily.

Another popular style is the bass-casting or dipsy sinker, which is an elongated egg-shaped sinker with a small barrel swivel molded into its head. These are usually available in small sizes, ranging from half an ounce to two ounces.

SNELLED HOOKS FAVORED

With a rig of this type most anglers employ snelled hooks. The hooks are snelled to 18 or 24 inches of stiff nylon leader material.

For species such as porgy, sea bass, tautog (often called blackfish), weakfish and others which range from one to four pounds on the average, a number 1 or 1/0 Eagle-Claw hook is fine. Some anglers in this section of coast prefer a Sproat hook or a Virginia hook, as well as a Beak hook. Whatever the hook style, make certain it is a good quality hook with a sharp point that will penetrate fast and a sufficiently large barb to hold the fish securely.

On the offshore grounds, where husky codfish, pollock, cusk and other cold-water species are the bill of fare, anglers employ larger hooks, finding the 5/0, 6/0 and 7/0 size more suitable for these large-mouthed fish.

The high-low rig we've just described is generally used from an anchored or slowly drifting boat. If the current is too fast, or if the boat drifts too fast because of strong wind, the rig will occasionally become entangled if the snelled hooks are attached to leaders that are too long. So be careful not to use leaders more than 24 inches long in conjunction with a rig of this type.

The high-low rig is a very popular bottom rig used by many anglers along all three of our coasts. It enables an angler to attach one high and one low hook to the rig with ease and to change hooks quickly as conditions warrant. It is made of a variety of materials and in many styles, but basically all fall within the same concept: to keep one bait right on the bottom and a second bait slightly off the bottom.

Porgies are fun to catch. They strike a clam bait with relish and give an excellent account of themselves when taken on a medium-weight general-purpose outfit. They're taken in great numbers by party-boat anglers along the Middle Atlantic states on up to New England, where they are often called "scup."

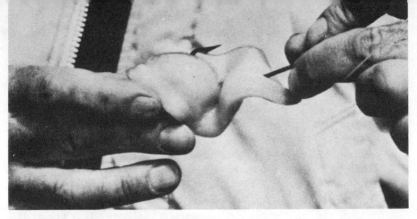

Along the middle and north Atlantic coast you'll find that clams are a favorite of the bottom fisherman. These plentiful bivalves account for bottom feeders the year round. Because of the tough meat of a clam it is best not to bury the hook in the flesh but to leave the point and barb exposed, so the hook can penetrate fast once a bottom feeder inhales it.

Summer Flounder Rig Differs

The summer flounder is one of the most popular summer species found along the Atlantic Coast (as is its close cousin, the southern flounder, along the Florida and Gulf Coasts).

Anglers who fish for this husky member of the flatfish clan usually employ a single-hook rig, for the flounder likes a moving bait. Most boatmen drift for them rather than fish from anchor. The single-hook rig is less apt to get tangled, which is why so many flounder fishermen use it.

The rig is built around a small three-way swivel. A size 4 swivel is fine. The swivel is tied directly to the end of your line. Onto one eye of the swivel tie a six-inch piece of lightweight monofilament, about 15-pound test. A loop is tied into the end of this short piece of monofilament, onto which a bank-style sinker is attached. Note that the piece of monofilament which is used to tie the sinker should be of a lighter test than the line you are using, so that should the sinker become fouled on the bottom the light line will break and you won't forfeit the whole rig.

As you'll be drifting or even slowly trolling at times, you'll find that bank sinkers in the three-ounce to eight-ounce size are most often the best to use.

Boats such as this are popular for sheltered-water bottom-fishing excursions. Here Art and Joan Cone and June Rosko prepare to shove off for a day of bottom fishing. Rental boats such as this are roomy enough for plenty of fishing tackle, an ice chest and lots of fish.

Captain Otto Reut of the charter boat First Timer unhooks a big Jersey fluke for Milt Rosko, Sr. The fluke, properly called summer flounder, was hooked while bottom fishing with a strip of fluke belly bait along the edge of Ambrose Channel leading into New York Harbor. Fluke of this size must always be netted, for they often thrash the water wildly as they are brought to boatside.

Onto the remaining eye of the swivel tie a 30-inch piece of stiff nylon leader material, onto the end of which is tied either an Eagle-Claw or Carlisle hook.

If using live minnows as bait, the Eagle Claw is preferred, whereas when using dead bait such as spearing, sand launce, strips of squid and the like, a Carlisle bait-holder hook is superior. The Carlisle bait-holder style is simply a standard long-shanked hook, with a small hook attached to the shank near the eye of the hook. The small hook holds the front part of the bait, and the large hook is imbedded well towards the back of the bait, where it quickly strikes home once a flounder takes it into his mouth.

Hook sizes from 3/0 on up to 7/0 are employed for summer flounders. The smaller sizes are appropriate for small bay flatties, while the bigger sizes are brought into use on the open ocean, where the fluke—as they are called in some areas—grow large.

SPREADER RIG HOLDS BAITS ON BOTTOM

A bottom rig which is extremely popular with anglers who fish for winter flounder along the middle and north Atlantic Coast is a spreader. This is nothing more than a stiff piece of wire with a loop on each end onto which snelled hooks are tied; the wire has a snap for a sinker in the middle, plus an eye to which you attach your line. This results in the entire rig resting right on the bottom.

Chestertown hooks are favored for the winter flounders, and these are snelled to about a foot of leader material, which in turn is looped onto the spreader. Hook sizes ranging from number 9 or 10 are fine for small bay flounders, while number 5 or 6 sizes are used for the big winter flounder found in the open ocean. Sandworms and blood-worms are the favorite baits, although clams produce well too.

Onto each of the end eyes of this flounder spreader the angler ties a snelled hook. His line is tied to the top eye while a sinker is slipped onto the bottom clip. When lowered to the bottom the entire rig rests right on the bottom, thus assuring that both hooks are in view of such bottom feeders as winter flounders.

Party boats that fish in northern climes usually have heated cabins. The Paramount II *out of Brielle, N. J., is typical of most packets in that it has heated cabins and a restaurant for those cold winter days when the fishing is slow.*

MULTI-HOOK RIG

Still another popular bottom rig used along many sections of sea-coast consists of a multi-hook rig, with two or three hooks attached to one leader. This is made up by attaching a hook to a three-foot piece of nylon leader material, and at one-foot intervals tying in with a blood knot additional hooks which are snelled to about a foot of leader material. A rig of this type is then attached to one eye of a three-way swivel, a bank-style sinker to another eye and your line to the remaining eye. This streaming multi-hook rig rests directly on the bottom, putting three baits right where flounders, porgies, sea bass, kingfish, ling, whiting and a host of other species can readily spot them.

INTERESTING RIG WITH TROLLING SINKER

While fishing in the Bahamas for grouper, and in the Gulf of Mexico too, we've employed a bottom rig which utilized a trolling sinker to good effect. The rig was made up much like a trolling rig, with a swivel on the end of the line, then a three-ounce or four-ounce trolling sinker, onto which was attached a four-foot or five-foot leader of number 8 or 9 stainless steel wire.

Onto the end of the wire a 6/o or 7/o Claw or Beak hook was attached, and the rig was baited with a small live baitfish. Any bait-fish works well, particularly in the Bahamas, for there is little fishing pressure for the bottom feeders and they're always anxious for a meal.

The rig is lowered to the bottow until the sinker bounces. Then it is quickly reeled up two or three feet. The reason for this is that there is a great deal of coral along the bottom, and regular sinkers would quickly become fouled. The torpedo-shaped trolling sinker seldom fouls, and yet is held several feet off the bottom, only the wire leader occasionally touches the coral.

When a big grouper or snapper strikes, it cannot cut the wire on the coral. If you put a lot of pressure on him you can lift him off the bottom, and he's soon your fish.

Skills Must Be Developed

Often catching bottom feeders is limited by the physical endur-ance of an angler. Frequently the fish are so plentiful that it's only a matter of dropping your line into the water and quickly pulling up a fish.

But there are occasions when bottom fishing requires all the finesse of offshore trolling or tangling with gamefish with a casting rod. So don't make the mistake of thinking it's going to be a push-over. Many over-confident anglers put in hours on the bottom grounds and come back with small catches to show for their effort.

Keep Terminal Rigging Minimal

An important consideration with any species, whether big game or bottom feeder, is to keep terminal rigging at an absolute mini-

The three-way swivel is a very useful piece of terminal tackle, for a wide variety of bottom rigs may be built around it.

mum. Often you'll see high-low rigs on a tackle counter that are a collection of beads, swivels, snaps and clips. These are made to look attractive and catch the eye of the fisherman. On the offshore grounds they're seldom as effective as a basic, simple rig with a minimum of components to get fouled on the bottom, or to let you down when you hook a lunker.

JIGS WORK WELL TOO

Throughout this chapter we've spoken of bottom fishing and discussed the rigs which are used primarily in conjunction with natural baits. Many bottom feeders, however, will take a jig worked in the depths, so we'll cover this interesting type of rig here; while it will take gamefish as well, it is most often used for non-game species.

The type of jigs we speak of here are not the bucktail jig which is popular with the gamefisherman and boat caster. The jigs used by bottom fishermen are of the diamond, tri-sided and butterfish types. They're usually molded of lead and then chrome plated. Some are even made of hammered stainless steel. They come in several types, some with hooks molded right into the body, others with treble hooks affixed with split rings.

In size the jigs vary from those weighing a quarter-ounce to huge 16-ounce models. The smaller models are used with light tackle in shallow water, while the bigger models are used to probe depths to 200 feet or more offshore.

Jigging Is Work

Jigging isn't as easy as fishing with a baited bottom rig. With a jig you've got to work, and work hard, but you can run up a nice score with bottom feeders if you do it properly.

The diamond jig can be used to coax many bottom feeders into striking. It must be worked with a vigorous tip action in order to be effective.

If you're using monofilament line you can simply tie your jig directly to the end of your line. If you're using Dacron or braided nylon line it's then best to tie a three-foot or four-foot nylon leader to the end of your line, attaching the jig to the leader. The connection between line and leader should be a small barrel swivel.

The accepted manner of jigging is to lower the jig all the way to the bottom and to retrieve it with a violent jigging motion of your rod tip. This sharp jigging and reeling motion causes the jig to dart toward the surface, then falter and dart toward the surface again.

Often bottom feeders are feeding on small baitfish just above the bottom, and when they see a shimmering jig they just can't resist it. This technique works very well with codfish, pollock, sea bass, mackerel, Pacific barracuda, Pacific yellowtail, weakfish, bluefish and almost all of the tunas.

Tube Teaser Helps Too

Many anglers improve the fish-catching effectiveness of their jigs by adding anywhere from one to five small teasers to their leader at intervals or from one foot to 18 inches. The teasers are fashioned of what is commonly called surgical tubing.

The tubing usually comes in neutral amber color, although red, yellow and black tubing produce well too.

The tubing teasers vary from an eighth-inch in diameter by two inches in length, to a half-inch in diameter by five or six inches in length. Within the center of the tubing is affixed a hook, ranging from small number 4 hooks for mackerel on up to 8/0 hooks for codfish.

As the rig consisting of a heavy jig and several teasers is jigged through the water it proves irresistible to hungry fish, for it resembles several frightened baitfish darting about. Surprisingly, more strikes are received on the teasers when they are used than on the jig proper.

While most jiggers use teasers made of surgical tubing or plastic tubing, we've seen many anglers employ strips of pork rind as teasers, as well as a tuft of feathers tied to a bare hook. All seem to work quite well by creating the impression that a scared group of little fish are trying to get away.

BOTTOM FEEDERS ARE TASTY

One thing that makes bottom fishing so popular with boatmen is the prospect of enjoying a fine seafood dinner afterwards. By far the tastiest fish in the sea are the bottom feeders. Indeed, no one could possibly dispute that lingcod from the Pacific's depths, flounder from the sandy bottom of the Atlantic, mangrove snappers from the Gulf, or Nassau grouper from the Bahamas are among the finest seafood dishes there are. Certainly few gamefish compare with the humble bottom feeder when it comes to gracing a dinner table.

Still another thing that makes bottom fishing so much fun is that it can be enjoyed by the whole family. It can be easy fishing, and bottom feeders are usually eager to cooperate in making a family's day on the water a great success.

Bob Rosko hooked this beautiful sea trout being held by Will Williams while drifting a shrimp across the bottom in the Gulf of Mexico off Yankeetown, Florida.

6 Boat Casting

THERE are many boatmen who love to fish, yet who never troll, bottom fish or chum. They're what might be termed dedicated casting enthusiasts, for they use their boats as casting platforms to reach spots and to position themselves within casting range of fish that otherwise might be inaccessible to their skill. Not only is there skill required to cast a lure or baitfish to a cruising fish, but even more skill is required when casting is done from a boat that may be tossing about on the ocean. Boat casters are a breed of angler who seem to develop. Initially most boatmen are content to do other types of fishing. But when they get in the company of casting enthusiasts they soon learn to enjoy the thrills which accompany effective casting, so that in reality they enjoy both the pleasures of casting and fishing.

Tackle Selection Up to Individual

There are many types of tackle which may be used for boat casting, as was discussed in an earlier chapter. The selection of either a multiplying, spinning or fly-casting outfit as the basic equipment is a selection which is entirely up to the individual.

Here, too, most boat casters progress from spinning through multiplying tackle, and finally to fly-casting tackle. The former is the easiest to master, while the latter is recognized by almost all boat-

163

men as being the ultimate casting tool in the hands of an experienced caster.

What makes casting so popular is the great personal satisfaction that comes from being able to handle a casting outfit properly. This, coupled with the fact that you're always doing something while casting, adds to the popularity of this fastest growing type of boat fishing.

Boat casting falls into three very distinct categories. There is offshore casting from a big boat or party boat far out at sea; then, inshore casting along the surf and jetties and while fishing in rivers, bays and tidal estuaries; and fishing from a small boat on shallow sand flats. Each has a type of excitement all its own.

OFFSHORE OFFERS THE UNKNOWN

Among some of the most exciting fishing a caster can enjoy is to fish on the offshore grounds most often frequented by trollers. In recent years a great many boatmen have employed trolling tackle to locate schools of feeding offshore gamefish, after which they shut down their engines to cast instead of troll.

We've employed this technique with great success in widely separated areas: for king mackerel in the Gulf, dolphin in the Bahamas and yellowtail off southern California. In each instance cited above, and in many more with other species, there was no sign of feeding fish on the surface. Only after several were hooked on trolled lures did we observe other fish in the area, after which casting tackle was brought into play with gratifying results.

Terminal Rigging Is Basic

There really isn't much to rigging up for offshore casting. Terminal tackle is kept to a bare minimum for practical casting. Whether using multiplying tackle such as a general-purpose boat or popping outfit, or a light or heavy spinning outfit, the terminal tackle remains basically the same.

Some anglers prefer using leaders which are prepared beforehand. These are made up in twenty-four-inch lengths, because if longer than this they would be difficult to handle while casting. Generally speaking, most offshore casters employ leader material which is somewhat heavier than the lines they are using, for they find the fish are less apt to sever a heavy leader with their teeth or to cause it to part should they wrap up in it.

Leaders are most often tied of nylon leader material in the range of 30-pound to 50-pound test. A small dual-purpose stainless steel snap is attached to one end of the leader to facilitate lure changing, while a small barrel swivel is attached to the other end, onto which the line is tied.

Some Tie Leader Direct

There are some anglers who feel the small swivel will cause a wary fish to shy away from the lure, so they simply fasten their leader to the line by using a blood knot.

Wire Best at Times

If you're fishing in an area frequented by such toothy offshore residents as barracuda, king mackerel and bluefish, it is often best to use a wire leader. These species will sever even a heavy nylon leader with their sharp teeth. Number 7 or 8 wire is usually sufficient for most casting situations. Monofilament should never be tied directly to a loop in the wire, for under great pressure the wire will cut through it. Instead use a small barrel swivel for your connection between leader and line. As with a nylon leader, a small dual-purpose stainless steel snap should be attached to the end of the leader to facilitate changing of lures.

Wide Array of Lures

Although the boat caster is limited in the types and sizes of the lures he may use, he still has a substantial arsenal from which to choose. A prime requisite of a casting lure is that it be of a size and weight which is easy to cast. Lures ranging in weight from half an ounce on up to two ounces are in the general range of those found to be best adapted to offshore casting.

Bucktail Jig Tops

Along each sector of coastline there is a lure which the casting fraternity rates as tops. The lure which most often gets top billing is the bucktail jig. For the bucktail jig is a versatile lure which may be worked just below the surface or sent into the depths with ease, and it has accounted for practically every offshore species you're apt to encounter.

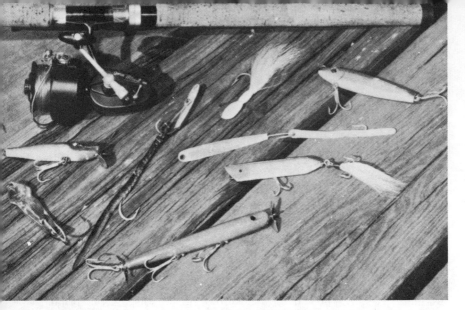

Pictured here are some lures favored by boat casters, including, from left to right: chromed spoon, subsurface swimming plug, rigged eel, propeller plug, metal squid with tail hook pork rind, bucktail jig, popping plug and a deep-running mirror plug. All of these lures will take a great number of gamefish when cast from a boat.

Both the bug-eye type bucktail jigs and flat, lima-bean shaped models produce well offshore. While they come in many weights, most offshore trollers settle on those weighing approximately one ounce, as these are an easy weight to cast. Hook sizes are usually 6/o or 7/o.

You can obtain bucktail jigs painted almost every color in the spectrum, but for all around effectiveness you need only include solid yellow, white, or red and white color combinations in your kit.

Quite often the action of a bucktail jig may be enhanced by the addition of a strip of pork rind. If fish are striking short, then tail-hook pork rind will catch the short strikers. We've occasionally added a strip of bait cut from the belly of dolphin, tuna or mackerel, which has resulted in more strikes than while fishing with the plain bucktail.

Popping Plugs Bring Strikes

Popping plugs in sizes from one ounce to one and half ounces, measuring four or five inches in length, will often drive offshore gamefish crazy. Most such plugs have a bucktail skirt which breathes as the plug is retrieved, causing an irresistible action. Popping plugs will draw gamefish from great depths, especially when they're retrieved with a whipping motion of your rod tip, thus causing the plug to create a lot of commotion as it is retrieved across the broad expanse of ocean.

Make certain you select plugs with sturdy construction, for offshore gamefish are vicious when they strike a plug, and they'll make kindling of poorly constructed plugs in one strike. Plugs constructed of cedar or plastic usually hold up best. Select only those with sturdy, extra-strong treble hooks made for salt-water use.

Finish doesn't matter too much in a popping plug, for the fish actually never get to see the top of the plug. With these plugs we'd be inclined to think the fancy color schemes are more to catch fishermen than fish, for we've frequently caught many fish while offshore casting with a plug that didn't have a bit of paint left on it, but had the tempting action which the fish couldn't resist.

Propeller plugs, mirror-type plugs, darters and swimming plugs are all used on the offshore grounds at times and bring strikes. It goes without saying that the wise boatman always carries a good stock of plugs to suit the fancy of the offshore adversaries.

Metal Lures Produce Too

Metal hardware such as hammered stainless steel jigs, small diamond jigs and block tin or chrome-plated squids work very well on the offshore scene. Spoons made of heavy-diameter stock and designed for casting also bring a share of strikes to the offshore caster.

Most metal lures come either plain or with bucktail or feathered skirts. Yellow, white, and red and white are the most popular colors. Those which are plain are usually dressed with a strip of pork rind to give them an added bit of flutter.

The bucktail jig when dressed with a piece of tail hook pork rind is a favorite of the boat caster. It may be effectively worked at all levels.

The popping plug is a favorite of boat casters. It works on the surface with its concave head pushing water ahead of it as it is retrieved. This surface commotion infuriates many fish who strike it out of sheer viciousness.

The hammered stainless-steel jig is a versatile lure. It works effectively when cast and retrieved slowly, or it may be jigged in the depths with good results. It is made in a wide variety of sizes to suit most fishing situations.

Claude Rogers is bringing aboard a big channel bass hooked by June Rosko while casting a hammered stainless-steel jig to a school of channel bass that was cruising just below the surface off the Barrier Islands of Virginia during the early spring.

Look for Signs of Fish

While locating offshore species by trolling and then breaking out casting tackle is fun, great sport can be enjoyed by just keeping alert for signs of feeding fish. Often the presence of nervous baitfish on the surface will disclose fish below. So will sea gulls diving to pick up pieces of small fish left by feeding gamefish. Close observation of flotsam will often disclose fish lying in the shadows beneath it.

Approach from Upwind

When you do spot activity on the surface, make it a point to approach the activity upwind or upcurrent. In so doing you can approach to within casting range and then shut down your engines, permitting the wind or current to carry you towards the feeding fish.

When you approach in this manner the boat will seldom startle the fish. Often you can drift right through without them even noticing you, if they're preoccupied with feeding.

As you approach the fish, make your casts to the edge of the school, for a fish will more readily observe a lure off by itself than one in the maelstrom of feeding fish and excited baitfish.

Seldom will you find fish on top chasing bait when they won't be receptive to some type of lure. Usually they are in such a feeding frenzy that they immediately seize anything that looks like food. This applies to yellowtail, albacore, bluefish, dolphin, barracuda and most other species which travel in schools, including the members of the tuna and bonito families.

With almost all offshore species a fast retrieve is important. Often you may look foolish reeling as quickly as you can turn the reel handle and jerking your tip wildly to cause the plug or bucktail to dart about, but this system will reward you with strikes while a slowly retrieved lure will seldom get the attention of the feeding fish.

Work Lures Deep

While few will dispute that catching offshore species on surface plugs is by far the most exciting sport there is, there are often times when it becomes necessary to probe the depths for feeding fish. Remember that for every fish you may observe feeding on the surface there may be dozens more in the depths.

The ladyfish is fun to catch on a light outfit. It will readily take almost any small artificial lure, jumping repeatedly when hooked. They are a poor table fish and most are released.

Lures such as bucktail jigs, hammered stainless steel jigs and metal squids are designed to work effectively at any level, and they'll work far deeper than even subsurface plugs.

Whip Retrieve Best

We've enjoyed best results while employing a whip retrieve while using bucktail jigs and other metal lures. A long cast is made, often right across any fish which may be feeding on the surface. As soon as the lure hits the water, line is stripped from the reel. This permits considerable slack, and the lure settles straight down.

At first you've got to try different levels. A good practice is to wait until you feel the lure has settled about ten feet, at which time you can start your retrieve, working the rod tip vigorously in a sweeping motion, causing the lure to dart towards the surface and then falter.

If a strike isn't received at this level, on the next cast permit the lure to settle a little deeper and repeat the same procedure. Keep probing deeper until you receive strikes, after which you can go back down to the same level and often receive strike after strike.

Apparently many gamefish find a level where the water temperature is to their liking, and they tend to congregate at this level, only moving to the surface or other levels to feed. But when a lure comes right through them, there are always one or two who find it too tempting to resist.

Go to Bottom

While most offshore casting is done for game species, there is good sport to be had by sending your jigs or bucktail jigs right down to the bottom. Many bottom feeders will take these lures, and if you're

June Rosko landed this prettily hued sea trout while fishing with Joe Sparrow and casting a small surface swimming plug along the marsh banks of Chesapeake Bay on Virginia's Eastern Shore.

The jack crevalle is a poor table fish, but a great fighter. Many south-
ern anglers deliberately avoid it when out fishing for edible species, for
if you hook a big one it takes a long while to land it. The one just landed
by June Rosko is about average size for Gulf Coast waters.

drifting over a shallow reef you can enjoy a mixed bag by permitting
your lure to settle right to the bottom and then starting your retrieve.

This technique will catch groupers and snapper, porgies, sea bass,
codfish, pollock and many other species which usually feed on or
close to the bottom.

Fly Casting Spells Excitement

Recently there has been a great deal of interest in salt-water fly
casting, with the result that many anglers now carry their long rods
well to sea, employing them to catch a wide assortment of offshore
species.

Best results are obtained with a fly rod when the fish are on the
surface and actively feeding. At such times you needn't worry
about a lot of wasted effort with blind casting, for you can usually
spot either single fish or groups of feeding fish and present your
streamers or popping bugs right to them.

Bear in mind that often a fly caster can employ a slower retrieve,
partly because the streamer flies he may be using will work, or
breathe, as he slowly retrieves them through a school of fish. This
breathing action of the hackles of the streamer makes it look very
much alive even when retrieved slowly with intermittent pauses.

SLOW DOWN FOR INSHORE CASTING

On the inshore grounds the boatman will find entirely different
species of fish, with substantially different techniques necessary

to catch them, even though most of the lures used are the same as those employed by the offshore caster.

Beginning in the open reaches of ocean, we find that many game-fish set up residence along the surf, around rocky jetties or break-waters and at passes or inlets which empty into the ocean.

All of these spots become prime areas for the boat caster to fish. Among the species which take up residence in such spots are striped bass, weakfish, snook, channel bass, tarpon, jack crevalle, sea trout, salmon and a host of small species such as ladyfish, blue runners and Spanish mackerel.

A great deal of the casting for these species is done blind, in that the fish are not visible on the surface or showing any signs of actively feeding. Through experience, however, the boatman knows that these species take up feeding stations at the mouths of inlets on a dropping tide, or off the points of breakwaters, or where there are deep cuts and holes along the surf.

Drift by Likely Spots

A favorite technique which we often employ is to situate the boat so that we drift parallel to a spot known to harbor fish. Here the tide and wind can often be used to good advantage. A word of cau-tion, however, when fishing along the surf or off rocky coastlines. Always make certain you situate yourself so that you're not carried in toward the surf or rocks. Frequently boatmen become so pre-occupied with casting that their craft gets carried in too close, which can become dangerous.

Always make certain to bracket an area with lots of casts. If two or three anglers are casting from the boat at the same time it is wise for each to use a different lure; one a plug, another a bucktail jig and the remaining angler a metal jig or squid.

Sometimes It's Wise to Anchor

There are times when drifting isn't always possible, either because of wind or current conditions, at which time it is wise to anchor. Frequently a boat can be anchored so that you can easily cover a broad area with little difficulty. This is particularly true at inlets or passes, along channel edges, or where rips and eddies form at a point of land.

If anchoring isn't possible because of water depth or rocky bottom, the boatman can often idle along slowly just off the spot he wishes to fish, while his companions cast in to the rocks or fast water at the mouth of an inlet. In fact, many boatmen cover a wide area by moving their boat in and out of gear every few minutes. In this way they bracket an area with casts, and if no hits are received, they just move ahead a short distance, continuing to cast until they receive strikes.

Protected Waters Differ

When a boatman enters the protected reaches of bays, rivers and estuaries, quite a different scene awaits him. Gone is the heavy water off the surf, or the swift currents and rips most often found off inlets and passes. The inshore waters have a serenity about them.

While the species landed are much the same in protected waters as those close to shore in the ocean, here again techniques vary. Where the ocean angler frequently employs heavy casting tackle because he has to contend with deep water, fast currents and often many obstructions, the angler who fishes in sheltered waters can often employ light casting tackle for he has fewer obstacles to contend with.

Creeks Provide Fast Sport

Some exciting casting sport is available in many creeks and estuaries which empty into coastal bays. Often big concentrations of gamefish move up to feed on the plentiful supply of baitfish which often seek the sanctuary offered along the marsh grass or mangroves which frequently line such waterways.

This type of fishing, with stripers, weakfish, snook, redfish and a host of other species the quarry, demands considerable skill, for the caster, whether using lures or flies, must be able to cast accurately right in close to the shore where the fish often lie in wait for food.

In such situations a slow, erratic retrieve often produces best results. It is best to cast your lure as close to the mangroves or marsh grass as possible, and to retrieve the lure away from the shore. In this way it appears to be a small baitfish swimming carelessly away from the protection which the grass and mangroves offer. The gamefish will often wallop it before it has a chance to move more than a couple of feet.

When using popping plugs it is often wise to cause the plug to pop with your rod tip and then permit it to rest for a few seconds. Then give it another pop with the rod tip, and let it rest again. This method will often drive gamefish crazy and they'll grab the plug out of sheer annoyance.

Always make certain to probe the depths of the creeks and estuaries with your lures. For frequently the gamefish will move from along the banks into the deep cuts and holes made by the tide and currents. Often a bucktail jig bounced along the bottom will bring exciting action, particularly on an ebbing tide when there is little water along the banks.

Fly casters can often probe these depths by using sinking fly lines and streamer flies or bucktails.

Fish Congregate Where Food Is

Often a broad expanse of bay or sound will be practically devoid of fish activity, while crammed into one small area there will be school after school of fish. The reason for this is that the fish congregate where the food is. Often fish will school up where a small creek empties into a bay, or beneath the lights of a dock or bridge at night. Where shallow flats drop off into deep water the fish will often take up station to feed on the small baitfish which swarm off the flats as the tide drops.

These boat casters are working a likely looking spot. Currents clash and waves break over submerged rocks. Spots like this often hold a great amount of baitfish which seek the shelter of the rocks, which in turn attracts many gamefish.

In fishing spots such as this you must be very careful not to make noise in the boat. For in shallow water fish spook very easily. Accepted methods of fishing such spots are to drift down with the tide, casting as you drift, or to anchor and then cast. Many anglers drift until a strike is received. Then they immediately anchor, which produces good results from schooling fish.

Smaller Lures

The lures most often used in protected waters are somewhat smaller in size than those used in the open reaches of the ocean. For most often the baitfish found in bays and rivers are smaller. This is particularly true where spearing, sand launce, pilchards, anchovies and sardines are plentiful in the bays and rivers. For with bait such as this forming the major portion of the diet of those fish in residence, it often becomes necessary to use lures in the three-quarter-ounce to one-ounce range. In fact, often anglers using quarter-ounce bucktail jigs will take such species as stripers, snook, sea trout and redfish when larger lures fail to bring strikes. Investigation of the stomachs of these species often discloses that they've been feeding on tiny fry or inch-long shrimp, which is why they were receptive to a small lure.

Much the same applies to plugs and metal lures. Try to have the lure match the predominant baitfish as closely as possible.

Many Cast Live Baitfish

While fishing both inshore reaches of the ocean and protected waters as well, many boatmen cast live bait to feeding fish. This is what might be called a combination cast and drift pattern, for the bait is most often cast well away from the boat and then drifted through a likely looking spot.

The most popular method of rigging up for live-bait fishing is to make up a leader two or three feet long, of 30-pound-test to 40-pound-test leader material. On one end of the leader a small barrel swivel is attached and onto the other end a hook is tied. It should be noted that some anglers prefer to fish without a leader, just tying their hook directly to the end of their line.

Favored hook styles for most bait-fishing situations is an Eagle-Claw or Beak hook, with the size tailored to the bait and fish in residence.

Occasionally a small clinch-on sinker is attached to the line where it meets the leader, to give added weight while casting and to take the bait deep. A plastic float may be added where it is desireable to keep the bait at an intermediate level.

Many Baits May Be Used

In the case of employing live baitfish, there are several ways in which they may be hooked. A popular method of hooking smaller baitfish such as anchovies, sardines and eels is to hook them right through the jaws. The hook is inserted in the lower jaw and out the upper jaw. This permits the baitfish to swim about in a natural manner and it is very easy to cast.

There are some anglers who find that hooking the fish through the eye sockets results in its being less apt to fall off the hook while casting. This method of hooking is particularly popular with pinfish, squirrel fish and grunts.

When using big baitfish such as mackerel and herring many anglers place the hook just under the skin of the back, just below and ahead of the dorsal fin.

Crabs may also be used as an effective live bait, and should be hooked through the body near one of the two points on their back. First break off their two pincer claws, but leave the swimming fins so that the crab can swim about in a natural manner. Live shrimp are often used while casting, and these are best hooked under the collar on their back. Many anglers prefer that the hook be concealed and place it completely within the shrimp instead.

Hesitate Before Striking

With all live baits it is important that you hesitate before striking. Most gamefish will first grab a bait in their jaws, holding onto it for several seconds before attempting to swallow it. If you strike at the first sign of a pickup, you'll often yank the bait away from the fish.

Instead, lower your rod tip and permit the fish to have slack line. In using very large baitfish it is often wise to let line pay off your reel, giving the fish ample time to swallow the bait before attempting to set the hook.

Many Ways to Keep Bait Alive

On party boats where live baits are used they are kept in live wells where the water is constantly aerated. Many private boats have built-in live wells in which the baits may be kept alive and active. Small boatmen who don't have live wells may keep baitfish

A live pinfish is a popular Gulf Coast bait that may be used for tarpon, snook, redfish and many other species. When hooked in this manner it may be easily cast and stays alive for a long while.

alive in wooden live cars, or they may employ ordinary round plastic trash cans placed in the boat. Care should be exercised to constantly change the water in any container that baitfish are kept in, for they quickly use up the oxygen and unless the water is changed they will die.

FISHING THE FLATS DEMANDS SKILL

Unquestionably the most difficult type of fishing confronting the boat caster is fishing the shallow sand flats of southern waters. These flats are frequented by large numbers of bonefish, tarpon, barracuda and other tropical species. At low tide most of the flats are completely exposed. As the tide rises, the water floods over the flats and the gamefish move onto them to feed on the abundance of crabs, shrimp and small baitfish.

A boat with a very shallow draft is necessary for this type of fishing. Most anglers who fish the flats employ outboard boats, although in some areas rowing skiffs are used.

Fish are extremely spooky when feeding on the flats, so it is important that you approach the area to be fished with caution. Most bonefish or tarpon anglers shut off their motors along the edge of the flats, and then proceed to pole their boats onto the shallow water areas.

A push pole is used to propel the boats. This may be nothing more than an oar, although most anglers who fish the flats regularly use a pole designed expressly for this type of fishing. It usually measures eight to ten feet in length and has a flat piece of wood fastened to the end which comes in contact with the sand or mud bottom. This small piece of wood prevents the pole from being pushed into the soft sand or mud.

The long length of the push pole permits ease in handling both the pole and boat. The boatman doing the poling most often stands either at the bow or stern as he pushes. One or two anglers are the maximum that can comfortably fish from a small boat on the flats.

Fish Must Be Sighted First

Fishing the flats has often been compared with hunting, for you never make a cast until you spot the fish. This is tedious work and requires deep concentration, for many of the fish blend in extremely well with the surrounding flats, particularly where there is a great deal of sea grass growing.

Experienced anglers develop a method of looking through the water which enables them quickly to spot the cruising fish as they swim along in the water, which is seldom more than one to two feet deep. Polaroid sunglasses are extremely useful in spotting fish, for they screen out reflected glare from the surface of the water.

Bright Sun Is Helpful

Cruising fish are most easily spotted on a bright sunny day, with little or no wind to disturb the surface of the water. On a cloudy or windy day, the spotting of fish becomes so difficult that many anglers don't even bother fishing.

When a fish is sighted the boatman poling must plan a strategy of placing the caster within casting range of the cruising fish. This often takes a few moments of observing the movement of the fish, so as to figure how to head it off.

If your approach is too close, or is noisy while poling, the fish will be startled and swim off the flats at a speed so fast you can hardly follow it. Movements must be slow both on the part of the person poling the boat and the angler as well.

Good Communication Is Necessary

Fish can hear sounds such as a banging tackle box in the boat or the push pole hit against the boat. But they can't hear you talking.

So it is wise to keep good communication between the caster and the person poling the boat.

A cast should not be attempted until the boat is first poled into position. Once the boat stops, the caster then takes over.

Light Spinning Tackle Favored

In the case of bonefish, barracuda and tarpon, light spinning tackle is by far the favorite, for casting with it is relatively easy. It is best to place your cast ahead of the cruising fish and off to the side, so that as the fish moves and you retrieve, the lure will come within the range of vision of the fish. This, naturally, is easier said than done. We usually try to place the lure about six feet to the side and ahead of the fish. Never cast beyond the fish, for as you retrieve your lure it will come up behind the fish and most certainly startle it.

Occasionally when the lure touches the water it will startle the fish. But if it isn't completely spooked it will quickly settle down and start looking for food again.

Plugs and Bucktails

When tarpon and barracuda are on the flats many anglers use popping plugs, propeller plugs and darters to draw strikes from these tough gamefish. Bucktails also bring many strikes. But these should be light in weight, with 5/0 or 6/0 hooks, for if they are too heavy they will dig into the bottom in the shallows and not work effectively.

Bucktail Favored for Bonefish

An eighth-ounce or quarter-ounce bucktail jig with a 1/0 or 2/0 hook is the favorite lure for bonefish. These come in models designed expressly for bonefishing, in that they are flat with a delta-wing shape, so that they wiggle when they are retrieved. Their design keeps them from sinking quickly, which keeps them just above the bottom. They come in many colors, with pink and pale brown being the most popular.

A slow retrieve with a slight movement of your rod tip to cause the bucktail jig to flutter produces best results. Some anglers let the jig settle deep and dance it along the bottom, which causes small puffs of sand or mud. This closely resembles a small crab scurrying along the bottom, which often results in a strike.

Bonefish Sometimes Travel in Schools

While fishing in the Bahamas we've frequently sighted big schools of bonefish cruising on the flats. These schools often numbered fifty or more fish, and often it was difficult to cast to them without spooking the entire school. Often we spotted a school coming along and would cast our bucktail jig well ahead of the school, permitting it to settle to the bottom. As soon as the school of bonefish approached the vicinity of the jig we started a slow retrieve, which often brought an immediate strike.

Shrimp Makes Fine Bait

Catching bonefish on lures is great fun, but occasionally the fish are spooky and they won't touch an artificial bait. At such times we've frequently employed a shrimp as bait with excellent results. The technique employed is much the same as with a lure, with the exception that after the cast is made the shrimp is left motionless on the bottom, being only twitched occasionally when the bonefish is within range.

Fly Casting Offers Thrills

Catching bonefish, tarpon and other flats marauders on a fly-casting outfit is considered by many to be the ultimate thrill in salt-water angling. It takes a great degree of casting skill and a deft presentation of the fly to get these flats residents to take a fly.

We've often recommended that boat anglers first develop the skills required to catch fish on regular casting tackle before proceeding to fly tackle. Once you get used to presenting a lure and learning the habits of these fine gamefish of the flats, it is then much easier to graduate to fly tackle.

The presentation of a fly such as the Pink Shrimp, Bonefish Bucktail or the Multi-Wing Streamer is much the same as presenting any other type of lure. The exception being that you've got to do so with a minimum of false casting and get the fly in front of the fish as quickly and accurately as possible.

The retrieve with a fly is accomplished by stripping line with one hand, while holding the rod with the other. Because of the floating line and light-weight fly, a very slow, lazy retrieve may be employed, thus presenting the tuft of feathers or bucktail in as lifelike a manner as possible to the cruising fish.

If the fish shows no interest in a slow retrieve, then try another cast and use an irregular retrieve, or sometimes a fast retrieve. As a general rule, however, you'll receive the greatest number of strikes with a slow, lazy retrieve.

Great Possibilities for Casting

Casting is but another of the many effective methods of catching fish from a boat. It requires a considerable degree of skill on the part of the angler to present his lure to a feeding fish and to work the lure so that it draws a strike. Although until recently casting tackle found limited application on boats, today you'll find it being used offshore, inshore and on the flats, catching gamefish of every size imaginable.

Salt-water fly casters catch a wide variety of species from small boats. Mark Sosin landed this streamlined cero mackeral on a fly tied of polar-bear hair with a sparse dressing of Mylar while casting off Walker's Cay in the Bahamas.

7 Fighting and Landing Your Fish

THERE are certain fundamental techniques for fighting fish which apply regardless of what type of equipment you use or the manner in which you hook your fish. Of paramount importance is setting your drag properly before a fish is hooked, so that excessive tension isn't put on the tackle.

All of the reels which we've discussed thus far, including multiplying, spinning and fly reels, have a drag system which may be either tightened or loosened, thus resulting in either greater or less pressure being necessary for a fighting fish to pull the line from the reel.

There are many proponents of the method of adjusting fighting drags on a reel with the aid of a scale. By using a scale and tying your line to it, you can adjust the reel's drag to any desired amount of drag pressure, from as little as one pound of pressure, on up to as tight as the drag can be adjusted.

While we've tried this method, we find it somewhat impractical under actual fishing conditions, for often a change of drag pressure is necessary, and it often becomes impossible to reset it exactly right.

KNOW CAPABILITIES OF TACKLE

Over the years we've learned that it is to your benefit to be thoroughly familiar with the tackle you are using, and to know just how much pressure can be put to a fish before having a failure of rod, reel or line. When we obtain a new outfit we frequently rig it up and tie the line to the fence in our back yard. We then walk off approximately 100 feet of line and put the reel in gear, or in the case of spinning tackle, close the reel's bail.

We then toy with the outfit, walking backwards with different settings of the reel's drag to see just what the various settings do to the rod and to see just how smoothly the drag functions. We've found this method to be almost foolproof, for when on the fishing grounds we then know that it would be foolish to tighten up the drag beyond a certain range for there would then be just too much pressure on the whole rig, which in turn could result in breaking the rod, parting the line, or ripping the hook from the fish's jaw.

Fighting Your Fish

It is a safe practice always to set your drag so that under moderate pressure it relinquishes line to the fish. Never fish with the drag so tight that it takes a great amount of pressure for a fish to take line. By the same token, don't fish with the drag so loose that there is little tension on the line and the fish swims off with yard after yard of line.

Small fish aren't difficult to land. Here Milt Rosko, Sr., reels a mackerel within a rod's length of his tip and simply swings it aboard. This is fine with fish of this size but shouldn't be attempted with heavy fish, as it puts too much strain on the tackle.

The rod should always have a comfortable arc to it while pointed upwards and fighting a fish. This arc helps in cushioning the run of a fish, it helps keep the line taut, and it also helps to tire the fish.

LET THE FISH RUN

It is a good practice with gamefish to let the fish use up its first burst of energy by fighting well away from the boat. When the fish is 100 yards or more from the boat there is little chance of it cutting your line off in the propeller or getting caught under the keel, or getting your line tangled with other anglers on board. Once the fish starts to tire you can apply a little more drag pressure and start to work it closer.

ALWAYS CHECK AFTER RESETTING DRAG

Here it is important to develop the habit of checking the drag immediately after you reset it. This is easily accomplished by holding the outfit in one hand, while you grasp the line with the other and gently pull line from the reel. Even when fighting a fish this isn't difficult, providing the fish has settled down and isn't ripping line from the reel.

A great many fish are lost by anglers excitedly tightening drags while fish are running. Although it may look like you'll run out of line, it is best not to worry about it and never to tighten the drag. Almost all fish will tire quickly once they've run off a couple of hundred yards of line. Remember that they're not only pulling all this line behind them, but fighting the drag and rod pressure as well, so the more line they get out the quicker they're bound to tire.

PUMPING HELPS

Usually you can bring a gamefish to the boat by employing steady rod pressure and slowly reeling as the fish gives in to the rod. But occasionally you'll hook big fish which run off a lot of line and which have to be pumped up from the depths.

Here the accepted manner of pumping is to reel up tight and lower your rod tip as you keep all the slack out of your line. Then slowly and smoothly lift back with your rod tip, raising it almost vertically as you pump. Then slowly lower the rod tip, quickly reeling as you do, so as to gain line. The procedure is to pump slowly and reel. Pump and reel, and soon the fish will be in range.

As you are pumping and the fish decides to make another run, just hold the outfit steady with the tip pointed upwards, and let the fish fight the rod as it makes another run.

BELT AND HARNESS GREAT AIDS

A rod belt is a great aid when fighting fish with light tackle and spinning tackle. A shoulder harness can be used in conjunction with the rod belt, or you can use the harness while fighting the fish from a fighting chair. The shoulder harness enables you to utilize your back and shoulders while fighting the fish, which takes a lot of strain off your arms and hands while pumping.

DIP ROD INTO WATER IF NECESSARY

When fighting a fish well away from the boat you'll seldom encounter much difficulty, but when you get it alongside the fish will

Pumping a fish is essential in order to get it out of the depths. Here the author lifts back with the rod tip, after which he will quickly lower it and turn the reel handle as he does, gaining precious line.

often go wild, vigorously attempting to gain its freedom. Often it will dive beneath the boat, at which time you should be prepared to lean over the side, literally thrusting your rod tip into the water, and walk the fish around either the stern or bow as the case may be. Often quick action such as this will save you from getting the fish fouled on the bottom of the boat, its rudder or propeller.

If you keep cool once a fish is hooked, which applies whether big-game fishing offshore or bottom fishing in a coastal bay, you'll have little difficulty in fighting it to boatside. Always remember to keep your tip up, reel quickly to keep the line tight should the fish swim towards you, and keep the drag on a moderate setting should the fish attempt repeated runs. By doing this you'll soon have the fish within reach of net or gaff.

Landing Your Fish

The techniques employed to land a fish are essentially the same whether you troll, bottom fish, chum or cast.

Ironic as it may seem, you can do everything right up to the moment you go to land a fish, and then through a single mistake lose it. Everyone who's spent a lot of time fishing from a boat has had the disappointing experience of losing a big fish; no matter how careful you are and how exact your timing is, you're bound to lose a few. But losses can be kept to a minimum if you go about landing them in the right way.

As we've said, each boat should be equipped with a good landing net and gaff. While there are many types of equipment which may be used to land a fish, the landing net and gaff are without a doubt the most popular pieces of equipment used for this purpose.

Knowing how to use these pieces of equipment, when to use them, and just when a fish is ready to be landed can be accomplished with ease, provided you put your mind to it.

NETTING ISN'T DIFFICULT

Netting any small or medium-sized gamefish isn't really difficult, yet we'd say that more fish are lost just prior to being netted than at any other time.

The major mistake that many anglers make is in trying to net their fish too quickly. Here it's important to remember that regardless of the fish you've hooked, you should let it do its fighting well away from the boat. If the fish expends its energy away from the boat, it's less apt to be difficult to net when it's played alongside.

Usually when fish are being fought 50 feet or more from the boat they have a tendency to stay in the water while fighting. These same fish, if pumped to the boat too quickly, might take to the air, thrashing the water white and fighting viciously to gain their freedom at boatside. The last-ditch bid for freedom, accompanied by several jumps and possibly a dive under the boat, is when the fish often breaks a line or leader or manages to shake the hook free.

So don't be too anxious to get the fish alongside. Just let it tire itself out before working it close.

If you are alone, make certain that the net is readily accessible, preferably lying across the gunwale. You'd be surprised at the number of fish that are brought to boatside before the angler realizes he has to drag the net out from under an oar or seat. In the interim, the fish often shakes free.

If you have a fishing companion with you, he should stop fishing and be ready to net your fish when it's alongside.

ALWAYS NET HEAD FIRST

The fish should always be drawn towards the mouth of the net head first. Often while being lead to the net the fish may charge off on another run. Don't attempt to stop him. Here's where your drag comes into play as the fish can take several yards of line without fear of anything breaking. Then just work it back in again.

Whatever you do, don't swing the net like a golf club. Many anglers make wild passes at fish, often knocking the fish off the hook.

Just gently lower the mouth of your landing net into the water and by drawing back on the tip of your rod, guide the fish right into the submerged mouth of the net. Firmly and without undue commotion, lift the net upwards and into the boat.

For the most part, reeling the fish to within a rod's length of the boat is usually perfect. Then just pull back with the rod and draw the fish into the net. Don't make the mistake of reeling the fish right up to the rod tip and then trying to net it!

UNHOOK FISH IN NET

Once the fish is safely aboard, hold the net suspended with the fish in it in one hand and reach in with your other hand and get a firm grip on the fish, either by holding it under the gills or with an eye socket hold. Once it's firmly in hand, remove the hook and put the fish right into the fishbox.

This technique of grasping the fish in the net is fine if you're using a single-hook lure. With a multi-hook lure such as a plug it's best to use a billy and with a single sharp blow settle the fish, so that its thrashing doesn't result in imbedding one of the barbs in your hand.

We've noted that many anglers make the mistake of turning the

Always lead a tired gamefish to net head first. Here the author leads a tired bonefish to the waiting net of Bob Stankus. The bonefish was hooked while fishing the flats of a small cay just north of Andros Island in the Bahamas. Moments after being netted the game fighter was released to fight another day.

net over and letting the fish flop around on the deck. Not only does this mess up the deck, but there's always the difficulty of getting hold of the fish again. Possibly, too, it might flip overboard, especially if you're in a small boat.

FOLLOW SAME STEPS IN GAFFING

Much of what we've said about fighting a fish before bringing him close enough for netting also applies to gaffing. Make certain the scrapper has used up all of his energy well away from the boat.

Most anglers employ a net for small and medium-sized gamefish, bringing the gaff into play for the heavyweights, although it may be used quite effectively on small fish as well.

When dealing with tough gamefish that are heavyweights, don't make the mistake of grabbing the line prior to gaffing the fish. Just guide the line or leader with an open hand.

DON'T HOLD HEAD OUT OF WATER

In our travels to all three coasts, we've frequently had party-boat deckhands ask us to impress people with the importance of not reeling fish to the surface until the deckhand is at their side with the gaff or net. The deckhands prefer that when the fish is reeled to the surface it is held right at the top and not reeled so that the fish's head is held half out of the water. A fish in this position is difficult to gaff or net, for it is often wildly thrashing, at which times it frequently shakes free.

The gaffing should be done with precision timing and in one swift motion. When the angler reels the fish to within a rod's length of the boat, he should stop reeling, and then guide the fish to the gaffer by lifting back slowly but firmly with the rod tip. In one smooth movement the gaffer should swing the gaff in an arcing movement, aiming toward the fish's head as it is led toward him. Remember that the fish will always continue moving forward and that if your aim misses the head area you still stand a good chance of getting the gaff into the back or stomach of the fish. Bear in mind that the fish isn't just waiting to be gaffed, but often thrashing around considerably, requiring quick, accurate movement on your part.

It takes force to sink a gaff into a fish, so don't give a half-hearted pull when you feel the point hit the fish. Pull hard, and as soon as you feel weight, continue in one movement and swing the fish over the gunwale and into the cockpit.

With the fish still on the gaff, use the billy club and settle the fish down promptly, for fish in the 50-pound to 100-pound class, especially wahoo, king mackerel, barracuda and other long, tough fish, can inflict serious injury to you by thrashing about, viciously snapping their jaws. Before you proceed to unhook the fish, it should be absolutely still. Many anglers make it a point to use a pair of side cutters, simply cutting the leader and leaving the single hook right in the fish's jaw. In all instances where a shark is brought aboard, the leader should be cut and the hook left in its jaw.

NO GAFF FOR SMALL BILLFISH

Most professional guides and experienced anglers do not gaff small billfish such as the Atlantic and Pacific sailfish, the striped marlin and white marlin. While most of these fish are released at boatside by cutting the wire leader, so that the fish can fight another day, there are times when an angler may want a billfish brought aboard to be mounted for his office or den.

A billfish that is to be brought aboard should be permitted to do all of its jumping and be thoroughly tired well away from the boat. For a wild, thrashing and jumping billfish at boatside is difficult to reckon with.

The technique employed by most good cockpit men is to wear a pair of cotton gloves and to grab hold of the leader as soon as it is within reach, after which they bring the leader in hand over hand until the fish's bill is within reach. Then they firmly grab hold of the long upper bill of the fish and in one swift pulling motion they literally drag the billfish aboard by its long bill. Some guides first use a billy and dispatch the fish while holding the fish's bill with one hand. This actually sounds harder than it is. Once you get the hang of it, you can bring a billfish aboard without too much difficulty. Most billfish of the type we're discussing here seldom weigh more than 50 pounds, although even 75-pound or 100-pound fish can be brought aboard employing this technique, providing your timing is correct.

Gaffing should be done with one quick motion. Here the author pulls a gaff into a big striper and quickly brings it aboard. The gaff handle should always be a comfortable length so that the fish can be easily reached as it is brought alongside.

Always be careful when you gaff a shark and bring it aboard. Never attempt to take the hook out of its mouth. Just use a pair of pliers and cut the leader, leaving the hook in its jaw. For a shark can inflict serious injury if you get your fingers in its mouth.

RELEASE FISH IF NOT NEEDED

Many fish which boatmen catch cannot be eaten and should be released to fight another day. Species such as the marlins and sailfish, the amberjack, bonefish and tarpon are great fun to catch but rather poor table fare. It is far better to release them at boatside than to kill them and later dump the dead gamefish off the dock for lack of anything better to do with them.

Also, there are many times when boat fishing becomes torrid. Fish frequently come flying aboard so fast and furiously that you soon have all the fish you can use. Then too it is wise to release those fish unharmed which you do not need.

All it takes to release a fish is to reach over the side with a pair of wire-cutter pliers and snip the leader close to the fish's jaw. The hook will either fall out or rust out in short order, with no bad after effects to the fish. With small fish it is a simple matter to handle them carefully with wet hands so as not to disturb their protective film, remove the hook, and then put them back in the water.

Moments after this photo was taken, guide Andy Heild placed a Woods Hole Oceanographic Institution tag in the sailfish being fought by June Rosko off Walker's Cay in the Bahamas and released it to fight another day. Tagging and releasing serves a dual purpose, by conserving our fine gamefish and assisting scientists in their research.

8 The Boatman's Favorite 50 Species

THROUGHOUT this book we've discussed many aspects of fishing from boats along the Atlantic, Pacific, and Gulf Coasts. Most of the techniques, tackle and equipment which are covered can be applied to fishing for a variety of species. We do feel that a conscientious boatman who takes his fishing seriously can, just by absorbing what we've already written, catch a lot of fish along any of our coasts as well as from the waters of many tropical islands close to home.

But we'd like to pursue coastal fishing just a bit farther and discuss the actual species which you're most apt to encounter as you fish from boats along the seacoast. For many species have certain characteristics which are peculiar to them alone, the knowledge of which could prove beneficial to you when you set your sights on them.

With that thought in mind we set out to prepare this listing of what we term the boatman's favorite 50 species. At first this list was swelled by half again as many names, but was pared down by deleting some species which had only local appeal, and by combining under a general heading the groupers, of which there are a great many subspecies. We also included the billfish in one heading, with the white marlin, striped marlin, Atlantic sailfish and the Pacific sailfish under this category because of the similarity of techniques which anglers employ while fishing for them. Sharks, of which there are many species, are also included under a single heading.

Naturally, whenever anyone sits down to make a listing there is a certain amount of personal feeling which enters into it. But we've tried to list those species which you're most apt to encounter when you go fishing from a boat, regardless of what type of craft it may be.

African Pompano

The African pompano is a rare species, but one which is prized by anglers who have landed this game fighter along all our southern coasts. Its range is wide; it is found in the Bahamas, Cuba and Panama, although seldom in any quantity.

It usually frequents areas where reefs are plentiful, for here it is able to find an abundance of food. It is a very pretty fish with a purple-blue back, blending into a silvery pearl color along its lower side. Its diet consists primarily of small fish, and it is most often taken while trolling along the reefs for other species.

Most African pompano which sports fishermen land range up to around 15 pounds, although occasional fish over 30 pounds have been landed.

They will strike most rigged baits, including mullet, balao and eels, as well as strip baits, and prefer the baits trolled at a moderate speed. While fishing off the Berry Islands in the Bahamas we succeeded in landing a 26-pounder, which proved to be a sterling fighter that required over half an hour to pump from the depths on light regulation-class tackle.

Small African pompano are occasionally caught by boat casters who ply reef areas with small bucktail jigs worked through the depths. The small fish are tough fighters too, using their broad bodies to make many sustained runs.

Albacore

The albacore is a far-ranging traveler that makes the Pacific Ocean its playground. It travels to Japan and the South Sea Islands, but sport fishermen herald its arrival off the Baja California peninsula during May or June. Albacore provide exciting sport during the summer as they move slowly up the California, Oregon and Washington coasts and on across the Pacific again. Only on rare occasions is it caught on the Atlantic Coast.

Seldom is the albacore found close to shore. Indeed, California party boats often leave dockside just past midnight in order to be on the albacore grounds by daybreak, for often a 50-mile or 60-mile trip out into the Pacific is required before the schools of albacore are sighted.

Albacore are usually fished for by chumming with live anchovies from party boats on the Pacific Coast, although many albacore are hooked by party boaters who troll while on the way to the grounds. When the trollers hook fish, the engines are quickly shut down and chumming operations commence.

Live anchovies are favored as chum, and most anglers employ a lively anchovy as hook bait as well. The trick when using an anchovy bait is to use a small, strong hook such as those designed expressly for albacore fishing. Many anglers use a number 1 or number 2 hook, which is small but extremely strong and offers no drag when hooked in the lips of a baitfish. When you have a strike, it is always wise to hesitate a second, permitting the albacore to take the bait firmly and move off with it, before you lean back to set the hook.

Albacore are extremely strong fish, with most that are decked weighing 15 to 25 pounds. It is foolish ever to try to stop the first line-consuming run of an albacore. Only broken tackle can result. Instead, let the fish run and tire itself out well away from the boat. Once its runs are of shorter duration, then, and only then, try to work it back within reach of the gaff.

Many small-boat men, particularly on private and charter boats, prefer trolling for albacore, for which they employ regulation-class tackle, with 20-pound and 30-pound class affording maximum sport. Albacore will take a variety of trolled lures, including Japanese feathers, spoons, chromed jigs, plastic-skirted trolling heads, strip baits and almost any other trolled offering that resembles a baitfish. They like a fast-moving lure tossed about in a churning white wake.

Some anglers employ casting tackle to tangle with albacore once a school is feeding around the boat. Even fly casters have caught these fine deep-water fighters on their long rods and tiny flies.

Amberjack

Brute strength is a characteristic which singles out the amber-jack among gamefish. This tough-fighting jack has a stamina that few fish can equal. So powerful is it that many anglers deliberately avoid it, because it just fights too hard!

It is most often found in tropical waters, usually around reefs or broken and irregular bottoms where there is a plentiful supply of food. We've caught them in the greatest numbers everywhere from North Carolina south and through the Gulf of Mexico. Off Bermuda great numbers of big amberjack are landed, as well as in the Bahamas and other southern islands. They are caught in the Pacific too.

Many anglers fish for big amberjack with extremely heavy tackle so that they can horse in the fish in a hurry. But the big amber is a fine fish on light tackle, which will test your skill to the utmost. We were fishing with Eddy Perinchief at Challenger Banks off Bermuda when she landed an amberjack that broke the 20-pound-class women's world record. The goliath weighed 83 pounds and 14 ounces and required a full 57 minutes to land on perfectly matched regulation-class tackle employing 20-pound-test monofilament line. It was a sterling angling accomplishment for Mrs. Perinchief, proving beyond doubt that the only way to fish for these fine gamefish is with light tackle.

Amberjack will readily take a trolled lure in the manner discussed for offshore trolling.

But the really big amberjack usually are caught on a live baitfish in deep water. Often the amberjack can be coaxed near the surface by chumming with small baitfish, and at such times they'll quickly take a live bait fished just below the surface. Favored bait used for amberjack in Bermuda is a live ocean robin about ten inches long. In Florida and the Bahamas a blue runner is a fine bait, although almost any live baitfish that is easily obtained may be used.

Size 7/0 or 8/0 O'Shaughnessy hooks are most often employed by light-tackle anglers, although Sobey or Martu hooks may be used if you're using 50-pound-class tackle.

Remember that amberjack are tough. They seldom fight on the

surface, diving extremely deep, at which time the only way to get them back to the boat is by rhythmically pumping them up. They never seem to tire, but steady rod pressure will prove their eventual undoing.

When chumming you often attract schools of 5-pound to 20-pound amberjack into the slick. Fish of this size are fine on casting tackle, and often they will strike a plug, bucktail or spoon which is cast while they dart through the slick looking for a tasty morsel.

Atlantic Bonito

The Atlantic bonito is the most plentiful of the bonitos found off the Atlantic and Gulf Coasts. It's often just called bonito or common bonito, and it saves many a day for the offshore troller. Often boatmen head offshore with their sights set on school blue-fin tuna, dolphin, white marlin, sailfish, wahoo or other fine game-fish, and find their only success with these species. The bonito is almost always around and in a cooperative mood, and often an otherwise unproductive day is turned into a rousing success by catching these fine hard fighters on light tackle.

On the average, bonito weigh four to seven pounds, though a few above this weight are taken each year. As a rule the bonito stays well offshore and is regarded as a blue-water species. Once in a while they'll stray inshore and occasionally come into the surf, where they chase baitfish right onto the sand. But for practical fishing look for the bonito well beyond sight of land. Seldom do bonito travel alone; they are most often in huge schools, some of which number in the thousands. While fishing off New Jersey and Long Island we've witnessed schools of bonito stretched as far as the eye could see.

When bonito are on top and actively feeding they're not too difficult to catch. Standard offshore trolling techniques are employed, with the fish preferring a fast-moving lure. Japanese trolling feathers in the half-ounce size are just about the most popular lure, although many bonito are taken on spoons, small strip baits, and small plastic baits made to resemble baitfish. Boat casters frequently take good catches while using bucktail jigs, wobblers and stainless steel jigs.

Never employ tackle heavier than 20-pound or 30-pound regulation-class on bonito, for with this light tackle you can enjoy maximum sport.

Occasionally bonito can be coaxed into a chum of ground menhaden, and they offer fine sport on light tackle. Make certain to use small hooks and conceal them well in baits of butterfish, sand launce or spearing, for the bonito has keen eyesight and will shy away from a small bait on a big hook.

Atlantic Mackerel

The Atlantic mackerel, which is called Boston mackerel and common mackerel in several parts of its range, is an extremely plentiful species found along the middle and north Atlantic Coast. It arrives during the early spring off the Virginia Capes and travels slowly northward, spending the summer in the cold waters of Maine and Canada, after which it heads south again in the fall, providing coastal anglers with fine fishing. During some summers there is a resident population of mackerel along the entire coast, due primarily to an abundance of baitfish.

Mackerel may be taken by many fishing methods, including trolling, chumming, and boat casting. One of the favorite methods is to attract the two-pound to four-pound mackerel to your boat with the aid of a chum of ground menhaden. Once the mackerel are attracted to the chum line, anglers employ small one-ounce to two-ounce diamond jigs rigged with several teasers above the jig. The jig is lowered into the depths and retrieved by alternately reeling and jigging vigorously with the rod tip. Often the mackerel are so plentiful that it's possible to catch them two or three at a time.

Anglers enjoy great sport by using light spinning outfits with small bucktail jigs or chromed wobblers. In fact, the mackerel will strike most any small bright lure. Trolling with light popping outfits is popular throughout New England and Maine, with any small lures producing more fish than you can imagine.

On occasions when mackerel become finicky, they'll swarm around your boat by the thousands, yet refuse to take lures. Then many anglers employ a small piece of bait cut from mackerel or herring, which is placed on a number 2 or 3 hook and drifted back into the chum. This often turns the trick.

For their size they're tough fighters and make great fish to go after when on a family fishing trip, for usually they are more than cooperative, providing plenty of action for all hands.

Billfish

Within this general category we include the smaller billfish which are within the sights of the small-boat man who employs moderately light tackle while trolling. These are the Atlantic sailfish, Pacific sailfish, striped marlin and the white marlin.

Although this manner of listing all these extremely fine gamefish together would make dedicated billfishermen shudder, we are doing so because we have found the techniques employed to catch all four species remarkably similar, whether fishing on the Atlantic, Pacific or Gulf Coasts.

The Atlantic sailfish is found in greatest numbers from the Carolinas south to Florida and along the entire Gulf Coast. There are great numbers of these high-jumping gamefish throughout the Bahamas and the many tropical islands south of them. The Pacific sailfish is fished for by gamefishermen off the southern coast of California, the Baja peninsula and south to Panama, sharing much the same range as the striped marlin. The white marlin is a resident of the Atlantic, ranging from Cuttyhunk south to Florida, and along the Gulf Coast. In the Bahamas they are very plentiful, as are they in the Virgin Islands, being caught in great numbers off the coast of South America, with anglers from Venezuela recently developing some fine sportfishing for the species.

Regulation-class tackle is by far the best tackle for these species, with 20-pound and 30-pound class being preferred. Techniques used are those discussed under offshore trolling, with the exception that artificial lures are seldom used.

Billfishing is unlike most other types of offshore trolling since these species are less plentiful than other offshore residents. They are usually far more difficult to attract to a trolled bait, and it is unquestionably more difficult to hook them.

Most anglers who pursue billfish do so with a passion, for it usually requires a great deal of time and patience before one becomes adept at billfishing. Many anglers are lucky to catch these species with little effort, while others work for years before they catch a billfish. We well recall our first offshore adventure for Atlantic sailfish. It took us precisely five minutes of trolling time to raise, hook and then land a beautiful seven-footer. We've fished for white marlin with many of the finest skippers all the way from Montauk to the Bahamas and beyond before finally hooking and landing one. During this time we put in over fifty days trolling for them, before landing our first. After that we could do no wrong and have caught many. The unbelievable part of this is that while preparing this book we caught our first striped marlin off Mexico's Los Coronados Islands within a half hour of putting the baits in the water the very first time we fished for them! A beautiful 113-pounder, measuring over eight feet in length!

The most popular method of catching billfish is to employ medium-sized baitfish which are rigged for trolling. Among the most popular baits are mullet, balao, sardines, mackerel, flying

Many experienced billfishermen release their fish rather than kill them. This wildly thrashing white marlin is being brought alongside to be tagged with a harpoon-type tag affixed to the end of the white pole to the right. The leader will then be cut, and the fish is no worse for the ordeal. When tagged fish are caught later marine scientists can study their growth rate and migrational pattern.

fish and eels, which are rigged on 7/0 forged O'Shaughnessy hooks. Many anglers also employ a strip bait cut from the belly of another fish, or a squid rigged either whole or as a strip bait.

A trolling pattern which is found to be very effective is to fish with four lines—two flat lines straight back off the stern, and two lines from the outriggers. Usually the boat trolls at a fast rate of speed, so that a good wake is thrown up, and so that the bait skips across the surface in an enticing, lifelike manner 50 to 100 feet behind the boat.

Seldom will a billfish strike a bait blind. Usually they'll surface behind the bait, look it over and then strike it. Sometimes the strike is almost instantaneous, while at other times the billfish may follow the bait for a full fifteen minutes before making up its mind.

The accepted hooking technique with billfish on the flat lines is to permit the fish to strike the bait with its bill. The angler immediately drops back line, permitting line to pay out from the reel for several seconds in order to give the fish time to get the bait into its mouth after having stunned it with its bill. The reel is then thrown into gear and the fish struck hard to set the hook in its bony, toothless mouth.

Baits trolled from the outriggers are fished in a somewhat different manner. As the billfish strikes the bait, the line flutters down from the outrigger, automatically giving the billfish slack line and time to mouth the bait. The angler waits until the line becomes taut as the boat continues moving ahead and then strikes.

There are, of course, many variations to this basic manner of trolling for billfish. Many trollers use huge fish-shaped teasers to attract the billfish from the depths, after which the teasers are hauled in so that the billfish will strike the trolled baits. Some anglers even fish for billfish with the aid of kites and live bait. Within this book it would be impossible to discuss all facets of billfishing. We might note that only through spending a lot of time on the water will you become adept at this exciting offshore sport.

We might add that before you become an experienced billfisherman you'll make many mistakes. Over the years we believe we've done more things wrong than right, usually dropping back when we should have reeled, or reeling when we should have dropped back, struck when we should have waited, and waited when we should have struck. We've reeled fast when we should have reeled slow and vice versa, run to the rigger line when we should have grabbed the flat line, and we still haven't caught a white marlin!

Blackfin Tuna

The blackfin tuna is one of the smaller tunas, seldom weighing more than 35 pounds, with an average weight in the range of 10 to 25 pounds. It is found in greatest numbers from Bermuda to Florida, with very little being known about its migrational habits.

It is an excellent light-tackle fish which responds well to a chum slick of ground fish or of small fish. It is wary when the water is clear, so terminal tackle and hooks should be kept as fine as possible, with extreme care being exercised to conceal the hook within the bait completely.

The blackfin tuna will readily strike a trolled lure, with best results being obtained at a fast trolling speed. Japanese trolling feathers and spoons are favored by most trollers, although big blackfin tuna will frequently strike strip baits and rigged balao and mullet.

It is a fine fish for 20-pound and 30-pound regulation-class tackle, whether trolling or chumming.

Bluefin Tuna

Bluefin tuna are world travelers about which very little is known. They are caught on all of our coasts and grow to a size in excess of 1,000 pounds. We'll confine our discussion to what are popularly called school bluefin tuna, those youngsters which range from 5 to upwards of 100 pounds. Fish of this size are excellent light-tackle gamefish that are a delight to catch on 20-pound to 50-pound regulation-class tackle.

There are two popular methods of catching them. Trolling is by far the most popular because of its convenience, although chummers who are adept at coaxing the bluefins into a slick also make substantial catches.

Tuna trollers find that the bluefins like a lure moving fast, often so fast that you wonder how the fish can ever swim fast enough to strike the lure. Japanese trolling feathers, cedar jigs, spoons and

*The bluefin tuna is a favorite of trollers and chummers on all our coasts.
The author landed this husky school tuna while trolling many miles
at sea off Mexico's Baja Peninsula.*

plastic baits all bring strikes when trolled close to the transom.
Most strikes will come when the lures are fished on either the
first or second crest of the waves being churned up in your wake.

When a fish is hooked you shouldn't rush to bring it aboard,
for often the hooked tuna will have several curious companions
watching its plight, and occasionally an entire school will follow
it. By holding the fish on a tight line, you can pump your rod
tips, causing the remaining lures to dance and dart in an enticing
manner, which will frequently bring strikes from other fish. Often
it's possible to hold a school of tuna off your stern for an hour
or more, providing a hooked fish is always kept in the water.

Chummers find that the bluefins respond very well to a chum of
ground menhaden or anchovies. When tuna invade a chum slick
they are often shy of the hook, so you've got to keep your terminal
tackle fine. Use 4/0 through 6/0 size Eagle-Claw albacore and tuna
hooks and conceal the hook as well as you can if using dead bait
such as chunks of menhaden, herring or mackerel. Live baits such

as small mackerel, anchovies and whiting bring strikes. The best method of hooking these baitfish is either through the lips or through the back just below the dorsal fin or under the collar of their gill.

Another effective bait is a chum bag. Often called a meatball, this bait is prepared by placing a hook and some ground menhaden within a small piece of a lady's hairnet and then securing it around the leader. When tossed into the water with several ladles of chum, the chum bag drifts down as a solid piece, and even the most cautious bluefin finds it difficult to resist.

When school bluefins are feeding on the surface you can often enjoy exciting sport by stopping the boat and casting metal squids, bucktail jigs and other lures to them.

Bluefish

The bluefish has a reputation of being among the most vicious fish in the sea. It has a mouth full of very formidable teeth which it uses to tear into schools of baitfish, often gorging itself to the bursting point, then regurgitating and wildly flailing into the helpless baitfish again.

It is without question one of the gamest fighters available to the inshore fisherman along the Atlantic Coast. It ranges all the way from Florida to New England, with peak fishing for the species occurring along the northern portion of its summertime range. It is also plentiful at times along the Gulf Coast, although the blues we've caught from Gulf waters seldom weighed more than 3 pounds, whereas along the middle and north Atlantic Coast fish in the 5-pound to 12-pound class are average.

Bluefish may be taken by sportfishermen in many ways. The techniques discussed under inshore trolling produce extremely well with the blues, although we must caution you not to go too light with tackle, as they are extremely tough fighters, testing your tackle to the limit. Favored lures used by trollers include spoons, Japanese trolling feathers, surgical-tube lures, plastic imitation eels and plugs. Some of the most fun-packed bluefish action we've ever enjoyed was when blues were chasing baitfish near the surface, which resulted in bonanza fishing.

Chummers off Long Island and New Jersey who use ground menhaden dock with perhaps the biggest catches of blues, particularly the party boats which specialize in this type of fishing, which is done on an around-the-clock basis. When chumming, a long-shanked hook of Eagle-Claw style is favored, the size of the hook being determined by the fish in residence, with sizes 5/o through 8/o being average. Favored bait while chumming include a chunk of menhaden, a small butterfish or piece of herring. Some anglers even use small live mackerel when they are available. Sand launce and spearing are good hook baits when small blues are plentiful.

Boat casting is still another fun-packed way of catching blues. Cast in the same areas frequented by chummers and trollers and use popping and swimming plugs, metal squids dressed with pork rind, and bucktail jigs through the depths. Blues are great fun on a fly rod if you can find them chasing bait on the surface. Both fly rod poppers and streamers will quickly bring strikes.

Bonefish

Fishing for bonefish is for the boatman who likes to cast. A peculiar trait of the bonefish is that it spends its time in the deep waters along the edges of tidal flats at low tide. As the tide starts to rise and flood the flats, the bonefish move into the shallow water to feed on the shrimp, small crabs and seaworms which are so plentiful on the flats, where the water is often only one foot to three feet deep.

Boatmen have found that a comfortable way to fish for the bonefish is to employ a small, shallow-draft outboard skiff, poling it across the flats while looking for feeding and cruising bonefish. A long push-pole is employed to push the boat quietly, for the use of the outboard or oars would spook the bonefish before you could ever get within casting range.

Bonefish are a silvery-hued gamefish, and it takes keen eyesight to spot them as they cruise along the flats in search of a meal. Ideal conditions for spotting the feeding fish are extremely bright sunny days with no wind. Anglers find that a pair of Polaroid glasses are most helpful in spotting the fish, as the polarizing effect of the glasses screens out the reflected glare of the water and enables you to look directly into the water.

By far the easiest way to catch a bonefish is on a live shrimp. The shrimp should be impaled on a 1/o or 2/o Eagle-Claw hook, and cast about five feet ahead of a cruising fish. When the bait hits the water it should be permitted to rest absolutely motionless, for the bonefish will find it quickly if he's looking for food. Keep movement in the boat to an absolute minimum, so as not to spook the fish. When the bonefish picks up the bait, you should strike it hard at least twice to set the hook in its very hard mouth. Once it's hooked you'll find yourself in for a real thrill, as a five-pound bonefish will often strip 100 yards of line from your reel in a single shot. Favored tackle for this type of fishing is a one-handed spinning outfit and six-pound-test to eight-pound-test monofilament line.

Bonefish will also strike a bucktail jig quite readily. Bucktail jigs weighing an eighth-ounce and a quarter-ounce are favored. Some are painted pink to resemble a shrimp, while others are of light brown with brown bucktail to resemble the small crabs which are so plentiful on the flats. Bucktails designed expressly for bone-fishing have a delta-wing effect, and may be retrieved very slowly with a jigging movement of the rod tip. Because of their design they do not dig into the bottom.

An extremely effective way to catch spooky bonefish is to cast the jig well ahead of the fish and permit it to rest on the bottom. As the bone approaches, give a slight jig of your rod tip. This will cause the jig to dart ahead, leaving a puff of sand on the bottom much the same as that made by a crab. The bonefish will quickly swim over to investigate, and the next time you cause the bucktail to dance by jigging your rod tip he'll be onto it in a flash.

Catching bonefish on a fly is without a doubt the ultimate method of catching this fine gamefish. But we must in all honesty say that it is far better for a beginner to catch his first few bonefish on live shrimp or bucktails while spinning before graduating to the fly rod. Some of the fly patterns recommended in our starter set are fine for bonefish, including the Blonde Bucktails and Bonefish Bucktail. Another fine fly which was designed expressly for bone-fishing is the Pink Shrimp.

Bonefish are most plentiful throughout the Florida Keys, in the Bahamas and the Virgin Islands as well as many of the West Indies. The farthest north we've caught them was in Bermuda, where we saw the largest bonefish, although there are fewer of them and they are more difficult to catch. In the Bahamas we've seen huge schools of bonefish during the course of a day's fishing, often casting to a hundred or more fish in a day. Hawaii too has a population of this fine scrapper.

California Halibut

The California halibut is a very popular bottom feeder, particularly with small-boat men who fish close to shore and with party boaters who fish off the California coast. Although most of the halibut landed by anglers are in the 5-pound to 20-pound class, there are times when a lucky fisherman has a 50-pounder take his bait.

California halibut are similar in their habits to the flounder of the Gulf and East Coasts, in that they prefer sandy bottoms, where they partially bury themselves and wait for an unsuspecting baitfish to happen by.

Because of this habit it is best to keep your bait moving constantly, so as to cover as much area as possible, thus presenting your bait to as many halibut as might be in the area you fish. The accepted method of fishing for California halibut is to drift live baits over sandy bottom. Most any small baitfish will do, although anchovies and small sardines are favored. Depending on the size of the halibut being taken, most anglers use hooks ranging in size from 1/0 to 4/0, with Eagle-Claw style being favored.

A peculiar habit of the halibut is to take a bait into its mouth and just hold onto it before swallowing it. Evidently the halibut just grabs the bait to kill it as it swims past, and then hesitates to make certain it is immobilized before attempting to swallow it. Because of this it is important that you hesitate for several seconds before attempting to set the hook. A sharp set-back with the rod at the first sign of a strike will just pull the bait away from the fish. Just wait and let the halibut get the bait well back in its mouth where the point and barb will have little difficulty in hooking the fish.

As halibut are primarily live-bait feeders, they'll strike a chromed jig worked near the bottom too. Most anglers permit their jigs to settle directly to the bottom, and then vigorously jig

Harry Bonner employed a live anchovy fished on the bottom to catch this California halibut. On a light popping outfit this biggest of the Pacific flatfishes gave a good account of itself.

their rod tip to cause the jig to rise several feet off the bottom and then falter. While the halibut generally lies in wait for food, it will quickly chase anything that looks like a meal, particularly a shiny jig.

Channel Bass

The channel bass was for many years the prize of the surfman alone. But as the popularity of boating grew, so grew the popularity of fishing for this bronze-colored gamefish from a boat.

Channel bass are found in great numbers from Virginia through to the Georgia Capes. These are primarily big fish weighing from 25 to 50 pounds or more, although there are appreciable numbers of small channel bass, which are called puppy drum, found in protected coastal waters. Throughout Florida and along the Gulf Coast the channel bass is most often called a redfish and in general is of much smaller size than those caught along the middle Atlantic Coast.

The channel bass is an extremely strong fighter. In spring it often moves into inshore middle Atlantic waters in great schools, often numbering fifty or more fish to a school. They cruise just beneath the surface, and on a clear sunny day they can easily be spotted by the alert boatman. A favored technique is to move up-current from the cruising fish, and to shut off the motor, and then to drift down to them, casting big hammered stainless steel jigs to the cruising fish. In casting, it's best to employ at least 17-pound-test or 20-pound-test monofilament line and a rod with plenty of backbone.

Boatmen who would rather not cast will find the channel bass receptive to a trolled spoon or hammered stainless steel jig. Attempt to skirt along the edges of the cruising fish, as by going right through them you're apt to spook them. Here it is wise to use a general-purpose rod and a reel loaded with at least 30-pound-test line.

Colonel Dick Crawford lifts a redfish out of the net for Bobby Rosko. The redfish, a local name for channel bass, is popular with Gulf Coast anglers, but seldom reaches the size of the channel bass caught by anglers fishing along the Barrier Islands and Outer Banks of the Atlantic. Note the distinguishing black spots on its tail.

During the fall the channel bass are seldom observed on the surface. Boatmen make their biggest catches in bay and ocean waters by anchoring on the shoals and along the sod banks frequented by channel bass and fishing with chunks of mullet, spot, or menhaden which are fished right on the bottom with a single-hook bottom rig. As the fish are usually very big, size 8/o and 9/o hooks are favored.

Throughout the southern part of their range, channel bass are often landed while bottom fishing with fresh shrimp, chunks of mullet or small live pinfish or squirrel fish. The redfish are also receptive to a cast lure, and many are landed from among the mangrove-lined estuaries while casting with bucktail jigs and plugs, using light casting tackle.

Cobia

Cobia are one of the toughest inshore gamefish found along the middle Atlantic and Gulf Coasts. Individuals weighing 30 to 40 pounds are by no means uncommon, and on a general-purpose boat outfit with 30-pound-test line it will often require a half hour or more to bring one of this weight to gaff.

In some areas they are loners, with only one or two fish cruising together, while in other areas they congregate in small schools of six or eight fish. We've observed quite a number of big cobia in the Chesapeake Bay and in the Atlantic off Chincoteague, Virginia, and we've seen several pods of the fish cruising just below the surface in many spots in the Gulf of Mexico.

The cobia, which has many nicknames, including sergeant fish, black bonito, ling and lemon fish, has a peculiar habit which is often its undoing. Just by slowly approaching buoys which mark channel edges you can often spot cobia finning just below them, waiting for an unsuspecting baitfish to happen by. Often these fish can be caught by carefully presenting a live baitfish such as a pinfish, small blue runner or a grunt to them. Often they'll show no interest whatever, so don't spend all of your time trying to catch those cobia which you can see.

Cobia will frequently strike a trolled lure, and many boatmen employ six-inch and seven-inch chromed spoons, which are sent to intermediate levels with the aid of trolling sinkers and trolled along channel edges or in spots cobia are known to frequent.

One of the most popular ways of catching cobia in the Chesapeake Bay, which should work equally well along the Gulf Coast, is to use live eels while fishing from either an anchored or drifting boat. The eels, preferably 12 to 14 inches long, are hooked through the head or lips with 7/o or 8/o O'Shaughnessy hooks. These are paid out on a live line with the reel in free spool, and invariably they head right for the bottom. They are permitted to swim about until a cobia spots them. After that you're in for a fighting treat, as they'll really test your tackle. Many cobia are also landed while bottom fishing over reefs using shedder crabs or large shrimp as bait.

Codfish

The codfish is a favorite of winter fishermen along the middle and north Atlantic Coast, because it is one of the biggest fish in residence during the cold-weather months. Very often the codfish is found well offshore, where he frequents open bottom as he searches for food, but more often he is found around reefs and wrecks of sunken ships which lie offshore in many areas along the Atlantic Coast.

When fishing for codfish over open or sandy bottom, the favorite technique is to use a conventional high-low rig with a general-purpose rod, drifting the bait across the bottom. In this way you cover a lot of area and as a result often catch more codfish. But while wreck fishing or fishing above reefs, you would loose too much terminal tackle while drifting, so the best approach is to anchor and fish your baits directly on the bottom.

Codfish will take a wide variety of baits. Their diet consists of crabs, mussels, lobsters, clams and the many species of small fish which frequent the waters around wrecks and reefs. Most codfishermen employ big sea clams for codfish baits, as these are readily available. We've known of codfishermen who quickly clean the first codfish they catch to remove the crabs which are often found in their stomachs, using them as hook baits. Subsequent cod were

Karl Osborne hooked this 56-pound cobia while casting a plastic rigged eel with spinning tackle off Destin, Florida. Cobia of this size have tremendous stamina, testing tackle and the angler's skill to the utmost.

The codfish is a favorite of middle and north Atlantic party-boat anglers. This beauty was landed off Montauk, Long Island, while fishing with a high-low bottom rig and a piece of clam as bait. They are a fine table fish.

also cleaned in order to obtain the crabs which are so plentiful along the bottom and constitute a major portion of the codfish's diet.

The codfish has a big mouth, so big hooks are in order, with 6/o or 7/o Eagle Claws being most popular.

As codfish frequently feed on small fish that are around wrecks, including cunners, tautog and sea bass, as well as herring and mackerel which swim at intermediate levels, they will very often strike a diamond, tri-sided or hammered stainless steel jig worked in the depths. The favored methods of jigging is to permit the jig—which may weigh anywhere from 3 to 16 ounces, depending on water depth and tidal flow—to settle to the bottom, and then to retrieve it with a whip retrieve, alternately jigging and whipping back with your rod tip. Teasers made of surgical tube are often rigged just above the jig, and frequently the codfish will hit the teaser.

Dolphin

The dolphin is without a doubt one of the finest gamefish available to the boat fisherman. It is found on the Atlantic, Pacific and Gulf Coasts, being most plentiful in the southern portions of its range, although during the summer months it often travels as far north as New England. The dolphin has been described by many as the prettiest fish in the sea.

Most dolphin are caught while trolling with regulation-class tackle and employing techniques discussed earlier under offshore trolling. They are most at home far from shore in the depths of the ocean. Seldom do they travel alone, but are often located in schools. The big dolphin often travel in small schools containing upwards of a dozen fish, while the one- to ten-pounders can often be observed by the thousands as they mill about on the surface chasing baitfish.

These prettily-hued fighters will strike almost any trolled bait you put before them. We've caught them on balao, mullet, eels and strip baits rigged for trolling, as well as on a wide assortment of lures including spoons, Japanese feathers and plastic imitation baitfish.

Dolphin have a habit of sticking close to a fish which is hooked and being brought to boat. If you delay boating one fish, it is often possible to hook a second or third dolphin in rapid succession. Often it's possible to catch dolphin by employing this technique until you're arm-weary, for the fish will continue to follow hooked dolphin, repeatedly striking any lures you put before them.

Big dolphin will jump completely clear of the water time after time when hooked, putting on a beautiful aerial display. They cannot be horsed into the boat, for they have a great deal of strength and will rip free or break tackle if you put too much pressure on them.

They have a habit of stationing themselves almost anywhere there is flotsam to be found offshore. Often you'll find a whole school of dolphin right under a couple of floating planks or along a weed line.

It is at times like this that it pays to ease up alongside the flotsam and break out casting tackle, for dolphin on a light rod can be a thrill that you'll long remember.

When they're cruising about under flotsam they're usually looking for a meal, for they know that baitfish frequently seek the protection of the weeds and other debris that is floating about.

Bucktail jigs, popping plugs, spoons and almost any other small lures will bring out the dolphin from beneath the flotsam in droves. Here too, by keeping one fish in the water you'll keep the other dolphin swimming close by, and you can get strike after strike.

We've often taken big dolphin on a fly rod, and are duty bound to admit that it is a thrilling experience. The Blonde series of bucktails, Multi-Wing Streamers and popping bugs will all bring strikes from dolphin that are in a feeding mood. When you hook one on fly tackle you can expect to get literally twice as many jumps from it than were it hooked on heavy trolling tackle. Twenty or more jumps per fish on the fly rod is nothing unusual, and these are the prettiest jumps you'll ever witness, for with the boat shut down the dolphin can display its jumping skills without being dragged along by the boat.

The dolphin is not only one of the prettiest fish in the sea, but one of the best fighters and jumpers you're apt to run into on the offshore scene.

Great Barracuda

Over the years the great barracuda has been painted as a sinister denizen of the deep by television and movie-script writers. But he's really not a bad individual, and great fun when taken trolling or casting.

The barracuda is found in great numbers close to shore and around reefs and cays in the Bahamas, off Florida and along the entire Gulf of Mexico. It's also found in great numbers off Bermuda as well as in the islands of the West Indies.

Barracuda will quickly take a trolled bait, such as mullet or balao which is intended for sailfish or white marlin, and unquestionably these "saber-tooths," as they have become nicknamed, are often sworn at by billfishermen who have their baits mangled by a rush from a big barracuda.

In addition to trolled baits the barracuda will hit a wide variety of lures, with spoons, plugs, trolling feathers and bucktail jigs being favored. Trollers who fish above the offshore reefs expressly for barracuda enjoy good results while trolling strip baits. These are cut from either dolphin, little tuna or bonito bellies, or fresh squid, and are trolled just below the surface with the aid of a small trolling sinker. Barracuda find them difficult to resist.

In tropical waters you're apt to find small barracuda almost anywhere. They'll be back in a small river where you're casting for tarpon, or offshore, while you're chumming for king mackerel, a 'cuda will often stray through your slick. They're a frequent visitor to the bonefish flats, and many an inexperienced eye has mistaken them for the bonefish. When you spot a cruising barracuda you can often tempt him with casting tackle. Surface plugs such as swimmers, poppers and propeller plugs work fine, as do bucktail jigs retrieved with a whipping movement of the rod tip which causes them to dart ahead and then falter.

Barracuda aren't considered edible by most anglers, and the greatest majority are released to fight another day. Extreme care should be exercised when unhooking them, as their teeth can inflict serious injury.

The great barracuda is found in Atlantic and Gulf Coast waters in great numbers. It has extremely sharp teeth and should always be handled with care. It fights well on light tackle and is taken via many methods, including trolling, casting and bottom fishing.

The Pacific barracuda differs considerably from the great barracuda of the Atlantic. It has a much longer and thinner body and not as formidable a set of dentures. It is a fine light tackle fish and readily takes live baitfish or a wide variety of lures.

Groupers

There are so very many groupers it would be impossible to include each individual species within a listing such as this. The groupers are, however, one of the major species caught by sportfishermen along the southern Atlantic Coast, along the Gulf Coast and in the Bahamas and other tropical islands as well.

Groupers are primarily bottom feeders, spending most of their time over reefs where there is a plentiful supply of food. Among the groupers which fishermen are most apt to catch are the jewfish, red hind, greasby, sickledfin, rock hind, Nassau, snowy, princess, yellowfin, gag and sea scamp. Some of these venture close to shore, but for the most part they are found in deep water, primarily around reefs.

The rock hind grouper is among the smallest groupers, averaging only 3 to 4 pounds in weight, while the giant jewfish grouper often weighs up to 500 pounds or more.

The groupers will strike lures and may be taken while employing casting tackle and bucktail jigs or chromed jigs. But by far the biggest catches of grouper are taken while using natural baits fished directly on the bottom. Chunks of mullet produce good results, as do large fresh shrimp. In fact, when you're anchored over a good grouper spot you can put a chunk of almost any fish on your hook and be assured of getting a strike.

A sturdy general-purpose boat outfit is essential when fishing for grouper in the 3-pound to 50-pound class. If you tangle with big jewfish you'd better lean towards 50-pound regulation-class tackle.

All groupers have big mouths, and hooks in sizes 6/o, 7/o and 8/o are most often employed. If live pinfish, squirrel fish and grunts are available, these make fine grouper baits, and should be hooked either through the lips, the eye sockets, or the fleshy part of their back just beneath the dorsal fin.

While groupers aren't considered a gamefish, they are a fine table fish, which is why so many people fish for them. They're caught primarily from party boats, although charter and private boats frequently stop to fish for groupers so that they'll have some good fish for the table.

THE BOATMAN'S FAVORITE 50 SPECIES

Jack Crevalle

The jack crevalle, much the same as the amberjack, is a fish which many people avoid because it just fights too hard! However, we certainly don't avoid a school of jacks when we spot them chasing baitfish near the surface, for we rate them as a great fighting fish which are certainly fun to catch.

Only once you've hooked a six-pound or eight-pound jack on a light one-handed spinning outfit can you appreciate the stamina which this fish possesses. They fight with a sheer determination to get away that is almost unbelieveable.

The jack crevalle is perhaps too easy a fish to hook, which is another reason many local anglers don't think too highly of him. When they're furiously chasing baitfish on the surface, they're almost certain to strike any bright, shiny lure you cast or troll past them.

The jacks will strike at spoons, wobblers, plugs, bucktail jigs and almost any type of feather jig. They are not a fish which is easily spooked, and you can bring your boat fairly close to them without fear of putting down the school.

While most of the jacks you catch will range from 5 to 10 pounds, there are many in southern waters which weigh 25 to 40 pounds, which will test your tackle to the utmost.

Jack crevalle aren't considered a good table fish, and most are released at boatside.

Kelp Bass

It is evident the kelp bass got its name because it has a habit of setting up residence around the kelp beds off the California and Baja California coast. This popular bass is by no means a heavyweight, usually averaging only three or four pounds, but it has a fighting heart, which makes it extremely popular with sport fishermen.

Seldom are kelp bass encountered at any distance from the kelp beds. Indeed, frequently a hook has to be fished right in among the holes in the kelp in order to get strikes. Although the major ingredient in the diet of kelp bass are the tiny shrimp which are found in great numbers among the kelp, sportsmen usually make their best catches while using live anchovies, small perch and other small baitfish.

Kelp bass readily respond to a chum line of live anchovies or other small baitfish and will quickly take a live bait when presented on a small hook and light leader. They will also move up in a chum line of chunks of herring or mackerel and will take a small strip or fillet of this bait fished in the slick. They can be fussy, however, and if a great deal of natural forage is available, they aren't apt to show much interest in dead bait.

By far the greatest majority of kelp bass are taken while chumming and live-bait fishing, but outboarders and small-boat men occasionally use light popping outfits and troll small jigs, spoons, bucktail jigs and feathers along the edges of the kelp to make fairly good catches of the hard-fighting kelp bass.

King Mackerel

The king mackerel is most noted by the exciting way in which it takes a bait trolled on the surface. They literally leap into the air a full ten feet or more, arching through the air and pouncing directly onto a bait. They never miss, and when they hit it you're certain to be in for some exciting sport, for they are fine fighters.

Found from the Carolinas south to Florida and along the Gulf Coast, as well as in most of the tropical islands of the Atlantic, the king mackerel averages 3 to 20 pounds, with most fish of a size sticking together in schools. They do grow big, however, with some in the 50-pound class being taken each year.

There are many methods employed to take the kings, or kingfish as many anglers call them. Small king mackerel are trolled for with Japanese trolling feathers, small spoons and strip baits, while the heavyweights are fished for with bigger baits such as balao and mullet.

Kings will readily respond to a chum slick of ground fish or finely diced pieces of mullet, mackerel or other fish. A favorite way of catching them is to troll until a school is located, then hold the fish around the boat with chum and employ small bucktail jigs tipped with a strip of fresh king mackerel. The scent of the fresh bait on

Kelp bass are a favorite of party-boat anglers on the Pacific Coast. Ernie Hous hooked this beauty while fishing on a twilight trip out of Oceanside, California, using a live anchovy as bait.

the jig, plus the fluttering action of it, is more than the kings can resist.

When kings are plentiful they'll often be seen chasing bait on the surface. At such times boat casters take the fine, deep fighters on surface plugs. With poppers and propeller plugs the king mackerel jump clear into the air before striking them, after which they disappear into the depths to fight.

King Salmon

Anglers who fish along the northern California, Oregon and Washington coastline look to the king salmon as their toughest ocean-caught gamefish. The heavy-bodied king salmon are the biggest of the salmons, with occasional kings being landed each year that weigh upwards of 50 pounds.

On the average, the king salmon caught by sport fishermen range anywhere from 10 to 25 pounds, with fish above that weight being the exception. By far the most popular method of catching the salmon is deep trolling. Often salmon trollers probe the depths between 100 and 200 feet, getting their lures and baits down by a variety of methods, including planers, heavy weights, wire line, and to a lesser degree in shallow water, trolling sinkers. Sinkers weighing one to three pounds are often used. These are released via a sinker

The king mackerel is a favorite of anglers in tropical Atlantic waters and in the Gulf of Mexico. Bob Stankus landed this one while trolling a mullet skip bait off Chub Cay in the Bahamas.

release mechanism when a strike is received, thus permitting you to fight the salmon without a heavy sinker.

Spoons, flashers and wooden swimming plugs are among the favorite lures used by salmon trollers. But by far the biggest catches are boated by those trollers who employ natural baits, with anchovies and herring being the most popular. Some anglers rig their baits on a single hook with a three-foot to five-foot leader. Others prefer tying in a second or trailing hook that simply swings freely alongside the bait, for they feel this hooks the salmon that might miss the primary hook.

When the king salmon move in close to shore off the mouths of rivers or are above shallow offshore plateaus, many nice catches are made while drifting. This permits the use of lighter tackle. Catching the salmon in depths of 30 to 50 feet proves far more enjoyable than in extreme depths, for the fish isn't subjected to a great change of pressure as it is pumped from the depths.

A favorite bait for this type of fishing is a plug cut from a herring or other small baitfish. The head is cut from the baitfish at about a forty-five degree angle, cutting away most of the stomach. The first hook of the rig is passed through the fleshy part of the baitfish just below the dorsal fins, while the second hook is slipped into the bait near the tail. As the bait is drifted along the bottom, the angler works it with his rod tip, causing the bait to rise off the bottom, flutter and settle back down. The technique accounts for many king salmon each year, particularly when the big kings move inshore.

Ladyfish

We're including the ladyfish here because it offers fine sport when hooked on a light casting rod. It's found in appreciable numbers along the southern Atlantic Coast and along the Gulf Coast as well. It is most noted because it jumps repeatedly when hooked. While

This is a favorite rig used by San Francisco anglers who troll for king salmon. The three-pound cast-iron sinker takes the anchovy bait into the depths and when a big salmon strikes the sinker release device causes the sinker to fall free, thus permitting you to enjoy the fighting quality of the salmon without the burden of having the heavy sinker on the line. This results in a lost sinker every time you hook a salmon.

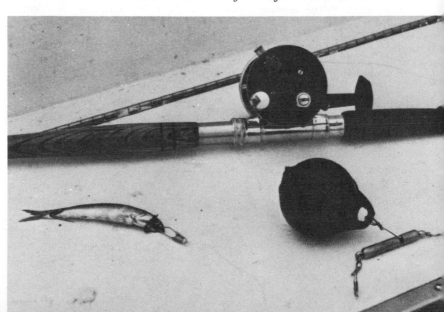

most specimens weigh only a pound or two, there are times when you might hook one double that weight and have your hands full.

The ladyfish is most often found in the protected reaches of rivers and sounds, although quite a few stray into the open Atlantic and Gulf. They are most often caught quite by accident while casting for other fish, but when hooked they perform beautifully, jumping into the air much like a tarpon.

Many people mistake the ladyfish for a bonefish, for at first glance they have very similar lines, with the exception that the ladyfish is much slimmer than a bonefish of comparable size.

Ladyfish take a variety of baits, including shrimp, small baitfish and chunks of fish fished on the bottom.

For maximum enjoyment you can't beat catching them on a small bucktail, jigged along with a whip retrieve. They are not considered good eating, and most are released at boatside.

Lingcod

The lingcod is not a species that would by any stretch of the imagination win any beauty contests. But what it lacks in outward appearance it makes up for in being one of the tastiest fish caught by West Coast anglers.

It is caught in fair numbers from Los Coronados Islands off Mexico on north, but the greatest catches are made from boats sailing from ports in the northern part of California on up to Washington and Oregon.

The lingcod is a bottom feeder that is most at home in deep water. It is not unusual to catch them in depths of 300 feet or more, although small lingcod often move into waters close to shore and are caught by small-boat men, particularly in the northern portion of their range.

The ganion rig is favored when the lingcod are in deep water, for it saves the angler the chore of just reeling in one fish at a time. Often the lingcod are mixed in with rockfish, at which times it is not uncommon to catch both lingcod and rockfish on the same ganion.

Lingcod aren't particular about what they eat, but there is little question that small live fish are preferred by them. In fact, many lingcod anglers will immediately bait their hook with any small fish

This big lingcod just lifted from the water on a gaff was hooked off the coast of Oregon. They are a plentiful bottom feeder highly regarded as one of the Pacific's tastiest fish.

that they may snag or catch while bottom fishing, especially if live bait isn't available on board. As a close second to live baitfish, chunks of herring, anchovies, mackerel and sardines may be used. Some anglers even use dead shrimp with fair results.

While the lingcod will strike a jig worked along the bottom, this method of fishing results in fewer strikes than while using natural baits.

They have a big mouth in relation to the rest of their body, so you seldom have to worry about using too large a hook. Suit the hook size to the general run of the fish being landed. Watch the lingcod's teeth. They're very sharp and can make a mess of careless fingers.

Little Tuna

The little tuna is found in great numbers from New England to Florida, along the Gulf Coast, and in the Bahamas and most tropical waters. It is a small tuna that is seldom over 20 pounds, with most averaging 10 to 15 pounds. For its size it is an excellent fighter.

It is usually taken trolling, and will strike much the same lures used for other tunas, including Japanese trolling feathers, spoons, cedar jigs and plastic baits. Frequently the little tuna wallop big baits trolled for billfish.

It will also readily respond to a chum of ground fish or fingerling baitfish. However, once it moves into a chum spread it is often extremely hook shy, cautiously looking over any bait before it takes it. Often it is best to conceal a 2/0 or 3/0 hook within a small baitfish and pack some chum around the baitfish and ease the bait into the water. As the chum separates from the baitfish the little tuna will often pick it up immediately.

When little tuna are chasing small baitfish on the surface, they often get so excited in their feeding frenzy that they'll take a cast lure. It is important if you try to catch them while casting that you use an extremely fast retrieve. A lure such as a bucktail jig or spoon works fine, but it's got to move fast, otherwise little tuna will seldom strike it.

Oceanic Bonito

The oceanic bonito is caught off all three of our coasts and is a fine light-tackle gamefish. It's often called skipjack. It is an extremely strong fish for its size, usually averaging 8 to 12 pounds. Big specimens are difficult to land, for the fish has an extremely weak mouth, which frequently results in the jaw literally being ripped from the fish while it is being fought. It is a blue-water fish and is most often found well offshore. It travels in big schools and can often be observed chasing baitfish on the surface. Butterfish, pilchards, anchovies, sardines, flying fish and squid constitute a major portion of its diet.

It will quickly strike a trolled lure. Best techniques are those discussed under offshore trolling, with 20-pound and 30-pound regulation-class tackle being more than adequate for these fish. While many oceanic bonito are landed on heavy tackle, it is indeed a shame, for on light gear they give a fine account of themselves.

Japanese trolling feathers are a fine lure for the oceanic bonito, as they closely resemble a small baitfish. Because of this species' very weak mouth, many trollers who fish expressly for them rig their trolling feathers with a double hook arrangement. A ringed O'Shaughnessy and needle-eye O'Shaughnessy hook in 7/0 sizes are employed. The needle eye is slipped through the ringed-eye hook, so that the latter rides in the curve of the needle-eye hook. The needle-eye hook is then twisted onto the leader wire, and both hooks are hidden in the feathers of the Japanese trolling feather. When an oceanic bonito strikes a trolling feather rigged in this manner, it usually gets the trailing hook well back in its mouth, and it's less apt to pull free than if it had a single hook in its weak jaw.

They'll also strike trolled strip baits, cedar jigs, bone squids, spoons and almost any lure that resembles a small baitfish.

Anglers who like to catch fish by casting will find the oceanic bonito fair game. They'll readily strike a small propeller plug when they're feeding on the surface, and bucktail jigs account for many. They're a fine fish for the fly caster too, as they frequently feed on the surface. With all casting tackle a fast retrieve is important.

Pacific Barracuda

The Pacific barracuda is considerably smaller in size than the great barracuda of the Atlantic Coast. It is caught in great numbers by California anglers who fish along the middle and southern California coast, as well as off Baja California. It is a fine gamefish which provides lots of thrills for anglers.

Most Pacific barracuda caught by boatmen weigh in the neighborhood of three or four pounds, although occasional individuals weighing ten pounds are landed during the course of a season.

They are most often found around offshore kelp beds, for around the floating seaweed there is usually a plentiful supply of food. They feed extensively on anchovies and small baitfish, and squid when these cephalopods are present.

By far the great majority of the Pacific barracuda are landed while fishing with live anchovies as bait. Because they are small in size and often in the company of other small gamefish, such as the Pacific bonito and kelp bass, anglers usually use small baits, number 1 or 2 hooks and light rods to take them. They respond well to a chum line of live baitfish, or to ground chum prepared from mackerel, anchovies, sardines or other forage species.

Pacific barracuda will also take a cast or trolled lure, but here too it is important to use a light spinning outfit while casting, or a popping outfit if trolling along the kelp beds from a small boat, for only in this way will you enjoy catching this long, extremely thin Pacific gamefish. Bucktail jigs, small spoons and chromed jigs worked vigorously in the depths will bring the most strikes.

Pacific Bonito

The Pacific bonito might well be termed the West Coast counterpart of the Atlantic bonito. Both are very similar in size and fighting characteristics and are extremely plentiful. The Pacific bonito, or California bonito as it is often called, ranges all the way from British Columbia down to Mexico, although it is found in greatest numbers in the southern portion of its range.

Frequently when albacore are not available or the prize yellowtail is not cooperative, anglers turn their attention to the bonito to fill the void. Most bonito average three or four pounds, although ten-pounders are landed occasionally.

The bonito is popular among party boaters because they can almost always catch a few to fill out their bags, while trollers know that before the day is over several of these torpedo-shaped adversaries are almost certain to grab the smaller lures trolled astern.

Pacific bonito prefer small fish, with anchovies and sardines making up the bulk of their diet. When they are observed feeding on the surface it is relatively easy to coax them to a chum of live anchovies and keep the small torpedoes swarming about the boat, quickly grabbing every anchovy tossed over as chum, as well as those with a hook in them.

If trolling, standard offshore trolling techniques apply, with this species preferring a lure moving at a good speed. Many trollers make a mistake of using too big a lure. Stick with lures in the three-inch to five-inch range with 7/o hooks and you should quickly receive strikes from this far-ranging bonito.

Casters too take a sizeable toll of bonito each year. Spinning and multiplying outfits are most often employed, with jigs, spoons and bucktails being the favored lures. Many fly rodders have employed streamers with fine results in recent years. This species is most cooperative, providing a good way to get experience with a fly rod in salt water.

Permit

Many light-tackle anglers rate the permit as one of the finest shallow-water inshore adversaries they can set their sights on. The permit have habits which closely parallel those of the bonefish. They frequent reasonably shallow waters close to shore, often moving in over the flats to feed.

Permit are extremely wary, sometimes traveling alone, although frequently you'll encounter small schools of them. By far the easiest way—if you could call it that—of catching them is to pole a small boat across shallow flats where permit are known to frequent on a flooding tide. They're most often found in the Florida Keys as well as in the Bahamas, although small numbers of them are taken in many tropical waters.

The ultimate sport is to employ a fly rod and small streamer for the permit, with spinning tackle and small bucktail jigs also proving a challenge. Many anglers enjoy best results with a one-handed spinning outfit and use a single live shrimp which is cast just ahead of the permit as it cruises along looking for a meal.

Permit are an extremely powerful fish which will test both tackle and angling skill alike. While most will average 10 to 15 pounds, each season sees several permit landed that weigh 30 pounds or more.

Anglers have been known to use pieces of shrimp as chum while anchored in the deep water right at the edge of the flats to coax the permit within range of hooks baited with live shrimp. But by far the most challenging method of catching them is while poling across the flats and making visual contact with the broad-shouldered adversary.

Pollock

Of the many fish which we've caught in our travels, we'd rate the pollock one of the hardest fighting non-game species we've caught. Actually a species that is most at home in cold water, the pollock fights extremely well. Pound for pound we'd say he outdistances some species which bear a gamefish label.

Although the pollock ranges as far south as the Virginia Capes, it is caught in greatest numbers from New Jersey north to the Maritime Provinces of Canada. In the southern portion of its range it is found during the late fall, winter and early spring, while throughout the northern part of its range is most often caught by sportsmen during the summer months.

The pollock is a fine cold-water fish that is caught in great numbers along the middle and north Atlantic coast. The one being brought aboard here was hooked while trolling in the rip just below Montauk Lighthouse. Wire line and a bucktail jig was the successful combination.

Pollock caught in inshore waters of bays and rivers usually average only a couple of pounds in weight, but those caught in the open ocean around wrecks and rock ledges and in tide rips often weigh 20 to 30 pounds.

Bottom fishermen catch great numbers of pollock while employing general-purpose boat outfits and high-low bottom rigs baited with clams. They also make fine catches while using diamond and trisided jigs worked near the bottom and at intermediate levels. Teasers attached just above the jigs also bring strikes.

Still another popular way to catch pollock is trolling. Often the pollock school up in tide rips at points of land and at such times trollers who fish their lines deep with the aid of trolling sinkers or wire or lead-core line score very well. Pollock strike spoons, Japanese trolling feathers, surgical-tube lures and heavy bucktail jigs. When they come to the surface while chasing bait, they provide great sport on casting tackle.

The pollock has often been called the "Boston bluefish" because of the similarity of its profile and coloration to that of the bluefish. During the cold-weather months they are the hardest fighting fish found along the middle Atlantic Coast, providing fine sport for party boatmen and private boatmen alike.

Porgy

The porgy is a favorite of bottom fishermen all the way from the Carolinas on up to New England. It moves inshore in great numbers during the summer months, where it takes up residence around mussel beds, wrecks, rocky bottoms and anywhere else there is abundance of natural food.

The big porgies, often called shad porgies or dinner plates, usually stay in the ocean, while the small porgies, called sand porgies, often invade inshore waters by the thousands. Big porgies usually weigh two to three pounds, although once in a while a lucky angler will land a four-pound beauty.

Porgies are primarily bottom feeders, and a general-purpose boat outfit or popping outfit is ideally suited to fishing for them. The favorite terminal rig used by porgy fishermen is a high-low rig, which is fished right on the bottom. The porgy will take a wide variety of baits, including seaworms, clams, squid, mussels and pieces of crab. Baits should be kept small, as a porgy has a small mouth. Carlisle or Eagle-Claw hooks are favored by most anglers, with the size tailored to the fish in an area; number 3 or 4 hooks are fine for sand porgies, while number 1 or 1/0 are often used for big sea porgies.

Throughout New England many anglers call the porgy "scup," and often these tasty bottom feeders are attracted by depositing crushed clams directly beneath an anchored boat. This practice is also followed by party boats, who find the crushed clams keep the porgies actively feeding, attracting more porgies to the area.

Rockfish

There are over 50 different species of rockfish living in the Pacific Ocean's depths off California, Oregon and Washington. Because of the great number of species, there are times when an angler seldom catches more than one or two of a single species in a day's fishing. Indeed, even many experienced party-boat skippers are at a loss to name each of the many varieties.

Those which are most plentiful include the vermillion rockfish, kelp rockfish and olive rockfish, plus the bocaccio, all of which are favored for the table.

Most rockfish live in depths of from 250 to 750 feet, and sport fishermen generally fish in the shallowest spots they can find the fish, for it becomes quite a chore reeling fish in from these extreme depths.

Because of the great depth of water, heavy sinkers are required to take the many-hooked ganion rigs to the bottom. Dacron line is favored because of its fine diameter and limited stretch quality, two important factors when fishing in such extreme depths.

Tough baits are essential, for a soft bait falls off the hook too easily, necessitating your reeling in too often to check the bait, which can become a chore because of the great time required to reel in so much line. Because of this, many anglers soak chunks of herring or other baitfish in table salt to harden them. Squid is favored as bait because it is tough and holds up well on the hook.

During the course of a day's fishing you're apt to catch rockfish ranging in weight from a half-pound to upwards of 40 pounds. Many anglers use a small rockfish as a hook bait to catch a larger rockfish. For the rockfish have very large mouths, and even a ten-pounder would have little difficulty in swallowing a one-pound rockfish.

While rockfishing is not great sport in the sense of the fighting quality of the fish, it is a lot of fun, because there is always a great variety of species coming aboard. The prime reason so many anglers fish for rockfish is that they are fine quality table fish.

Sea Bass

The sea bass is a bottom feeder found along the middle and north Atlantic Coast in great numbers. It is caught in southern and Gulf Coast waters too, but not in as great quantity or large size.

They rank among the favorite bottom feeders of the coastal party-boat angler because sea bass are usually eager to take a bait. On a good day it doesn't take too much effort to catch a sizeable quantity of them.

The favorite method of taking them is by bottom fishing, employing a high-low rig with a pair of snelled Eagle-Claw hooks in 1/0 or

Walt Reed hooked this double-header of big sea bass while fising above a wreck off Chincoteague, Virginia. Small pieces of squid fished on a high-low rig proved to be the right combination for this tasty bottom feeder.

2/o size. The sea bass frequent bottom strewn with rocks, pilings or wrecks, for they find an easy meal in the mussels which cover such debris. Favored baits include strips of squid, small pieces of clam and bloodworms or sandworms.

When sea bass are present and in a hitting mood, it's often a simple matter of letting the rig directly to the bottom and waiting until you feel a hard yank on the line. You then set the hook and pull in the frisky bottom feeder.

Most sea bass caught in the northern part of their range average around two pounds, although off the Virginia Capes where there is little fishing pressure we've caught a great many sea bass in a day's fishing that weighed a solid three to four pounds.

Occasionally sea bass move up in a chum spread intended for other species, and quite a few fair-sized specimens are landed quite by accident while bluefish chumming. When fishing above a wreck, the fishing can often be improved by lowering a chum pot loaded with ground menhaden, or by crushing clams and dropping them overboard to entice the sea bass to the area.

Sea bass are a fine table fish, which makes them popular with party boatmen and other bottom fishermen.

Sea Trout

The sea trout is a favorite of inshore anglers, for it is found in greatest numbers in the protected waters of bays, rivers and estuaries. It does move into the Atlantic Ocean and the Gulf of Mexico, but seldom strays far from shore.

It prefers weed beds, for here it finds an abundance of shrimp, small baitfish, crabs and the other marine life on which it feeds.

The fish we call sea trout here goes under a wide variety of names. It's called spotted weakfish, spotted trout, spotted sea trout and speckled trout in various parts of its range. Occasionally it strays as far north as New Jersey, but is found in greatest numbers from the Chesapeake Bay south and along the Gulf Coast.

Most sea trout anglers drift across weedbeds in small boats, employing live shrimp or seaworm baits which are placed on 1/0 or 2/0 Eagle-Claw hooks. Sometimes a float is employed to keep the bait from fouling in the weeds, but most often it is permitted to drift with the current as the boat drifts across the weedbed.

Sea trout will readily take an artificial bait, and many boatmen prefer this method of fishing over using natural baits. The technique is to drift across the weedbeds, casting lures as you drift. Favored for this fishing is either a light popping outfit, or a one-hand spinning outfit, although some anglers even use fly casting tackle and streamers or popping bugs. Favored lures of the casters are small subsurface mirror-type plugs, lightweight bucktail jigs, and surface and subsurface swimming plugs.

Most sea trout average one to three pounds in weight, although it's not uncommon to catch fish in the five-pound to seven-pound class in southern waters. Often these heavyweights are called "gator trout" by the natives who specialize in fishing for them.

Shad

For many years the shad was strictly a fish caught by commercial fishermen in nets. But in the past decade its popularity as a sport fish has grown tremendously. Each spring shad enter fresh-water rivers to spawn. As they move through coastal rivers and bays to reach fresh water, boatmen enjoy bonanza fishing for several weeks, for frequently the shad rest in brackish water before proceeding up-stream to accomplish their spawning chores.

At such times small-boat men can catch the shad by either trolling, casting or jigging. The techniques employed on the Atlantic and Pacific Coasts are remarkably similar, with a small lure called a shad dart being by far the most popular, accounting for many thousands of shad each spring. The shad dart resembles a small bucktail jig and weighs only an eighth-ounce. Some are painted bright colors with bucktail skirts, while others are chromed plated. Some have feather skirts.

Most often the shad move through the rivers traveling right along the bottom. It is necessary to get the shad darts very deep in order to get strikes. A favorite shad rig is to tie a small three-way swivel to the end of your line. Next comes a six-inch dropper off one eye of the swivel, onto which a small bank-style sinker is tied. Onto the remaining eye of the swivel a three-foot or four-foot piece of nylon leader material is tied, onto the end of which is tied a shad dart. Mid-way between the shad dart and the swivel, a second shad dart is tied in dropper fashion, giving you a two-hook rig. The entire rig is permitted to settle right to the bottom and then trolled and jigged through areas frequented by shad. Some anglers prefer drifting instead of trolling, while others anchor and jig their shad darts.

When the shad migration is in full swing, it is not uncommon to catch a half dozen or more five-pound to six-pound shad. They are great fighters and jump repeatedly when hooked. While providing great sport on the rod, the shad and its roe is a delicacy on the dinner table.

Sharks

Because there are so very many different species of sharks found in our coastal waters, we will only mention those which are most often encountered by sport fishermen. It should be noted that there are many more species in our waters, many of which provide excellent sport on rod and reel. By far the greatest fighter of all the sharks is the mako, which jumps repeatedly when hooked. Others which give a good account of themselves on the line include the hammerhead, porbeagle, spinner, thresher, tiger and white shark.

Sharks are not too difficult to catch, and until recently there has been little sport-fishing pressure for them. But during the past few years quite a few boatmen have turned to shark fishing because it enables them to catch a really big fish, and to do so at practically any time.

Captain Jim Seddan grabs the leader wire as he brings a big hammerhead shark alongside his charter boat while trolling off Miami Beach, Florida. Rather than tangle with him Jim simply cut the wire and turned the shark free. This is a wise practice, for a big shark can do a lot of damage if you attempt to bring it aboard while it is still full of fight.

It is surprising how few people realize that literally thousands upon thousands of sharks are in residence in almost all of our coastal waters just a few miles from shore. These sharks may be taken by a variety of methods, but by far the most popular is by either trolling or chumming, with the latter being by far the most effective.

Sharks are most receptive to a natural bait, and each year sees many of them taken on rigged baits such as balao, mullet and mackerel.

In chumming, the favorite technique is to use ground menhaden or other oily fish and to chum in an area where sharks are frequently observed cruising about. Once the sharks invade the chum slick, it is a relatively easy matter to get them to take a bait. Some anglers use live baits which are caught from the bottom, although a chunk of dead fish often works just as well. Hooks used with sporting regulation-class tackle should be at least 10/0 in size, with Martu or Sobey styles being favored. While sharks may be landed on 20-pound and 30-pound regulation-class tackle, it becomes less of a chore when you use 50-pound-class tackle on sharks in the 100-pound to 250-pound class.

We must impress upon you the importance of being extremely cautious in handling sharks when you fish for them with sporting tackle. They are unbelievably dangerous, staying alive many hours after you catch them. The hooks should never be removed from their mouths. Instead, just cut the leader. Many anglers who fish for sharks for sport prefer not to bring them aboard, but simply release them at boatside by cutting the leader.

If you should want to bring one aboard, the best procedure is to gaff it, and while still holding it on the gaff in the water, put a rope around its tail and secure the rope to a cleat on the boat. In that way you won't have a nasty shark thrashing around the cockpit. Many boatmen use a pistol or rifle to shoot sharks before bringing them aboard, while some anglers dispatch them with a billy club. Whatever method you may select, always remember that many hours after it has been landed a shark is still potentially dangerous.

Sheepshead

The sheepshead is the southern angler's counterpart of the tautog, or blackfish, of the north. It is found in greatest numbers from the Carolinas south and is especially plentiful along the Gulf Coast.

They set up housekeeping extremely close to pilings, rocks and underwater debris such as wrecks and old bridge abutments. When the water is clear, they can often be observed swimming about within a couple of feet of the pilings and rocks by the dozen, while the surrounding bottom discloses hardly a fish.

Because of this habit, it is extremely important that you fish your baits very close to such spots. This may mean losing an occasional rig because of fouling on the bottom, but it'll result in far more strikes. Anglers use a regular southern bottom rig with an egg-shaped sinker and small Eagle-Claw hooks in sizes ranging from number 2 to 2/0.

Favorite baits include shrimp, sand fleas and small pieces of crab. Sheepshead strike extremely fast; you've got to react quickly and lift back with your rod tip to set the hook. Most sheepshead weigh from one to three pounds, although there are times when you might hook a five- or six-pounder. Be prepared to apply as much pressure as your outfit will stand, for a big one will quickly dart into a crevice in the rocks or around a piling, snagging your line.

Silver Salmon

The silver salmon is one of the West Coast angler's favorite game-fish. It is found in greatest numbers from northern California up to Alaska. While it ascends coastal rivers to spawn, the major fishing effort for this fine scrapper is in the open reaches of the Pacific, for it is in the open ocean that these fish feed extensively and grow to respectable size.

There are records of silver salmon weighing in the 25-pound to 30-pound class being landed. But fish of this size are the exception, with the average being in the five-pound to eight-pound class. Anything over ten pounds is a respectably large trophy.

By far the biggest catches of silver salmon are made by trolling in deep water far from shore, employing deep trolling devices such as planers and underwater outriggers, and a modified variation of the underwater outrigger which consists of a heavy lead ball that takes the trolling rig deep but is immediately detached when a strike is received.

While deep trolling often produces fine catches, it is not as sporting as trolling for the silvers closer to shore, or above shallow reefs, or where several currents clash forming a tide rip. In a tide rip the salmon often cruise to within a few feet of the surface, feeding on herring and other baitfish which are swept along by the tide.

Unquestionably the most popular bait used for silver salmon is a herring fillet. The fillet is cut about eight inches long by two inches wide, and tapered to a point at the tail. It is rigged on a double hook, with the fillet being attached to only one of the hooks, while the second or trailing hook swings freely near the tail of the fillet. As this rig is trolled through the water it spins and flashes, quickly attracting the prettily hued silvers. For average size silvers a 2/0 or 3/0 Eagle-Claw hook is fine.

Some anglers attach wobblers or flashers to their line just ahead of the herring fillets, as they find the flashing action brings more strikes.

Snappers

Within the snapper family are a great many species that find favor with boatmen. They are found in all tropical waters off our southern Atlantic Coast and along the Gulf of Mexico. Those which find favor among sport fishermen are the mutton snapper, mangrove snapper, red snapper, lane snapper, schoolmaster snapper, yellowtail snapper, giant snapper and blackfin snapper.

Perhaps the three most popular snappers with sport fishermen are the mangrove, yellowtail and red snapper.

The yellowtail snapper is a reef dweller that is a tough fighter for its size. It's found in great numbers around reefs and ledges, but occasionally comes into protected bay waters. The yellowtails that are found near heavily fished areas are usually small, weighing only one to three pounds. But those that are found around far offshore reefs, and in areas off Bermuda and the Bahamas which are seldom fished, often weigh six to eight pounds. They are found in many tropical waters, especially off our southern Atlantic and Gulf Coasts.

The yellowtail snapper will readily take a small bucktail jig worked right above the reefs when presented on casting tackle. It will also take almost any small natural bait fished on the bottom, including hogmouth fry, pilchard and shrimp.

A favorite way to catch yellowtail is to chum for them. Once a school is attracted from the reef into a chum slick you can often catch them until arm-weary. Size 1/0 or 2/0 Eagle-Claw hooks are fine when chumming and using small baitfish as hook baits. Occasionally a small clinch-on sinker may have to be added to your line, especially if a strong tide is running.

Yellowtail snapper is a fine light-tackle fish, and nothing heavier than a one-handed spinning outfit or popping outfit is required. Care should be exercised not to fish with too tight a drag, for often heavier reef species such as grouper are encountered while chumming for yellowtail.

The mangrove snapper is a resident of many creeks and estuaries in southern waters, being particularly plentiful along the Gulf Coast, the southern Atlantic Coast and in the Bahamas. Not big (it seldom weighs more than a couple of pounds), it's a very smart fish which will test the wits of boatmen.

Mangrove snappers frequently travel in small schools, and if you can find them in a feeding mood they'll take shrimp readily. Small bucktail jigs perform well when worked through a school of snapper, with a whip retrieve resulting in more strikes than a steady retrieve. Hooks on both jigs and bait rigs should be small, number 2 or 3 being fine sizes.

Mangrove snapper are a fine table fish, which has resulted in their wide popularity with boatmen.

Another fine table fish, one which is caught in extremely deep water, is the red snapper. In fishing for this deep-water resident of the Gulf and Atlantic tropical waters, the minimum type of equipment used is a general-purpose boat outfit. Light tackle isn't practical, for often you have to fish in water at least 100 feet deep, often several times that depth. To get down to the bottom requires heavy sinkers which often weigh upwards of a pound or more.

Most anglers use a high-low bottom rig, often rigging four hooks or more, so that it is not necessary to be constantly reeling in to check the bait. Favored baits include pilchards, chunks of mullet, shrimp and almost any small forage species native to the area being fished.

While fishing for red snapper you'll often catch other species of snappers, almost all of which are rated as excellent table fare.

Snook

Snook are a favorite of the small-boat men, for they frequent areas usually accessible to outboarders. They are most at home in mangrove-lined creeks and estuaries which flow into the Gulf, although substantial numbers are caught along the southern Atlantic Coast as well.

Casting tackle is by far the favorite tool of the snook fisherman, who pursues this hard-hitting, tough-fighting jumper into waterways often so narrow that 30-foot to 40-foot casts are more than ample. Because of the heavy growth close to shore where the snook lie in wait for food, such as under the overhang of mangroves, most casters prefer to use surface lures. The surface lures never get caught on bottom obstructions, and the strike of a snook taking a surface lure is a thrill in itself. Popping plugs produce many snook, as do surface darters, propeller plugs and mirror-type plugs. Fly casters employ popping bugs with good results, particularly on small snook.

In open water bucktail jigs are often brought into play for snook, as are small spoons.

Trollers account for many snook while trolling in rivers and the open Gulf. The inshore trolling techniques discussed earlier apply to this type of fishing, with big spoons, rigged needlefish, rigged eels and swimming plugs producing many fine catches of big snook each season, particularly along the southwest Florida coast.

Many snook in the 10-pound to 30-pound class are taken while bottom fishing with live baitfish. Favored baits include pinfish, squirrel fish and grunts, which are hooked either through the eye sockets or the lips and permitted to swim along the bottom in tide rips, off points of land, and in the passes and inlets which lead into the Gulf and Atlantic. For this type of fishing a regular southern bottom rig with an egg-shaped sinker is employed, utilizing a 6/o or 7/o Eagle-Claw hook for the big hook bait.

Spanish Mackerel

The Spanish mackerel is a favorite of the inshore small-boat fishermen throughout Florida and along the Gulf Coast. While not a big gamefish, averaging only about two pounds, it's a plentiful scrapper that provides a great deal of sport for those anglers who fish close to the shore and in the sheltered waters of bays and sounds.

At times the Spanish mackerel is as plentiful in southern waters as is the common mackerel in northern waters, and much the same techniques may be employed to catch it. The Spanish mackerel will respond to a chum of small pieces of mullet, mackerel or other baitfish. Once you get them in your slick, they'll take almost any small shiny lure, or you can fish for them by using small pieces of bait.

Many anglers fish for the Spanish mackerel in bay and sound waters by just drifting along, using a plastic float on their line and a live shrimp fished three or four feet under the surface.

When the Spanish mackerel chase bait on the surface, the boat caster can load up. A one-handed spinning outfit or a popping outfit is ideal for this species, for with light gear you can enjoy maximum sport.

Occasionally in open water the fish will settle very deep, and at such times it is difficult to catch them near the surface. Trolling with wire line often pays off handsomely then. Small spoons, wobblers, chromed jigs and Japanese trolling feathers produce best for the trollers.

Striped Bass

The striped bass is without a doubt one of the most popular salt-water gamefish caught by boat fishermen in the United States. It's found on both the Atlantic and Pacific Coasts, where it delights anglers. Greatest catches are made from the Carolinas north to the Maritime Provinces of Canada on the East Coast, while West Coast anglers enjoy fine sport from San Francisco north to Washington.

The striped bass, which is called striper, rock, linesider and squid hound in various sections of its range, is basically an inshore feeder which prefers bay, river and estuarial waters as well as the open ocean close to shore. He's quite at home in the surf and around jetties and breakwaters.

Of the many fish in the sea, the striped bass have perhaps the most unpredictable disposition. This, to a great degree, is why so many anglers seek these husky striped battlers, for it never ceases to be a challenge to catch them.

What adds to the striper's popularity is that it may be taken by such a wide variety of angling methods. Considerably more methods are employed than with most coastal fish.

If you like inshore trolling you may employ the tackle and techniques discussed earlier, for the striper will readily strike a trolled lure along the surf, around jetties or along submerged offshore reefs.

The Spanish mackerel is a favorite of Florida and Gulf Coast anglers. It will readily take a small piece of almost any bait and is very receptive to small shiny lures. A fine fighter when landed on a one-handed spinning or light popping outfit.

The Atlantic mackerel is the northern anglers' answer to the Spanish mackerel. Found in great numbers from the Virginia Capes on north, it responds well to a chum line of ground menhaden and will strike a wide variety of small lures.

He also frequents tide rips and inlets emptying into the ocean, where trollers often make excellent catches. The troller in a small boat who prefers the solitude of coastal bays, rivers and creeks will also find the striper cooperative and great sport on a light popping outfit. Among the standard trolling lures in the arsenal of the small-boat trollers are both surface and subsurface swimming plugs, bucktail jigs, spoons tipped with pork rind, surgical-tube lures, plastic rigged eels, and natural rigged eels. The size of the lures employed will depend on the size of the stripers in residence. Tiny half-ounce bucktails are fine for 5-pound school bass, but foot-long bunker spoons and plugs of the same length are necessary when stripers in the 40-pound to 50-pound class are around.

Stripers are also receptive to natural baits, either fished on the bottom or drifted with the tide from a boat. Each year many fine catches are boated while drifting seaworms in tidal rivers or where rips form at a point of land. The bass will readily strike a live mackerel or sardine fished on a live line from an anchored or drifting skiff just a short distance from the shore. They'll also take a clam bait fished directly on the bottom, as well as many other baits which may be native to a particular area.

Chummers also account for many fine bass catches each year. The stripers respond well to a chum spread of ground clams, and a chum line of live grass shrimp is something they can seldom pass up. Light popping outfits are in perfect order for chumming. Hooks are tailored to the baits being used and the size of the bass being taken, with 1/0 and 2/0 Eagle-Claw hooks being ideal for school bass, while hooks in the 3/0 through 6/0 size often prove most practical when bass 15 pounds or larger are constantly being caught.

When bass are located feeding on top, just about the most exciting way to catch them is while casting. When they're chasing sand launce, mullet, anchovies, baby mossbunkers and other small baitfish on the surface they'll readily hit a popping plug, propeller plug or slowly retrieved surface-swimming plug. Even bucktail jigs produce when the bass are on top, as do small spoons, feather-tipped metal squids and hammered stainless steel jigs.

Small wonder that the striper's such a popular gamefish with boatmen. In some areas of his range he's cooperative through a full ten months of the year, spending only the cold winter months in a dormant stage on the bottoms of deep holes in coastal bays.

In 1966 we wrote *Secrets of Striped Bass Fishing,* which was published by The Macmillan Company. The entire book is devoted to the popular striper, and understandably goes into far greater detail than we could possibly go into here. For the serious boatman who is aroused by the unpredictable nature of the linesider, we feel the book would prove helpful in improving your catch of this fine gamefish.

Summer Flounder

Because the summer flounder and southern flounder are so similar in habits and habitat we felt it wise to include them together. For only in the eyes of the trained marine biologist is there any marked outward distinction between them. On researching the difference—for we could never tell one from the other—we found that the southern flounder has anywhere from 8 to 12 gill rakers, while the summer flounder has anywhere from 14 to 17 gill rakers. For all practical purposes, let's say they're the same!

The summer flounder, which is called fluke in the northern portion of its range, is most plentiful from the Chesapeake Bay north to New England, while the southern flounder is found in greatest numbers along the southern Atlantic Coast and along the Gulf Coast.

Flounders spend most of their time in the shallow waters near shore, where they often literally bury all but their head in the sand bottom, waiting for an unsuspecting baitfish to happen by. They will, however, readily chase baitfish, often leaping clear of the surface as they chase salt-water minnows, spearing, sand launce and other forage species in a tidal estuary.

The two most popular methods employed to catch flounders are drifting and trolling.

In drifting, a standard single-hook bottom rig is employed. Carlisle or Eagle-Claw hooks are the most popular, with sizes in the 3/0 through 7/0 range being used most often, though of course this is dependent upon the general run of fish.

Most anglers drift across sandy or adjacent to rocky bottom for fluke, for the bigger flounders often prefer to lie in the sand among the rocks, where they find baitfish and other food is very plentiful. Favored baits include live salt-water minnows, strips of squid, strips of flounder belly, spearing, sand launce, shrimp, and almost any other bait found along the bottom.

Trolling is particularly effective when fishing for flounder in the protected reaches of bays and rivers, where the water is often shallow. Much the same bottom rig is used as for drifting. Slow trolling proves advantageous, as you're able to cover two or three times the area you would cover if you were just drifting. Trolling is difficult in shallow water with a big boat, but outboarders can get their craft right in along the marsh banks, where the water is often only a couple of feet deep. There they register fine catches while slowly trolling their baits along the bottom.

In addition to providing good sport, the flounder is a fine-flavored fish, among the mildest tasting in the sea.

Tarpon

The tarpon takes honors as being the best aerial performer within range of the small-boat man or inshore fisherman. Tarpon are found in great numbers along the south Florida coast, through the Keys and along the entire Gulf Coast down into Mexico. Each season sees a few small schools of big tarpon move as far north as the Virginia Capes. The tarpon provides sport for every type of angler, using a light spinning outfit for three-pound tarpon in a tidal estuary or trolling with regulation-class tackle in the open Gulf for 150-pounders.

Small tarpon are usually found in the protected reaches of bays and estuaries, often frequenting the same type of brackish water as snook. Most tarpon stay in these waters until they reach a weight of 15 or 20 pounds, when they move down into the big rivers and bays and then into the open Atlantic and Gulf.

All types of casting tackle are employed to catch tarpon. Plugs and bucktail jigs are the favored lures, with the size used dependent upon the tarpon being sought. As the tarpon are most often observed rolling on the surface, one can readily tell the size of the fish. Fly casters enjoy great sport with big tarpon when they are feeding on the flats. Big streamer flies are the most successful lures.

Many casters find the big tarpon are easily fooled with a live offering, and they quietly ease up on a school of surfacing tarpon and cast a live blue crab or a pinfish into the feeding fish. Seldom is such an offering passed by.

Occasionally tarpon will refuse lures, and at such times natural baits must be brought into play. In the passes and inlets, where the water is swift and deep, a favorite method is to fish a pinfish or grunt on the bottom, while either drifting along with the tide or anchored. Some anglers even use a chunk of fresh mullet with good results.

For this type of fishing a southern bottom rig with an egg-shaped sinker is employed. The sinker is often attached to the leader or swivel with soft copper wire, so that when the tarpon jumps the sinker is thrown off and doesn't fly about as the fish is being fought.

Tarpon are primarily a gamefish, with little table value. As such, most anglers release these high-jumping fighters at boatside so they may fight another day.

Tautog

Throughout some portions of its range from Virginia to the Maritime Provinces the tautog is known as blackfish. This plentiful bottom feeder is cooperative from early spring until fall and is found in great numbers around rocks, wrecks, breakwaters, bridge abutments and almost anywhere where mussels, sand fleas, crabs and other such food is available.

The tautog is a difficult fish to hook, primarily because it has a rather small mouth and strikes a bait very fast. Often a newcomer to tautog fishing has his bait repeatedly cleaned from his hooks because of the lightning-fast strike. A regular high-low bottom rig is fine for tautog. A bank-style sinker should be employed, as this is less apt to become fouled on the bottom than other sinkers. Eagle-Claw hooks are fine as are Sheepshead-style hooks. Blackfish range in weight from one pound to upwards of 15 pounds and vary in size in different areas, so it always pays to have an assortment of hook sizes with you.

Among the favorite baits used by blackfishermen are green crabs, fiddler crabs, sand fleas, clams and seaworms. The bait should be small and the hook concealed within the bait. You must have extremely fast reflexes to hook blackfish; the best procedure until you develop a feel for their strike is to lift back sharply with your rod tip the instant you feel them take your bait.

The tautog is a favorite of bottom fishermen along the middle and north Atlantic Coast. Linda Rosko hooked the nice one just swung aboard by her father while fishing with a sandworm bait in Buzzards Bay, Massachusetts. Tautog, often called blackfish, strike very fast and it takes lightning-fast response to set the hook.

Boatmen often anchor off stone breakwaters and use a chum of grass shrimp to coax the blackfish out from the rocks. This is practiced in only a few areas, but should work no matter where blackfish reside.

Wahoo

The wahoo is without doubt one of the fastest, hardest fighting gamefish found in the sea. It is caught in substantial numbers off all our coasts and prefers warm southern waters.

It is primarily a troller's fish. Most are taken while trolling skip baits on the surface, with such baits as balao, mullet, flying fish, sardines and eels bringing the most strikes. Strip baits are a good skip bait for wahoo too, as are several of the new plastic imitation fish which work on the surface. In addition to these baits wahoo frequently strike trolling lures set out for smaller game, including Japanese trolling feathers, bone squids, spoons and cedar jigs.

The average wahoo landed by trollers ranges from 25 to 50 pounds, although fish in the 100-pound class are not uncommon.

They are very tough fighters and will test your tackle to the utmost. It is wise to never try to rush the fish to boat, for they have tremendous stamina and will smash tackle if too much pressure is applied during the initial stages of the fight. Stick with 20-pound and 30-pound regulation-class tackle for maximum sport.

Weakfish

We include the weakfish in this listing in hopes that this fine gamefish might someday return in numbers sufficient to warrant serious angling for it. Over a score of years ago, weakfish were extremely plentiful along the middle Atlantic Coast. Because of a number of factors including possible overfishing by sport and commercial fishermen, particularly at its spawning habitats, the weakfish caught today are most often small in size and few in number.

In some areas, particularly southern New Jersey and in the Chesapeake Bay, there are still sufficient schools of weakfish to warrant serious fishing. They respond well to a chum line of grass shrimp, and will take shrimp, seaworm, shedder crab and fresh squid baits.

Often during the fall weakfish school up just offshore, and nice catches are made while using bucktail jigs and light spinning tackle. Diamond jigs often produce good catches too, with the weakfish showing a marked preference for any lure predominately yellow in color.

In the northern part of their range, throughout New England, weakfish are often called squeteague or squet, while the big weakfish weighing over five pounds are often called yellowfins or tiderunners. The big fish seldom move in big schools as do smaller weakfish. Often in the fall it is possible to catch the tiderunners while bottom fishing with seaworm or shedder crab bait, particularly at the mouths of creeks and estuaries, where the weakfish move in to feed on shrimp and small baitfish on a dropping tide.

White Sea Bass

The white sea bass is a very popular gamefish found in the shallow waters off the California coast from San Francisco south to the Baja

The author just netted this weakfish for Bill Perry, who landed it while chumming with grass shrimp in the upper reaches of Chesapeake Bay near Chesapeake Beach. On light spinning tackle the weakfish is great fun.

The white sea bass is a favorite of California anglers. It is often caught in great numbers at night and responds well to a live anchovy fished in a chum line. A fine light tackle fish that often grows to large size.

California peninsula. It's also found in appreciable numbers in the Gulf of California. Inshore coastal waters often produce appreciable numbers of white sea bass for rod-and-reel anglers, but the heavy-weights in the 20-pound to 40-pound class often stick to the shallow spots several miles offshore, where there is always a plentiful supply of sardines, mackerel and anchovies and their favorite dish, live squid, to satisfy their appetite.

Daytime fishing produces many nice catches, but you can be certain of almost doubling your catch if you fish after dark. Once the sun goes down, white sea bass seem more active and are easier to coax to bait. They respond well to a chum line of live baitfish, but by far the best results are obtained if you can locate a school of squid and keep them under the lights of your boat while drifting across shallow offshore waters at night. The squid is a favorite of the white sea bass, and once they find a school of these cephalopods they feed extensively.

It is often possible to use a long-handled dip net, quickly scooping squid into it when they are darting around beneath a light hung low over the water at night. Another method of catching these prime baits for white sea bass is to employ a weighted treble-snag hook. This is simply cast into the school of squid and jigged vigorously until a squid is impaled on the hook. The whole live squid should be used as a live bait. Best results are often obtained by fishing with the squid away from the lights, for the single squid swimming alone proves extremely tempting to a cruising white sea bass that moves into the area.

While live baits are favored, the white sea bass will hit a trolled spoon, feather or strip bait. Boat casters also find times when white sea bass are receptive to chromed jigs, bucktails and spoons.

Winter Flounder

The winter flounder is a very popular member of the flatfish clan which frequents the waters of the Atlantic Coast from the middle Atlantic states on up to the Maritime Provinces. In the northern part of its range it is caught in bays and rivers during the summer months, but throughout the rest of its range it comes inshore during the late fall and stays right through the winter, retiring to the ocean depths as the waters warm.

The average winter flounder caught by sport fishermen weighs about a pound. But what they lack in weight they make up for by being plentiful. Often it's possible during the height of a run to catch several dozen of these tasty bottom feeders in a day's fishing.

Because of their size, it is important that light tackle be used in order to obtain maximum enjoyment. A bay or popping outfit is ideal, for with a light rod you can feel even the lightest pull of the small flounders as they mouth your bait.

The winter flounder has a very small, rubbery mouth with no teeth. Because of this, small hooks and small baits must be used. Chestertown hooks in number 8 or 9 sizes are best for all around fishing. These are most often employed with a spreader which permits the use of two hooks, both of which rest directly on the bottom.

Favored baits include sandworms, bloodworms and small pieces of clam or mussel.

Winter flounders readily respond to a chum line, and the angler who employs a chum pot filled with ground menhaden, clams, mussels or even dog and cat food will enjoy better sport than the angler who doesn't attempt to attract these small bottom feeders. Best results are usually obtained while fishing from an anchored boat. Some of the biggest winter flounders caught along the Atlantic Coast are landed on the grounds located off Block Island, Rhode Island. In these fertile waters the flounders often average three to four pounds, with occasional flatties being landed that weigh over six pounds.

Yellowfin Tuna

In various parts of its range you'll hear the yellowfin tuna called Allison tuna, but scientists agree that this is a single species which, much to the delight of sport fishermen, is caught along the southern Atlantic, Gulf and southern Pacific Coasts. They're also caught in the Bahamas and as far north as Bermuda, where a substantial sports fishery exists.

These are considered by many to be the hardest fighting of the tunas and an excellent light-tackle fish. They are ideally suited to 20-pound and 30-pound regulation-class tackle. While it may take an hour or more to land a big yellowfin on such tackle, it is a thrill, to put it mildly.

Unfortunately, yellowfin tuna infrequently travel in big schools. Because of this many of those which are landed are hooked quite by accident. Often they are taken on heavy tackle being fished for other species. They'll readily take a trolled lure, with small yellowfins responding to Japanese trolling feathers, cedar jigs, strip baits and spoons. Big yellowfins, those from 50 pounds to a couple of hundred pounds, take skip baits such as sardines, mullet, balao and eels.

Yellowfins will respond to a chum of ground fish or of small fingerling baitfish. When they move into a chum spread they are often hook-shy, so best results are obtained by carefully concealing the hook within the bait being used. When they are available, such live baits as ocean robins, pilchards and almost any small forage species will quickly bring strikes. Tuna and albacore hooks in 5/0 through 7/0 size are fine for average-sized yellowfins.

Yellowtail

Of the many species of fish which roam the wide expanse of the Pacific Ocean, the yellowtail is perhaps one of the most popular. Without it the party-boat fisherman would often be at a loss during the summer months. Its range is from Monterey Bay south to the waters of Baja California, with the biggest catches being made from the offshore islands of southern California.

The finest yellowtail fishing occurs during the summer months, when party boats and charter boats make big catches. The most popular method of catching them is chumming, although trollers also account for many fine fish.

Yellowtail respond best to a chum of live anchovies or sardines. Often when a school of the yellows is chummed up, they swarm about the boat by the dozens. It is not uncommon for them to go on a feeding spree, chasing the frightened small baitfish and taking a live baitfish on a hook with little hesitation.

Many anglers use a general-purpose boat outfit while chumming for yellowtail, although a number of party-boat regulars prefer a long spinning rod, as they are better able to cast a live anchovy bait away from the boat. Light monofilament lines are a must for this type of fishing, for the yellowtail are very wary and will shy away from other types of line.

Most proficient boatmen tie their hooks directly to the end of their lines, using number 1 or 2 Eagle-Claw or Beak hooks, which hold the bait well yet penetrate fast into the yellowtail's jaw. The anchovy or sardine baits are hooked either through the lips or through the eye sockets, so that they may swim about in a natural manner.

When a school of yellowtail moves around the boat, it is important that you cast your bait as gently as possible, to keep from having it rip off the hook while casting. Often it is wise to keep your reel in free spool or the open bail, so that line can be paid out and the bait-fish permitted to swim away from the boat. Drags should be kept at a medium to soft setting, so as not to snub the fish when it takes the bait.

There's no mistaking when a yellow takes the bait, for it will take off on a run that will clean a great deal of line from your reel. Seasoned boatmen let the yellowtail run without too much pressure until they slow down. Only then do they start to apply heavier drag pressure and start to pump the fish back toward the boat. For it is far better to let the fish tire itself away from the boat than to have it swimming wildly close aboard, where it might well tangle other lines.

What makes the yellowtail so popular is that fish in the 10-pound to 20-pound class are by no means uncommon. Often still bigger fish are brought to gaff.

Some of the biggest yellowtail are boated by trollers who are out after albacore. The big ones often cruise around the kelp beds and will strike at Japanese trolling feathers, bone squids, chromed jigs and spoons. They'll also strike a strip bait and sardine or mackerel rigged as a skip bait.

Yellowtail are a fine table fish. While many are used in their fresh state, some anglers find them a gourmet's delight when smoked.

In Conclusion

We have included within the covers of this book as much information as possible about fishing from boats. While we are hopeful that a great deal of it will prove helpful to both the newcomer and the veteran who fishes from boats, we must honestly say that within one book it becomes difficult to cover adequately all there is to know about fishing from boats.

We are hopeful, however, that by using this as a primer, boat fishermen may be able to apply techniques and methods used throughout various coastal areas to their own particular fishing locale. For often a new technique may be the difference between a day of poor fishing and one where a blitz ensues.

It is important, we believe, to point out that fishing from boats as we know it is solely for the enjoyment and relaxation which it brings. We feel you'll enjoy boat fishing more by having the right tackle and knowing how to use it. You'll have more fun catching fish, and catch more fish too, when you absorb as much as you can about the great sport of fishing coastal waters from a boat.

Glossary

Anchovy By far the most popular of West Coast baitfishes. Considered a major food source of almost all Pacific gamefish.

Bait Any type of food that a fish will eat when placed on a hook; includes most natural food found in the sea, such as small fish, clams, shrimp, crabs, mussels and seaworms.

Baitfish Almost any small fish which can be used as bait for larger fish.

Ball-bearing swivel A swiveling device with ball bearings that is used to join line and leader, thus preventing a spinning or twisting lure to cause the line to twist.

Barrel swivel A swivel with two eyes, used to join leader and line.

Billfish Any of the fish with a bill, such as the sailfish and marlins.

Block tin squid A lure molded of block tin with a shape of a small baitfish. It usually has a flat top and round or square keel.

Blue water A term applied to the deep blue color of the ocean waters many miles from shore.

Bone squid A lure made of plastic and shaped much like a small round bottomed boat with a flat top and either a single or double hook.

Bottom feeder A species of fish that does most of its feeding on or near the bottom of coastal waters.

Braided line A line braided of Dacron or nylon.

Breaking fish Fish which are splashing on the surface, often chasing baitfish, but sometimes just playing.

Bucktail jig A molded lead lure with an eye to fasten your leader on the top of its head. The hook is molded into the lure and tied around it is a skirt of bucktail.

257

Butt   The lower section of a rod, often referred to as the handle. Most often made of hickory, aluminum and specie cork or composition cork over a fiberglass shaft.

Casting   The skill of using rod, reel and line and synchronizing the movement to throw a lure or bait to a target, in most cases a fish, with smooth precision and accurate presentation.

Cedar jig   A trolling lure made of a piece of cedar in the shape of a cigar. The cedar is attached to a lead head. A hole through the center of the lure is used for the leader and hook. When trolled the lure glides through the water with an action pelagic species find irresistible.

Charter boat   A fishing boat which is chartered for a private group, usually numbering four to eight anglers, although in some areas boats accommodating 25 or more anglers are available.

Chum bag   A mesh bag or onion sack in which chum is placed and then suspended over the side of the boat.

Chumming   Attracting fish within range of your boat by dropping pieces of food into the water, which sets up a chum line. As the fish pick up the food they continue to move to the source, eventually taking your baited hooks.

Chum pot   A wire basket, usually with a lead bottom, in which ground chum is placed and lowered to the bottom.

Clinch-on sinker   A sinker which may be placed on your line and securely clinched in place by bending over two small lead ears around your line after having recessed the line in a slot in the sinker.

Current   The movement of the water, most often caused by wind or tide.

Deboner   A metal tube which is inserted into a baitfish's mouth and used to completely remove the backbone by cutting around it as the deboner is pressed through the length of the fish's body around the backbone.

Diamond jig   A four-sided lure made of lead and chrome or nickel-plated. It is widest at the center, tapering to a point at each end. The leader is attached to an eye at one end while a treble hook is most often attached on the other eye.

Double-line   When after big fish many anglers double the end ten or fifteen feet of line, in affect doubling the strength of their terminal end, which proves advantageous when landing big fish.

Drift   To permit a boat to be carried freely by tide or wind.

Eddy   A spot where a miniature whirpool occurs, such as on the down current side of a bridge or the leeward side of a rocky promontory.

Extension butt   A small extra butt which may be added to the butt of a fly rod once a fish is hooked to give extra leverage while fighting a fish.

Fathom   A measure of depth equivalent to six feet.

Fillet   A bone-free piece of fish.

Fishing machine   A boat designed expressly for a specific type of fishing, with all other considerations secondary.

Fishing rod   A piece of equipment, designed expressly for catching fish. It may vary in length from five to ten feet and have an action which provides maximum sport while fighting a gamefish.

Flats   Extremely shallow water, especially those areas which are exposed at low tide and flood as the tide rises.

Flotsam   Miscellaneous floating objects, about, around and under which gamefish often congregate.

Fly line   A line designed expressly for fly casting. Unlike other lines, a fly line is made to a specific weight and tapered for a specific type of casting, so it in turn balances with the rod, reel, leader and flies to be used. They are made to float on the surface or weighted to sink into the depths.

Forage species   Any of the many hundreds of small fish found in ocean waters on which other fish feed.

Foregrip   A hand grip located above the reelseat on a rod. An angler fighting a fish usually holds onto the grip while pumping. Often called a forward grip.

Gaff   A large, strong hook attached to a handle, which is pulled into a fish as it is brought alongside, thus enabling an angler to bring a fish aboard quickly.

Gamefish   Those species that are great fighters are usually afforded this title.

Ganion rig   A deep-water-bottom fishing rig popular on the West Coast on which six and sometimes more hooks are fastened. Often all the baits are taken, thus enabling the angler to reel in several fish at one time.

Gimbal nock   A fitting affixed to the butt section of a rod. Usually made of chromed steel, with two slots that fit into a rod holder, chair gimbal or rod belt, thus keeping the rod in an upright position at all times.

Green fish   A fish which has been brought to boatside too quickly and is still full of fight and thrashing about wildly as an attempt is made to boat it.

Ground fishing   A term applied to fishing for bottom feeding fish in some areas.

Guide boat   A specialized type of fishing craft used by a guide who can accommodate only one or two anglers on board. During the course of a day the guide's total effort is towards having his anglers make a good catch of gamefish, usually on light tackle.

Hammered stainless steel jig   A flat jig made of stainless steel, with a shape similar to an elongated knife handle, and having a finish as though hammered with a ball-peen hammer.

High-low rig   A basic bottom rig to which is attached two hooks, one of which is fished about two feet off the bottom and the other directly on the bottom. Most popular on the East Coast.

Inboard-outdrive   A boat with an inboard engine and an outboard-type propulsion unit.

Inlet   A spot where a small body of water meets a large body of water; where a river flows into an ocean or a creek into a bay. Often called a pass or breachway, especially where it joins a bay or sound with the ocean or gulf.

Jigging   Enhancing the action of a lure or bait by vigorously working your rod tip, causing it to dart ahead and falter. This technique may be employed at most any time, while trolling, chumming, casting, drifting or bottom fishing.

Kelp   A type of seaweed abundant in the Pacific Ocean, around which great schools of fish congregate.

Landing net   A cone-shaped mesh bag attached to a strong metal hoop which is attached to a sturdy handle. A fish is guided into it and brought aboard with the landing net, thus enabling an angler to successfully net the fish at the crucial moment when it is boatside.

Lead core line   A line of braided nylon, with a thin lead core that takes it deep.

Leader   A piece of nylon monofilament, stainless steel wire or cable, usually less visible and of finer diameter than the line being used; between line and lure or bait.

Leaning on a fish   Applying as much pressure as the tackle can stand to bring the fish to the boat.

Levelwind reel   A reel having a mechanism that moves back and forth as line is retrieved, laying the line evenly on the reel.

Live well   A tank in which baitfish are kept alive. Usually water is circulated in the well to keep oxygen in the water so that the fish will not die.

Lunker   A big fish of any of the larger species.

Lure action   The movement of a lure in the water so that it appears lifelike. A lure or bait not working properly is often said to have poor or no action.

Minnow   A general term used for many small baitfish, particularly of the killifishes, a major baitfish.

Mirror-type plug   A plug made of plastic, with the shape of a small baitfish. So designed that it gives a mirror effect due to metallic inlay within the plug body.

Monofilament line An extruded, or solid line made of nylon monofilament.

Multi-hook rig A bottom rig with two or three hooks attached to one leader.

Multiplying reel A reel whose spool turns as the reel handle is turned, thus retrieving and storing line on the reel. Often called a conventional reel.

Outrigger A long pole attached to the boat; it is lowered to a 60-degree angle as you troll. Trolling lines are attached to the outriggers via a clothespin attached to a line and pulley on the outriggers. The outrigger serves a dual purpose, as it keeps the baits far from the boat and helps their action by causing them to skip about. When a fish strikes a lure fished from the outriggers it pulls the line from the clothespin and the angler is free to fight the fish.

Party boat A fishing boat which sails daily, with anglers paying their fare on an individual or per head basis. Often called head boats in many areas.

Pilchard A popular silvery baitfish found in great numbers along the south Atlantic and Gulf Coasts.

Planer A metal or plastic device designed to pull your lure deep as it is trolled through the water.

Plastic float A modern version of a cork float, used to keep a bait from sinking too deeply.

Plug A lure made of wood or plastic, painted to resemble a baitfish. Made in many styles that work on the surface and down deep.

Pod of fish Approximately six to twelve fish feeding together.

Poling Propelling the boat across shallows or flats with the aid of a long wooden pole designed expressly for this purpose.

Popping bug A plastic- or cork-bodied lure which floats on the surface at rest and is used by fly casters. When retrieved it has a splashing action which many gamefish find irresistible.

Popping plug A surface plug with a concave head that throws water ahead of itself as it is trolled or retrieved.

Pork rind A tough, pliable rind of pork which is attached to many lures to enhance their action. It comes in many shapes and colors, but is seldom more than one-eighth inch thick.

Propeller plug A cigar-shaped plug or one shaped to resemble a small fish with a propeller fore and aft to create commotion as it is drawn through the water.

Pumping The systematic raising of your rod tip, then quickly lowering it and simultaneously reeling in line as you bring a fish to the boat.

Reef A group of rocks or coral lying on the ocean bottom, often extending close to the surface of the water.

Reel drag   A mechanism on a reel that can be set to desired pressure, permitting a fish to pull off line from the reel when that pressure is reached, thus preventing the line from breaking.

Reel seat   A metal seat located on the butt section of the rod, on which the reel is placed and held firmly by a screw-locking arrangement. Often made of anodized aluminum for light rods, but of heavy, hard-chromed construction on heavy-duty rods.

Ring guide   Four to ten ring guides are mounted on a rod tip to distribute the strain. The circular ring through which the line runs is made of hard-chromed stainless steel, tungsten carbide or agate.

Rod belt   A belt worn while fighting fish. It has a cup or tube, with a pin to accommodate the gimbal nock or butt of a rod, and prevents an angler from injuring his stomach.

Roller guide   Several are mounted on the rod tip to guide the line and they have small rollers on which the line runs smoothly.

Rubber-cored sinker   A sinker having a core of rubber, which may be slipped on and off your line by simply twisting the rubber core around your line or leader.

Run   The period of time when a fish is taking line from your reel as it swims away from you.

Sand launce   A popular baitfish found in great numbers along the middle and north Atlantic coast. Often called sand eel.

School of fish   A large number of fish congregated in a small area.

Sea weed   A leafy green or brown vegetation which is found in varying amounts and varieties in almost all salt waters.

Seaworm   A general term applied to any of several varieties of marine worms found along our seacoasts.

Shoulder harness   A vest-like harness from which two belts are snapped to harness lugs located on large-size reels. The harness takes the strain off your arms while fighting fish, permitting bulk of the pressure to be placed on your back.

Shrimp   A small marine crustacean found in many areas along our coasts and a fine natural bait.

Sinker   Any one of many different-shaped weights designed to take your lure or bait deep. Usually molded of lead, although cast iron is popular for heavy sinkers on the West Coast.

Skip bait   A bait such as a strip bait, balao, mullet or eel which is trolled so that it skips on the surface in an enticing manner.

Slick   An oily patch on the surface of the water which may be caused by the oil from chum, residue from feeding fish in the depths or from food regurgitated by feeding fish.

Snelled hook   A hook which has a short piece of leader material, about 8 to 12 inches long, attached to it, ready to slip on to a swivel or rig.

Spinning reel   A reel whose spool is fixed and does not turn while casting or retrieving. While casting the line slips off the side of the spool and while retrieving the line is wound around the spool with a bail mechanism.

Split ring   A metal ring, split so that it may be used to attach hooks to wobblers, plugs and metal jigs.

Spoon   A lure made of a flat, somewhat curved piece of metal in the shape of a fish. When drawn through the water it has a twisting, lifelike action that resembles the antics of small fish.

Spreader rig   A bottom rig made of stiff wire which can accommodate two hooks, both of which rest directly on the bottom.

Streamer fly   A fly tied on a long-shanked hook to closely resemble a small baitfish.

Strike   The moment when a fish takes your lure or bait. Also, the act of setting back to set the hook at the moment of the strike.

Strip bait   A strip bait is usually cut to a torpedo shape and has an attractive action when trolled. It may be cut from pork rind, fresh squid or the belly of dolphin, tuna, bonito and other such species.

Stripping line   Pulling a fly line through the guides while retrieving or casting.

Surgical-tube lure   A lure made by slipping a hook inside a piece of surgical tubing. When drawn through the water it has a shimmering action fish find irresistible.

Swimming plug   A plug with a side to side or swimming motion that is caused by a wobble plate at its head. Made in surface and sub-surface models.

Tail-hook pork rind   A piece of pork rind with a small hook permanently attached to its tail section. This hook accounts for fish that may strike but miss the hook of the lure to which the pork rind is attached.

Teaser   A large lure without a hook, trolled from an outrigger to tease gamefish, which after striking it take a bait with a hook in it as the teaser is pulled away. Very effective with billfish. Another teaser is a small tube, feather or pork rind lure fished several feet ahead of your primary lure. Ofter a fish strikes the small teaser instead of the primary lure.

Terminal tackle   That equipment tied to the end of your line. Includes swivels, clips, snaps, lures and leaders.

Three-way swivel   A swivel with three eyes. Your line is tied to one eye, a sinker to the second and a snelled hook or leader and hook onto the remaining eye.

Tide   The tide alternately rises and falls twice in each lunar day. This causes currents, often called tidal flow. The flood tide causes greatest depths in ocean waters, while the ebb tide results in the lowest water.

The rise and fall are greatest during the period of the new moon and full moon.

Tide rip   A spot where several currents clash, or where a fast-moving current in deep water clashes with a shoal.

Tip top   Is actually an end guide which is built on a metal tube that is cemented onto the tip end of the rod.

Trailer boat   Any small boat, usually outboard or inboard-outdrive powered, that is placed on a trailer and towed behind a vehicle to various launching spots.

Trolling   Drawing your lures or bait through the water on long lines while proceeding slowly under power.

Trolling feather   A lure with a lead or plastic head and a full-feathered skirt. A leader is run through the head and a hook attached so that it is concealed in the feathers. Often called a feathered jig on the West Coast.

Trolling sinker   A torpedo- or keel-shaped sinker with an eye at each end. Usually placed between line and leader while trolling to get your lures deep.

Wake   The churning white water thrown about as your boat moves ahead.

Whip retrieve   Retrieving a lure while simultaneously whipping your rod tip to give the lure an exciting action.

Wire line   A soft, solid line of Monel wire, used to get lures deep. Brass lines are occasionally used.

Wobbler   A lure which closely resembles a spoon. Most wobblers have a free-swinging treble hook attached to the body via a split ring.

Working lures   In order to bring strikes a lure must move through the water in a lifelike manner or work. A lure is made to work by trolling or retrieving it at an ideal speed for the particular lure.

Index